THE BRITISH ARMY OF THE RHINE

THE HISTORY OF MILITARY OCCUPATION

Edited by John Laband and Ian F. W. Beckett

A list of books in the series appears at the end of this book.

THE BRITISH ARMY
OF THE RHINE

Turning Nazi Enemies
into Cold War Partners

PETER SPEISER

UNIVERSITY OF ILLINOIS PRESS
Urbana, Chicago, and Springfield

All Illustrations Courtesy of the Council, National Army Museum, London.

Library of Congress Cataloging-in-Publication Data
Names: Speiser, Peter, 1975– author.
Title: The British Army of the Rhine : turning Nazi enemies into Cold War partners /
    Peter Speiser.
Description: Urbana : University of Illinois Press, 2016. | Series: The history of military
    occupation | Includes bibliographical references and index.
Identifiers: LCCN 2016002822 | ISBN 9780252040160 (hardcover : alk. paper)
Subjects: LCSH: Great Britain. Army. British Army of the Rhine. | Germany—
    History—1945–1990. | Great Britain—Foreign relations—Germany (West) |
    Germany (West)—Foreign relations—Great Britain | British—Germany—History—
    20th century.
Classification: LCC DD257.2 .S65 2016 | DDC 943.087/4—dc23
LC record available at http://lccn.loc.gov/2016002822

For Quinn and Zoe

CONTENTS

PREFACE

The focus of this book is on the attempt by the postwar British Labour and Conservative administrations to use the British Army of the Rhine (BAOR) as a tool to improve relations with the German civilian population during the early stages of the Cold War. The original contribution to knowledge lies in the evaluation of the efforts made by both the British and the German administrations to transform the BAOR from an occupation army to a protecting force and utilize its presence to strengthen German integration into the Western defense against communism. Although historians have evaluated the BAOR's role in Germany from a strategic and military perspective, the political and social contexts resulting from the presence of nearly eighty thousand British troops and their families during the early period of postwar German sovereignty have been largely neglected. This study considers not only the official contacts between the British armed services and the Germans but also the more individual levels of contact, including living conditions of troops, social interaction, and points of friction between soldiers and civilians.

The book argues that the success of the transformation of the BAOR from a force of occupation to a tool of integration depended on two factors: the receptiveness of the German population to the new role of the BAOR and the attitudes of the British military in conducting their new relationships with German civilians. It examines the German perceptions of the British armed services by analyzing hostile incidents between troops and civilians as well as comparing the popularity of the British military with that of the other occupying powers in the young Federal Republic of Germany. Furthermore, it seeks to establish the extent to which the widespread unwillingness of the British military to engage with Germans, evident in 1948, was transformed by the mid-1950s. This entails the analysis of the representation of Germany in British media and popular culture as an influence on troops in the BAOR as well as initiatives taken by the services themselves to improve relations.

The main findings of the book are that although significant changes were implemented by the British administration to improve relations, the BAOR was not an effective tool to strengthen the Anglo-German partnership. This was partly due to the organizational structure of the military but also due to a widespread reluctance by British troops to engage with the German population. Despite some local successes, the main achievement of the British and German administrations throughout the period in question was not an improvement but, rather, the prevention of a deterioration of relations between British servicemen and German civilians in a crucial period of German integration into the Western defense against communism.

ACKNOWLEDGMENTS

I would like to express my personal thanks to friends and colleagues at the University of Westminster who made invaluable suggestions, commented on parts of the text, or contributed in other ways, in particular Mark Clapson, Patricia Hogwood, Helen Glew, Tony Gorst, and Martin Doherty. I would also like to thank Richard Coopey for his advice and encouragement. Any errors that remain are entirely my own.

I am also grateful to librarians and archivists who assisted, especially the staff at the National Archives, Kew; the British Library Newspaper Archive at Colindale; Kirsten Hoffmann of the Landesarchiv Niedersachsen, Hannover; the Landesarchiv Nordrhein Westfalen, Düsseldorf; the Politisches Archiv des Auswärtigen Amtes, Berlin; the Bundesarchiv, Koblenz; the Mass Observation Archive, University of Sussex; the County Durham Record Office, Durham; the BBC Written Archive Centre, Reading; and the German Historical Institute, Holborn.

I furthermore owe gratitude for the friendly advice and support from a number of museums dedicated to the British armed services. I am particularly grateful to the staff of the Royal Engineers Museum, Gillingham; the National Army Museum, Chelsea; the Imperial War Museum, Southwark; the Royal Artillery Museum, Woolwich; and the Royal Signals Museum, Blandford Forum.

ABBREVIATIONS

BAFO	British Air Forces of Occupation
BAOR	British Army of the Rhine
CCG	Control Commission for Germany
CDU	German Christian Democratic Party (*Christlich Demokratische Union*)
COS	British Chiefs of Staff
CSU	Christian Social Union of Bavaria (*Christlich Soziale Union*)
EDC	European Defence Community
ERP	European Recovery Program
FO	British Foreign Office
FRG	Federal Republic of Germany
GDR	German Democratic Republic
GSO	German Service Organisation
ISD	Information Services Division (Foreign Office)
JSLO	Joint Services Liaison Officer
KPD	German Communist Party (*Kommunistische Partei Deutschlands*)
NA	National Archives
NAAFI	Navy, Army, and Air Force Institutes
NATO	North Atlantic Treaty Organization
NDR	Northern German Broadcasting Company (*Norddeutscher Rundfunk*)
NORTHAG	Northern Army Group (NATO)
NRW	North Rhine-Westphalia (*Nordrhein Westfalen*)

PLO	Press Liaison Officer
RAF	Royal Air Force
SPD	German Social Democratic Party (*Sozialdemokratische Partei Deutschlands*)
TAF	Tactical Air Force
TASS	Telegraph Agency of the Soviet Union (*Telegrafnoye agentstvo Sovetskovo Soyuza*)
UNESCO	United Nations Educational, Scientific, and Cultural Organization

THE BRITISH ARMY OF THE RHINE

INTRODUCTION

> If we are to give the Germans a sense of community with the
> West something more must be done by the Services than through
> purely professional contacts and cooperation. A real sense of
> community must be fostered not only at work but in normal
> human relationships as well.
> —J. M. Fisher, British Information Services, Bonn, to R.A.A. Chaput
>   de Saintonge, German Information Department, Foreign Office,
>   London, 16 March 1956

Like its predecessor after the First World War, the British Army of the Rhine
(BAOR) was stationed in Germany in 1945 as an army of occupation in
enemy territory. However, the advent of the Cold War, the creation of the
Federal Republic of Germany (FRG), and the establishment of the North
Atlantic Treaty Organization (NATO) in 1949 led the Rhine army to evolve
"into something quite different."[1] For the first time in the history of the
British army, the BAOR was now permanently stationed in Germany and
constituted the British contribution to the defense of Western Europe against
communism. This contribution brought not only British soldiers to the British Zone of Occupation but also thousands of their wives and children, who
often spent years living among the German population. At its peak in the
1950s the BAOR employed nearly eighty thousand troops in the British zone
of Germany.[2] This troop deployment included the British army as well as
the British Air Forces of Occupation (BAFO). This book focuses on the role
and experience of these BAOR troops in the Federal Republic of Germany.

The country these troops were stationed in transformed rapidly, from
the Nazi enemy of 1945 to a Cold War ally of the 1950s. At the Paris
Peace Conference in May 1952, West German sovereignty was officially
restored and the Allied occupation of the Federal Republic formally came
to an end. In the eyes of British foreign secretary Ernest Bevin, the role of
western Germany had very quickly changed from that of Britain's biggest
enemy in 1945 to that of a key ally against the much bigger threat of the
Soviet Union.[3] There was, however, considerable reluctance among sizeable
parts of the British public, as well as many members of both the Labour

and Conservative administrations, to put any trust in Germany, let alone a rearmed Germany, so soon after the Second World War. Nonetheless, despite a suspicious public and a very often German-phobic press, both Labour and Conservative governments aimed at improving relations with Germany, above all for the sake of the Washington-led defense of Europe against communism. As a consequence, the relations between the BAOR and the Germans came under intense scrutiny, as the British forces were now "stationed in Germany by agreement with a sovereign government and not by virtue of their victories in war."[4] According to the plans of British policy makers, the British Rhine army was to be turned into a means for strengthening the alliance between London and Bonn. The main function of this book is to analyze this attempt, which has been largely overlooked by historians, to utilize the BAOR in order to improve Anglo-German relations during the early Cold War.

This study provides an evaluation of the political and social impact of the British attempt to transform the BAOR from an occupation force of the defeated Nazi Germany to an alliance partner of the Federal Republic of Germany, which joined NATO as a full member in 1955. The book begins in 1948, when it became increasingly evident that the western zones of Germany would merge into a semi-sovereign state; it ends in 1957, when the generally good political, economic, and cultural cooperation that had been established between Britain and Germany in the decade after the war began to deteriorate. This deterioration was due to, among other factors, the question of British entry into the European Economic Community (EEC) and the German unwillingness to continue to cover the cost for the stationing of the BAOR.[5]

This work thus aims to establish the extent to which the BAOR, nearly eighty thousand strong by 1954 and geographically spread over the former British Zone of Occupation, provided an effective tool for the improvement of Anglo-German relations in a crucial period of the Cold War. The first part of this analysis focuses on the difficulties encountered by both the British and the German administrations during attempts to come to a better understanding between the BAOR and the German public. The second part considers the degree of success achieved in the political, economic, and individual contexts. It is important to shed new light on this key aspect of Anglo-German diplomatic, military, and social relations after 1945 and to evaluate its impact on the wider context of European integration after the Second World War.

As pointed out by Anne Deighton, a professor of European international politics, who has a particular interest in Anglo-German international relations after the war, it is hardly surprising that Germany was disliked by the majority of the British public and by "many elites in political life and in Whitehall for many decades to come."[6] This widespread antipathy was still strikingly evident as late as 1989 when the question of German unification arose.[7] "Popular representations of Germany even to this day are powerfully conveyed in Britain through the showing and reshowing of old Second World War films; the popular press needs very little prompting before it indulges in outbursts of chauvinistic attacks on Germany."[8] Caused by two world wars, this widespread unpopularity of Germany in Britain was particularly understandable in the decade or so after the Second World War. Many public and political figures had personal memories of war, and thousands had lost family members and friends. Still others had seen their homes, streets, and town and city centers damaged or destroyed by the Blitz.[9] Therefore it would be surprising if resentment toward the Germans was not also felt by many of the members of the British Army of the Rhine who were stationed in Germany after the war.

Yet despite all of this, by 1956, little more than a decade after the defeat of Nazi Germany, the British government had invested millions of pounds and considerable diplomatic efforts to achieve their aim of integrating the Federal Republic into the Western defense against communism. Although the main driving force behind such efforts came from Washington, DC, it was at least partly due to British diplomacy that the three West German Zones of Occupation received Marshall aid, and Britain's considerable military efforts helped to end the Soviet blockade of West Berlin. Furthermore, London played a key role in the creation of the new West German armed forces when the Korean War heightened the fear of a communist attack on Western Europe. It was also in large part due to British foreign secretary Anthony Eden's efforts that by 1955 Britain and West Germany were members of two formal alliances to defend Europe against communism: NATO and the Western European Union. Finally, for the first time in history, Britain stationed its troops—the BAOR—on German soil indefinitely as part of a combined Western European defense effort. There was therefore a remarkable inconsistency between government policy and at least parts of British public opinion.[10] Also, unsurprisingly, "the British press frequently reacted with incomprehension to government policy."[11] Caught between the two extremes, the BAOR would have to side with government policy rather than public opinion if it was to play its role in the process of transforming the relations between Britain and Germany from victor and vanquished to alliance partners. British concerns about political stability in the newly established Federal Republic and the financial burden the British armed services placed on the German population did not make the task of the BAOR easier, leaving the British services in Germany in a unique and challenging position.

Attempts by the civilian element of the British administration, the British Control Commission for Germany (CCG), to foster better relations between occupation troops and German civilians began soon after the war. Early initiatives ranged from the instructions given by the British military governor in Germany, Sir Brian Robertson, to British officials in Germany in 1947 to accept the Germans as a "Christian and civilized people," to an encouragement of contacts between German and British children. They also included joint participation in sports and games.[12] However, Robertson had no authority to force his views on the BAOR.[13] As a result, the army, at least initially, had very different ideas regarding fraternization, and three years after the cessation of hostilities, there was "no great desire evinced to associate much with Germans."[14] A key question is to what extent this reluctance was overcome between 1948 and 1957 among the various ranks of the BAOR and which attempts were made to transform the initial unwillingness of British personnel to engage with Germans. In this context it is important to consider the difference in attitudes between officers and ranks, regular soldiers and National Servicemen, as well as the army and the Royal Air Force (RAF). It is furthermore vital to consider the German perspective, as there was a marked contradiction in reactions to the armed forces by the German population. On the one hand, there were complaints from many quarters about the impact of the continuing occupation by foreign troops on housing shortages, maneuver damage, and crimes committed by soldiers. On the other hand, there was widespread fear of the consequences that a reduction of the same forces would lead to in the context of the Cold War. It is this striking disparity that requires further investigation.

British Aims and Expectations: The BAOR in Context

The main focus of this book is to examine the relationships between the military, political, and social contexts in which the BAOR operated. A successful demonstration of a new attitude toward the German population by the British forces arguably served as a useful contribution to a number of short- and long-term British security interests, with regard to both Germany itself and to the defense of Europe. This issue concerned both the military and the social contexts of relations between the BAOR and the Germans, as British military objectives in Germany were closely connected to the behavior and actions of British troops on the ground. The evaluation of the role of the BAOR's presence in the context of a number of key issues, including the rearmament of the Federal Republic, is therefore vital. A remilitarized Germany was considered a necessity by the chiefs of staff, even before the outbreak of the Cold War, but opposed by sizeable portions of both the British and German public. The BAOR also posed an easy target for anti-Western propaganda from both the left and right of the political spectrum in Germany.

Furthermore, the questions of British and German contributions to the European defense system as well as continued German payments for the upkeep of the large number of BAOR bases were issues that had an impact on the BAOR's position vis-à-vis the German population.[15] On the one hand, German participation in European defense eased Britain's burden by dividing the task of defending Europe among a larger number of contributors.[16] On the other hand, a rearmed and sovereign Federal Republic posed a threat to the continued German financial contribution to the upkeep of the BAOR, while making the task of controlling Germany potentially more difficult. Good relations between troops and Germans were important once West Germany had entered NATO and Britain had agreed to the first ever peacetime commitment for a permanent involvement of British forces on the European continent. This had been the decisive factor in convincing the French to accept German rearmament.[17] A hostile German population was a potential threat to continued German payment for the upkeep of the BAOR, as well as the stationing of the troops themselves as part of the European defense system. Hence the social context of public opinion was a uniquely important arena that intersected with military intentions.

The political context of this book examines the use of the BAOR to improve the relations between the British and German governments. Arguably the BAOR also constituted an important political asset for Britain. As previously noted, the political relationship between Britain and Germany changed from one of victor and vanquished to one of two sovereign states. By the early 1950s London attempted to use the BAOR to support the pro-Western government of the Federal Republic. British policy toward Germany was more aimed at British European interests, the containment of the Soviet threat, and the "special relationship" with the United States in general rather than the improvement of Anglo-German relations in particular.[18] However, in order to achieve these British aims of simultaneously controlling Germany and containing the Soviet Union, the BAOR was an important tool, and therefore friendly Anglo-German political relations were crucial. A negative image of British troops among the German population potentially played into the hands of those political forces in Germany, which were against a close alliance with the West, particularly after the release of Stalin's notes on German unification in March 1952. The role the BAOR played in the tense political climate of the early Cold War in Europe requires consideration here.

On a social level, which includes the values and perspectives, or the subjectivity, of the British soldier, this study aims at determining to what extent anti-German sentiment among groups and individuals in the BAOR might have hindered the process of Anglo-German reconciliation. Hostility toward Germany would be expected to be even stronger in the BAOR than among the general British public, as many British conscripts may have lived through the Blitz as children and many officers might have personally fought against the German *Wehrmacht*. British servicemen were also more likely than the rest of the population to show an interest in cultural products featuring the British war effort against Germany. Fictional literature and war films, produced in large numbers throughout the period in question and, as will be seen, popular among troops, would have particularly influenced their views. Perhaps unsurprisingly, one British Foreign Office paper argued as late as 1954 that "the attitude of the Forces in general and the Army in particular towards the German population has been unsatisfactory" and that more should be done to improve relations.[19]

It is these official efforts to facilitate better relations, taken at the different levels of the British administration in London and Germany due to the initial reluctance of the army to engage with Germans, that require investigation. The large number of bases all over the British zone in cities like Hamburg, as well as in more rural areas like Bielefeld, poses an opportunity to examine the relations between soldiers and civilians in various different social and geographical settings. Furthermore, different military leadership in different bases may have influenced relations between the BAOR and the Germans. It is important in this context to consider the RAF's contribution to the British military presence. The British forces in Germany also included the Second Tactical Air Force, which posed additional problems to local relations due to noise from low-flying aircraft and the use of bombing ranges in Germany. The example of the German island of Heligoland, which had been evacuated by the British in 1945 and used as a bomb target, was the most notorious case here.[20] The British forces also have to be evaluated in the context of the other occupying powers in Germany, particularly the Canadian, American, and French troops.

The BAOR as British ambassadors? Divisional brass bands parades such as this one by the 1st Battalion The Buffs (Royal East Kent Regiment) at Dortmund were often very popular with the German civilian population.

The BAOR in the Existing Literature and the Structure of This Book

Despite the significance of the subject there has been no publication focusing on the specific issue of the British Army of the Rhine and its potential role as a tool for the improvement of the newly found Anglo-German partnership and its relations with the Germans. It is striking, for instance, that in the historiography of the British army after 1945, the issue of conscription has attracted far greater interest than the presence of eighty thousand British troops in Germany.[21] As David French points out, there are two reasons for this lack of historical interest in the BAOR. Primary sources for the period after 1949 are relatively scarce, and, more important, since the BAOR "never actually embarked upon the war for which it prepared, historians have nothing dramatic to describe and analyze."[22] It is this lack of historiography, particularly with regard to the political and social aspects of the British military presence in the Federal Republic, that this book intends to address.

The first chapter of this book outlines the development of the BAOR in Germany during the period in question in terms of size and organization before analyzing its role in British policy toward Germany. Graham Watson and Richard Rinaldi's recent work makes a useful contribution to outlining changes in location of regiments and their organizational history.[23] When considering British occupation policy and the German reaction to it, both British and German publications cover the period between 1945 and 1949 in general in far more detail than they do the first half of the 1950s. This also applies to individual relations between Britons and Germans.[24] Likewise, the later period between 1955 and 1961 has been dealt with recently, for example, by Sabine Lee and Daniel Gossel.[25] Memoirs and biographies of high-ranking British and German diplomats and military personnel of the time provide some useful contributions on those aspects of occupation policy that are relevant to this study.[26]

Also explored in the first chapter of this book are the broader context of the Cold War, British military strategy, and the BAOR's role. Despite the obvious importance of Anglo-German relations in the context of the making of postwar Europe, generally the coverage of the bilateral political and cultural cooperation between 1948 and 1957 is relatively sketchy and has only recently begun to attract wider scholarly attention. This is partly because the significance of bilateral relations in postwar Europe was reduced by the increasingly close European-wide cooperation in the context of the Cold War. Anglo-German relations were particularly affected by this trend. Germany's desire for rehabilitation and supranational collaboration within the EEC also increasingly contrasted with Britain's focus on intergovernmental trade relationships envisaged by the European Free Trade Association (EFTA). As a result, neither considered "the partner across the Channel a top political priority."[27]

Regardless of how vital bilateral Anglo-German political relations were throughout the 1950s, from a military or security perspective there is a widespread consensus in the existing literature on the importance of the British contribution of forces to the Continent. In matters of security and defense policy, Britain aimed for a strong and united Europe to withstand communism, albeit in an Atlantic framework rather than a European one. Germany was a crucial factor in this regard.[28] Britain's unprecedented contractual commitment in October 1954 to station four divisions and a tactical air force on the Continent was arguably the only firm commitment of this kind in the entire history of Britain's postwar defense policy.[29] The various potential aims of the stationing of the BAOR in Germany have been touched upon in a number of publications on Britain's security and defense policy since 1945. Gottfried Niedhart points out that apart from being an advanced defense of the British Isles,[30] the BAOR increasingly constituted a vital tool for achieving the long-term goal of "*Sicherheit für Deutschland*" instead of "*Sicherheit vor Deutschland.*"[31] Beatrice Heuser's work on Britain, West Germany, and NATO shows that "Britain went further than any other country bar the USA by unilaterally committing forces to Germany." She demonstrates that the BAOR was to support the inclusion of "West Germany into the Western Union (recast to become the Western European Union) and into NATO."[32] Furthermore, Olaf Mager stresses the important fact that stationing the BAOR aimed far more at preventing a change of US defense strategy and a domestic destabilization of the FRG than calming French fears of a resurging Germany.[33] What has been neglected so far is the potential impact of relations between the BAOR and the Germans on attempts to achieve the above aims. In contrast, the closely related issue of German rearmament has been documented in great detail, most recently by Spencer Mawby. His work also covers the development of British policy toward the arming of West Germany, "from the entry into force of the Occupation statute in September 1949, up to the recruitment of the first volunteers at the end of 1955."[34]

It is important to highlight the controversies the BAOR created within the British administration when other interests clashed with the idea of using the armed services to foster Anglo-German relations. This entails an examination of the views of both the Labour and Conservative administrations of the new Germany in chapter 1. Anne Deighton's recent article on Britain's policy toward German rearmament demonstrates that when considering Britain's security policy, "the anti-German strand of opinion was more easily recognisable but less powerful for decision-makers than the imperial and post-imperial strand." As a result, "Cold War priorities for strategic reasons were stronger than anti-Germanism."[35]

The relationship between the BAOR and the British civilian administration in Germany in 1948 also requires further analysis. Patricia Meehan has demonstrated how the BAOR and the CCG, quickly nicknamed "Charlie Chaplin's Grenadiers" or "Complete Chaos Guaranteed" by the army, were soon just "as far apart from each other as from the Germans."[36] Furthermore, Meehan highlights that army personnel were generally reluctant to socialize with Germans and that according to the CCG, there had to be "re-education *of* the Army before you can start re-education of the Germans *by* the Army."[37]

The second chapter of this book examines the portrayal of Germany and its people in Britain in order to shed light on the views that would have influenced young Britons joining the BAOR. The focus is on media that are likely to have been encountered by young British men, such as the British press, nonfictional as well as fictional literature, and war films. The chapter also highlights the impact of grassroot level initiatives on the perception of Germany. Finally, it considers the impact of Germany's economic recovery on British opinion. With regard to cultural and more personal relations between the BAOR and the Germans, a number of relevant publications point to factors that potentially influenced the view of the general British public toward Germany and that of individual soldiers stationed in Germany. Sabine Lee, for example, highlights the anti-German feelings expressed by the Labour left with regard to British public opinion and parts of the press.[38] Furthermore, public opinion, at least in the early postwar years, mostly favored the Soviet Union due to the wartime alliance and the slow acceptance of the emerging Cold War.[39] Apart from useful works by Evgenios Michail and Ruth Wittlinger that highlight these broader trends in overall British public opinion on Germany,[40] a relatively large number of accounts of particular nongovernmental groups and prominent personalities (as opposed to general mass opinion) and their efforts toward and experiences with the Germans in the immediate postwar period can be found in secondary literature.[41] Many of the army conscripts going to Germany perhaps had a predefined opinion of Germany and its inhabitants. What Jill Stephenson terms the "peculiarities of British history" may have led many a Briton "to regard continental Europeans, with their border disputes, wars [. . .] and changes of political regime as unreliable, unenlightened and backward; [. . .] the implication is that there was a gaping gulf between the British way of life and European traditions and practices—without much doubt left about which is superior."[42]

This may certainly have applied to the period immediately after the Second World War. Walter Lippmann's *Public Opinion* (1929) highlighted that "for the most part we do not first see and then define; we define first and then see. In the great blooming, buzzing confusion of the outer world we pick out what our culture has already defined for us, and we tend to perceive that which we have picked out in the form stereotyped for us by our culture."[43] These stereotypes were to an extent furthered by the British film industry during the 1950s. For instance, Richard Falcon's article on the portrayal of Germans in British films points out that the "industry seemed largely preoccupied with appealing to audiences via heroic World War Two narratives."[44]

The focus of chapter 3 is on the German perspective of relations with the BAOR. It analyzes the changing expectations of and demands by the German civilian population as well as federal and *Land* (state) administrations during a period of fundamental changes in Anglo-German relations. Attempts to use the BAOR in order to undermine German cooperation with the West are scrutinized along with German efforts to counter these threats. Economic, political, and social contexts are explored here. Furthermore, relations between Germans and NATO soldiers of other allies are scrutinized in order to provide a comparison. When considering the occupation forces of the Western powers, the problems created by the presence of American troops have been highlighted by John Willoughby. His work focuses on the threat to US authority in Germany posed by the disorderly behavior of American troops and the resulting initiatives that prevented a deterioration of relations in the period between 1945 and 1948.[45]

Chapter 4 is an exploration of the BAOR's own attempts to adapt to the changing nature of Anglo-German relations between 1948 and 1957. This involves constraints caused by the organizational structure of the British armed services in Germany, the impact of service accommodation on levels of contacts, official attempts by military units to improve relations in local towns, and the experiences of individual officers and ranks. A comparison of RAF and army initiatives, as well as attempts to minimize negative publicity caused by incidents, is important here. Secondary source material on the official relationship between the British army and the Germans is limited and so far covers only the period immediately following the German surrender in May 1945. Patricia Meehan provides useful insight into this period and establishes that, unsurprisingly, relations got off to a rather cool start.[46]

Relatively few accounts of officers and conscripts in the BAOR and their experiences in Germany are available in secondary sources. John Ramsden provides insight into some individual experiences of British soldiers in Germany after 1945. He also points out that many British servicemen quickly replaced their anti-German attitudes with "a lighter vein of humour and tolerance," despite the army leadership's best efforts to prevent further fraternization.[47] Some servicemen found the Germans in some of the areas where they were stationed quite easy to get along with.[48] In addition, B. S. Johnson's collection of accounts comments on how boredom takes over in an army during peacetime conditions. This in itself, at least for some soldiers, was a motivating factor for fraternization.[49] However, most of the recollections of servicemen in Germany during the 1940s and 1950s tend to focus on army life rather than on the contacts made with the local German population. It is the latter aspect that this work aims to address.

Chapter 5 is titled "'How the army of a democratic nation should behave': The British Administration and the BAOR." It discusses the attempts by the administration in London and on the ground in Germany to influence the BAOR in order to use it as a tool to tie the Federal Republic into the Western system of defense. This includes the use of the BAOR to strengthen the Konrad Adenauer government, to promote British values, and to control Germany at a time of increasing independence of the young Federal Republic. To a large extent, it also involves mitigating problems created by the presence of the BAOR. This chapter, which constitutes the focal point of the study, examines the crucial period of the mid-1950s, when German sovereignty fundamentally changed both Anglo-German relations in general along with the position of the BAOR in Germany. Existing publications that prove useful for the exploration of these issues are scarce, but Yvonne Kipp's recent book presents for the first time an analysis of the British foreign secretary and later prime minister Anthony Eden's attitude and foreign policy toward Germany between 1951 and 1957 in its entirety, therefore providing a valuable addition to the wider topic addressed here.[50]

The concluding chapter evaluates the efforts made by the BAOR and the British administration to improve Anglo-German relations by utilizing the presence of the armed services. It also sheds light on whether German sovereignty did change the position of the BAOR vis-à-vis the German population and administration in the period immediately after Federal German sovereignty was established. Finally, the chapter answers the question of whether or not the BAOR was able to effectively adapt to serve its new policy purposes.

CHAPTER I

Britain, the Cold War, and the BAOR
Policy Makers, Strategy, and Organization

> We have never doubted that many of the bad old nationalistic
> elements in the community have survived. [. . .] However, it is
> not in Parliament that [they] do harm. It is on the street corners
> and in public meeting places that they work upon the humiliated
> pride and dormant brutality of the German people.
> —United Kingdom Delegation Brief, The London Conference,
>   May 1950

It was doubts about the reemergence of German nationalism among the British administration at the highest levels, as expressed in the brief cited above, that led to the consideration of using the BAOR as a force to foster democratic elements in Germany. However, these doubts also provide fascinating insights into the mind-sets of British policy makers. It is therefore important to shed light on some of the revealing attitudes of the highest-ranking staff of the Foreign Office in London and the British High Commission in Germany before progressing on to the armed services themselves and the initiatives introduced by the civilian administration in Germany to improve relations with the Germans. After all, it was these attitudes that helped to shape and implement British policy toward West Germany. Many members of the British civilian and military administration stationed in Germany at the time of the creation of the Federal Republic had had firsthand experiences with Nazi Germany before and during the war, and their approach toward the Bonn republic was heavily influenced by these experiences. It is important to consider the attitudes of some of the senior British personnel in Germany before moving on to mass public opinion and its impact on the British military in the next chapter. The antipathy toward German nationalism, combined with the determination to pursue a pro-German policy, influenced the British administration's view of the BAOR as both a factor and a potential problem for Anglo-German relations.

The second theme that emerges is that of the nature and development of the British troop commitment in Germany. British military strategy in the broader context of the Cold War, the organizational structure of the British military presence in Germany, and the adaption of the BAOR to political change in the context of Anglo-German relations are crucial elements to the understanding of how the armed services could be utilized as a tool for improved Anglo-German relations. After a brief outline of the wider strategic and military context of the Cold War, this chapter establishes the structure and responsibilities of the British civilian administration in Germany before addressing the question of what Foreign Office expectations of the BAOR's role in Anglo-German relations were prior to 1949. The analysis of the British administration and its relations with the BAOR and the Germans also considers the significant changes in the relation between occupiers and occupied resulting from the establishment of the Federal Republic. Finally, in order to understand the value of the BAOR as a tool for better relations between Britons and Germans, the political functions of the BAOR require analysis. This also entails an exploration of political controversies over the size of Britain's troop commitment as well as friction caused between different government departments over policy direction with regard to the BAOR.

Nazi Germany, the British Administration, and the Federal Republic

Despite the consistently pro-German policy Britain pursued in order to integrate Germany into the western alliance system, it is evident that many Foreign Office officials harbored the same fears, resulting from two world wars, of a return of German militarism that were common among the upper echelons of British society.[1] The Labour Foreign Secretary Ernest Bevin "hated the Germans and refused to visit Germany,"[2] whereas in 1949 the British high commissioner Sir Ivone Kirkpatrick commented on the German "truculence and arrogance which makes him impossible to deal with."[3] Anthony Eden had described the Germans as "brutish monsters beneath a veneer of civilisation" as early as 1919.[4] Ten years after the war, the British ambassador Sir Frederick Hoyer-Millar warned that "the German political consciousness is beginning to re-awaken," the sense of guilt for the war was faint, and the German character had not fundamentally changed. "The spirit of national egoism has, for a second time, survived defeat and occupation." Furthermore, the German character was "volatile and basically unstable."[5] Suspicions of the German character among the highest circles in London were certainly widespread and lasted well into the mid-1950s.

Kirkpatrick was aware of the difficult position of the British military in Germany. And he saw himself as someone who was uniquely well placed to understand the context in which the BAOR would operate. At this point it is worth considering his long-standing relationship with Germany and its people. During the First World War Kirkpatrick was wounded in action but then, at the age of only nineteen, found himself heading a ring of British spies in the Netherlands.[6] Having been employed by the Foreign Office since 1919, Kirkpatrick gained detailed knowledge of and insight into the workings of the fascist states of Italy and Germany during the interwar period. He served first in Rome and then in Berlin from 1933 to 1938. Moreover, he accompanied then prime minister Neville Chamberlain to the infamous meetings with Hitler during the 1938 Munich crisis. These meetings had filled him "with such a physical repugnance" that he unsuccessfully asked to be excused from having to attend any more sessions of the negotiations.[7]

Whatever his attitudes toward the Federal Republic were, they were undoubtedly influenced by his experience with Nazi Germany, as "this time proved the most formative part of his career."[8] According to his memoirs, in 1937 Kirkpatrick "was told with some truth that I must be prejudiced by dislike of Germany." In his view, "This was scarcely odd because the spectacle of a nation preparing ruthlessly to impose its will must be alarming and distasteful."[9] When war broke out again in 1939, Kirkpatrick initially resumed work in the field of intelligence and propaganda, which he had carried out in the Great War. His role in the European services of the British Broadcasting Corporation (BBC) led him to interview Adolf Hitler's deputy Rudolf Hess after the latter's misguided attempt at diplomacy had ended with a plane crash in Scotland in 1941.[10] From 1944 on he became one of the most experienced and distinguished members of the Foreign Office. He formed the British Element of the Allied Control Council, tasked with governing Germany after the war; served as political advisor to General Eisenhower; and in 1949 became head of the German section of the Foreign Office. This impressive rise through the ranks then culminated in the post of British high commissioner in Germany from 1950 to 1953 and head of the Foreign Office thereafter.[11]

The Allied High Commission in the Federal Republic, which Kirkpatrick headed, was based in the very hotel where Neville Chamberlain had stayed during the 1938 meetings with Hitler. A constant reminder of the past was that Kirkpatrick's office was in the same apartment where Chamberlain had stayed.[12] His views of the Federal Republic were just as much influenced by the past as by the present. On the one hand, his relationship with German chancellor Konrad Adenauer was very cordial, and, according to his memoirs, in 1953 Kirkpatrick found it "a wrench to leave Germany, where I had made many friends and [. . .] had been so intimately connected with every phase of the national life."[13] On the other hand, as mentioned above, in 1949 he had also commented on the "truculence and arrogance" that he considered part of the German character.[14] Furthermore, as late as 1959 Kirkpatrick believed "it would be folly to suppose that in no circumstances can Nazism, even if in a different form, ever raise its head in modern Germany."[15] It has to be noted that not all leading members of the British administration in Germany were as reluctant as Kirkpatrick to leave the past behind when dealing with the Germans. Particularly Sir Brian Robertson, the military governor and Kirkpatrick's predecessor as UK high commissioner, was instrumental in "guiding the social and democratic advancement of a future ally." Despite his experiences of two world wars, he formed a genuine friendship with Adenauer and tirelessly worked toward closer Anglo-German relations.[16] According to Lord Langford, "Adenauer was not a man who readily showed his emotions. But there was a break in his voice when he told me how much he would miss Brian Robertson. . . . He had found him a true friend of Germany."[17]

It is not surprising that many key members of the British administration tasked with fostering Anglo-German relations were themselves often doubtful whether the "German character" could ever be changed for the better. In many cases their personal contacts with Germans both before and during the war influenced their views in the postwar period. Naturally this had an impact on both the perception of the need for a tool such as the BAOR and the envisaged likeliness of its success.

British Military Strategy, the Cold War, and the Transformation of the BAOR

The dramatic events of the early Cold War period in Europe and the accompanying deterioration of relations between the two emerging blocs had a significant impact on British defense policy and therefore also led to changes in the size and role of the BAOR in Germany. The initial task of the BAOR in 1945, as in 1919, was to act as an army of occupation. Prior to the First World War the British army had been accustomed to "garrison the Empire, and only went onto the continent of Europe in wartime as expeditionary forces."[18] As a consequence, the army was a relatively small force that, in contrast to many of its European counterparts, did not regularly make use of conscription and fought many of its campaigns in far-flung parts of the empire rather than on the Continent. As Colin McInnes points out, "The two World Wars had proved the exception to the rule for both the Army's experience of war and its place in British defence policy" by forcing the British to engage "with well-armed, well trained, well-equipped and highly organised armies" in Europe, "fighting in mass campaigns involving hundreds of thousands of men."[19] When war ended, the army normally demobilized and returned to the task of policing the empire, and this desire to end conscription and disengage from Europe was certainly still evident after the Second World War. However, this is not what happened after 1945. Although the postwar period eventually did see the end of conscription and renewed involvement in Africa and Asia, the "focus was increasingly drawn towards Europe," and "the conflict that came to dominate defence policy and Army planning was that of a large-scale, high intensity war against the Soviet Union in Europe."[20] The nature of this new threat demanded that the army was in a constant state of readiness to strike at very short notice, and in order to guarantee this level of preparedness, Britain introduced peacetime conscription in 1948.[21] During this period British defense policy was forced to adapt to the advent of nuclear weapons and to extend its commitment in the increasingly unstable Middle East.[22] Of course large-scale demobilization of British soldiers in Germany did take place after 1945, due to strong pressure from the British Treasury to cut defense spending as quickly as possible. However, the occupation of Germany that was agreed on at the 1945 Potsdam Conference and, soon thereafter, the emergence of the Cold War prevented the disbanding of the British Expeditionary Force in Germany. The 21st Army Group instead became the British Army of the Rhine in August 1945.

In 1945 the BAOR consisted of "three corps districts with several divisions." Each corps was made up of up to 450,000 men and each division numbered up to 150,000 men. However, after the end of the war most British units were demobilized, and "by January 1947, the British troop presence was reduced to three divisions."[23] Only thereafter was the BAOR increasingly expanded and turned into a permanent military force in Germany. The 1947 National Service Act, introducing universal conscription in peacetime for an indefinite period for the first time in British history, meant that the ranks of the BAOR were now also filled with National Servicemen.

These young Britons made up for the shortfall in recruitment among regular soldiers after 1945.[24]

By May 1947, Whitehall, the British civil service, was convinced that the Soviet Union was "the potential enemy."[25] It was the task of Clement Attlee's Labour government to develop political and military strategies to counter this threat. Whereas military considerations involved "questions of strategy, bases and force levels," the political response focused on the creation of defensive alliances.[26] In a European context the first step in this process was the 1947 Anglo-French Treaty of Dunkirk. This treaty was extended in 1948, when Foreign Secretary Ernest Bevin created the Western Union, bringing together Britain, France, and the Benelux countries in the Brussels Pact. The alliance was given a more military character with the establishment of the Western Union Defence Organisation.[27] However, it was US involvement and the creation of NATO in 1949 that constituted the most important deterrent against communist aggression on the Continent.[28]

As David French points out, the "Attlee government never seriously considered that they might be able to roll back the tide of communism."[29] However, since British expectations were that the Soviet Union would be unable to launch a military attack on the West before 1957 due to the severe losses sustained in the Second World War and US superiority in nuclear weapons, the Soviet threat in Europe was perceived to be of a political and economic nature rather than a military one. As a consequence, until 1950, "Britain continued to give the Middle East the highest strategic priority, while Europe was only part of our overall strategy."[30] This overall defense strategy, with its main focus on the defense of the British Isles, "the maintenance of sea lines of communications and the defence of the Middle East," was reflected in a stagnation of troop numbers in Germany.[31] In 1947 the Imperial General Staff, the minister of defense, the secretary of state for war, and the secretary of state for air along with the military governor of the British Zone of Occupation therefore agreed that "the figure of about 55,000 should be regarded as the absolute minimum size of the Army which should be maintained in Germany in the foreseeable future."[32] However, even in 1947 this figure had been accepted by the military governor only "under great pressure. The need is really for larger forces."[33] Britain's containment policy in Europe during this period aimed at increasing the political strength of Western Europe rather than troop numbers.

Events such as the 1948 Czech coup and the Berlin blockade increasingly challenged the British perception of the Soviet threat in Europe not being primarily of a military nature. The Soviet Union successfully tested its first atomic bomb in 1949, and communism appeared to be spreading on a global scale. In June 1948 a communist-inspired insurgency erupted in Malaya, in

December 1949 the Chinese civil war ended in communist victory, and in February 1950 the new Chinese government signed a treaty with Moscow.[34] These developments in Asia had a direct impact on the BAOR and British strategic thought as to the defense of Europe. In March 1950 the chiefs of staff raised concerns over French morale in case of a Soviet attack and suggested a guarantee to the French that two British divisions would be sent to the Continent immediately should war break out. Soon thereafter they argued that "the defence of the UK required holding the enemy on a line as far east in Europe as possible."[35] This was a clear break from the earlier plan to counter the Soviet forces in Europe with only "about two divisions and a tactical air force of some 141 aircraft," and partly in response to pressure from Britain's allies, London agreed to increase its armed forces in Germany.[36] As a consequence, the number of troops in Germany would now be determined by two factors. The first was to "support the prestige and authority of Military Government in the British Zone of Germany." The second was "to act as part of the covering force behind which the military resources of the Western Union can be mobilised in the event of war with Soviet Russia."[37] Although the importance of nuclear weapons for military planning increased considerably during this period, the Labour government nonetheless assumed that conventional ground troops would continue to play the decisive role in a European conflict in the foreseeable future. The main responsibility for a counterattack against the Soviet Union therefore rested on the British army and the RAF.[38]

It is this context that explains the expansion of the BAOR, which in January 1948 "totaled 11 armoured regiments and 14 infantry battalions (exclusive of those in Berlin)."[39] British troop strength in Germany rose steadily thereafter, particularly following the outbreak of the Korean War in June 1950. The impact of the Korean War was significant, as it led to the transformation of NATO from merely a political alliance to a military one, headed by General Eisenhower as "the alliance's first Supreme Allied Commander in Europe (SACEUR)."[40] The rapid development of nuclear weapons on both sides of the Iron Curtain also further changed military strategy. Earlier plans to withdraw from the Continent and then launch a repeat of the Allied invasion of Normandy in 1944 were now obsolete because the danger of a nuclear attack on the invading forces was considered too great. Troop numbers on the Continent therefore had to be increased in order to prevent the Red Army from overwhelming the Allied forces until reinforcements arrived, and the BAOR "had to be held in a higher state of readiness" due to the envisaged speed of a Soviet attack.[41] This shift in Britain's defense strategy led to the increase of troop numbers on the Continent from two to four divisions by 1952.[42] The rise coincided with the increase of the US military presence in Germany from one to five divisions as a result of NATO's new "forward strategy."[43] Whereas in September 1950 there were 44,000 British personnel in Germany, this number increased to 50,000 by December and to 52,000 by January 1951. Numbers thereafter grew by an average of 5,000 per month up to April and reached 65,000 by July 1951. The US contingent now stood at 81,000.[44] At the same time, the total number of French troops in Germany was 55,000. Allied troops therefore amounted to a combined total of 186,000 "as against an estimated total of 320,000 Soviet troops in the Soviet zone of Germany."[45] It was primarily conscription that allowed for this expansion of the BAOR. Despite the Labour government's commitment to reduce defense expenditure by withdrawing from expensive overseas commitments, the threat of a Soviet invasion of the Continent and the subsequent need for a large army hampered these efforts. The rearmament program launched to fight the Korean War placed further strains on the British economy, and the negative impact of rearmament on postwar economic recovery contributed to the downfall of the Labour government in 1951. Unsurprisingly, the incoming Conservative administration was determined to cut defense expenditures, and the reduction of the size of the BAOR was part of this plan.[46]

The Queen's birthday parade 1957 at Wuppertal, attended by large numbers of soldiers and civilians, was a highly visible demonstration of the British military presence at its peak.

At its peak in 1956, the BAOR was made up of four divisions containing twenty-one battalions of infantry and sixteen armored regiments, totaling seventy-seven thousand troops.[47] However, by this time the British military believed that West German membership of NATO and German rearmament would enable Britain to implement the troop reduction demanded by the Treasury. As early as 1952 the chiefs of staff had "emphasized deterrence over defence in Europe," and "priority was therefore accorded to nuclear weapons."[48] This shift away from conventional forces toward nuclear deterrence added a strategic element to the economic argument for the withdrawal of parts of the BAOR. Particularly the advent of American hydrogen weapons suggested that "the *military* importance of our forces on the Continent" was considerably diminished and that the threat of a limited conflict in Europe appeared increasingly unlikely, making the BAOR an exclusively political force.[49] It is this context that made the idea to use the BAOR as a political tool for Anglo-German rapprochement increasingly plausible.

Britain's worldwide defense commitments continued to negatively affect an already struggling economy. Declining levels of trade with the empire and the lack of competitiveness with the rapidly recovering European economies in general and the Suez debacle and the sterling crisis of 1957 in particular led to an increasing determination to significantly cut the number of troops in Germany.[50] Bonn's growing reluctance to foot the bill for Allied troops in Germany further exacerbated British financial difficulties. A significant reduction in military spending now appeared unavoidable and "the commitment to maintain 77,000 men on the continent was by 1956 looking increasingly untenable."[51] In 1957 the government also announced the end of National Service, with no more call-ups after 1960. In line with the overall reduction of British forces worldwide, the "BAOR was to be reduced from 77,000 men in 1957 to about 44,900 men by 1963."[52] This drastic step, however, was met with a barrage of opposition from Britain's European allies, which led to a significant reduction of the planned cuts of the BAOR. One of the main reasons for the resistance to British troop reductions was the unexpectedly slow pace of German rearmament. The Germans themselves were likely to regard troop reductions as a sign of waning British commitment to the defense of the Federal Republic. There were also fears among Britain's European allies of a "nuclearization of NATO."[53] As a result, the now all-volunteer BAOR only saw a reduction in size to approximately 55,000 men by 1959. Despite strong economic and strategic arguments in favor of a significant troop reduction, "alliance politics mitigated against this," and it was only in the following decades that more significant reductions were achieved.[54]

Although never considered strong enough by the commanders in chief to successfully stop a Soviet attack on western Germany, the BAOR significantly grew in numbers during the period in which a war scenario similar to that in Korea appeared the most likely. This increase in size was in part politically motivated, as French and American troop contributions were directly connected to the British commitment in Germany. Above all, the BAOR was an expression of the political will to defend the Federal Republic, regardless of military realities. "Germany has to be convinced of the growing strength of the West and its ability to defend her on the Elbe," and "the reinforcement of troops and provision of heavy equipment suitably deployed and in evidence" was to be the visible proof of British determination.[55] Once the immediate threat of a conventional war in Europe receded, the BAOR was mainly used as a political tool in a European context but, as the following chapters demonstrate, above all, on an Anglo-German level. It was the organizational structure of the armed services and their widespread physical presence throughout the entire British zone that turned it into a resource for establishing close contacts with the population of its host country.

The Organizational Structure of the BAOR

Although known as the British Army of the Rhine, the area of the BAOR occupation "extended well beyond the Rhine into northwest Germany."[56] The organizational structure of the BAOR was constantly fluctuating due to the changing size and role of the armed services. The number of principal garrison cities in Germany exceeded twenty-five, which were spread throughout the two federal states, or *Länder,* of North Rhine-Westphalia and Lower Saxony.[57] The BAOR headquarters were relocated twice, first to Bad Oeynhausen in North Rhine-Westphalia, and then, in October 1954, to Rheindahlen near Mönchen Gladbach. The division into administrative districts of the BAOR area of operation also varied considerably over time. In 1948 the area the British military controlled was divided into two separate entities—Hamburg District and Hannover District. Rhine District, initially the third component, had been transformed into headquarters for Rhine army troops in 1947.[58] However, this organizational structure was adapted to the growth in size of the BAOR as well as the advent of NATO, and the "Rhine District seems to have reappeared by 1952, along with a new Lübbecke District."[59] Yet by 1957, when troop reductions were under way, all districts had been merged, leaving only the Hannover and Rhine districts. The BAOR's main supply headquarters were located at Düsseldorf, and its communications headquarters were at Emblem in Belgium.

Troops relocating to Germany passed through Emblem to be dispersed to their various bases. Since the BAOR was now under NATO command, it was commanded by a four-star general based in Rheindahlen, which also served as the headquarters of the RAF.[60] The three armored divisions of the BAOR were spread over twenty different locations throughout North Rhine-Westphalia and Lower Saxony. The increase in size of the BAOR in the wake of the Korean War led to the creation of a new division (11th Armored) in September 1950. The 6th Armored Division was formed in the United Kingdom in 1951 as a reserve, but due to the aforementioned strategic changes, which demanded a larger troop presence to prevent the Soviets from overrunning West Germany and France, it was relocated to Germany in 1952.[61] During this period from 1951 to 1956, when the BAOR was at its peak in terms of its size, it was made up of four divisions and nine brigades.[62] Although this constituted a considerable increase in numbers, in the mid-1950s these BAOR divisions essentially still employed much of the same equipment and organization that was used to defeat Nazi Germany ten years earlier. The reduction of the size of British forces in Germany announced in 1956 led to the disbanding of the 6th Armored Division and a complete reshuffling of the remaining units, resulting in the BAOR being made up of the 2nd Division, 4th Division, and 5th Division by 1958.[63]

As the military requirement for the BAOR throughout its existence was constant readiness for a Soviet attack, frequent exercises took place all throughout the British zone. The physical presence of the armed services in the British zone was further highlighted by regular patrols of the border with East Germany from 1949 on. This, together with the frequent reorganization of the forces and their high number of garrisons, provided for regular contacts with the local population.

The British Administrative Presence
in Germany before 1949

Up until 1949 the effort to use the BAOR as a tool for German integration was largely led by the Control Commission for Germany (CCG). This division of the British presence in Germany into civilian and military elements, and the resulting internal organizational problems between the BAOR and the CCG, promised to constrain the integrative ability of the BAOR, quite apart from any problems arising over contact with local Germans. After the cessation of hostilities, the CCG, under the auspices of the Foreign Office, soon took over governing of the British zone from the army, and, although ultimately responsible to the secretary of state for war, a junior minister was appointed to oversee the administration "of an organisation approaching some 50,000 members."[64] John B. Hynd, Labour MP for Sheffield and chancellor of the Duchy of Lancaster, headed the newly established Control Office for Germany and Austria from October 1945 until April 1947.

It was the organizational structure of the CCG that led to widespread resentment toward the civilian administration among members of the BAOR from the very beginning of the occupation. Although the CCG was initially organized along similar lines to the British Civil Service, it had to adapt in order to coordinate its activities with those of the services, as it was now tasked to participate in a military occupation. As a consequence, all CCG employees in Germany were provided with an "honorary military rank." "A former private or corporal might return to Germany with the equivalent rank of warrant officer and the right to claim equivalent privileges."[65] The fact that it was now also possible for civilians who had spent the war at home to receive higher ranks, better pay, and better accommodation than soldiers who had fought their way through Germany created hostility. This quickly resulted in the two British presences in Germany being "almost as far apart from each other as from the Germans."[66] As late as 1948 the CCG complained that "all efforts made by CCG to meet the Services, and to invite their interest and co-operation, have all too often met with a cold and uncompromising reception."[67] Attempts by the British civilian administration to impose its will on the BAOR and change the army's relation with the Germans was therefore beset with difficulties from the outset. This became evident when early CCG attempts at reeducation of German civilians in Britain were hampered by the BAOR. The Foreign Office sent selected Germans on training courses to England and asked the army to accommodate these people in Hannover while waiting for the train to the Hook of Holland. The BAOR refused point-blank and would not be influenced—even by the Foreign Office—as it was "considered highly undesirable that Germans should be accommodated in a transit camp with Service personnel, from a disciplinary, security and morale point of view."[68]

During the early period of occupation up to 1948 the CCG was increasingly pushing for closer contacts between the British and Germans in order to promote democratic reeducation, whereas the army was consistently dragging its feet. Soon after 1945 the CCG drew up plans to reeducate the German population with the goal of eliminating Nazism and fostering democratic thinking. In May 1947 the new attitude toward the Germans was officially communicated in an instruction stating that British personnel should treat the Germans as members of the "Christian and civilized race [. . .] whose interests in many ways converge with our own and for whom we have no longer any ill-will."[69] Once again the army had different views on this issue. An army document regulating social contacts with Germans in 1947 began by defining Germans as "all persons, who, during the war, lived in Germany of their own free will" before adding "there will be no entertainment of Germans for purely social reasons by units in Messes or Clubs."[70]

The pace of reconciliation was to increase once it became clear the western zones would emerge into a semi-sovereign state in 1949 and the end of Allied authority drew closer. The civilian administration now deemed it necessary to use all personnel, including the armed services in the British zone, to foster Anglo-German relations. So as early as 1948 the CCG "examined in great detail all fields of potential Army-German association—social, sporting, educational and welfare—with a view to producing practical proposals by which the Rhine Army can assist the CCG in its task of re-educating the Germans."[71] Crucially, in early 1948 the army command finally accepted, at least in principle, the necessity of gradually changing its approach toward the German population. According to the regional commissioner of North Rhine-Westphalia, "The Army Commander had decided that closer contact with the Germans was now desirable and that he proposed to set an example in this direction himself."[72] It was therefore noted with relief by the CCG "that Rhine Army policy is now positive."[73] However, because of the initially hostile attitude of the British forces toward closer relations, the CCG now considered it essential to implement changes carefully and only gradually, especially when considering social matters. "It is probable that there is some resentment on the German side."[74] The task of turning the BAOR into an asset for Anglo-German relations was clearly going to be a difficult one for the Foreign Office.

It was this formal and organizational approach dictated by the CCG that was to dominate early BAOR efforts. It was unrealistic to convince the BAOR to take any radical steps. The reluctant attitude of the British military was still very much evident at this point, as they claimed it was "unwise too rapidly to turn on the tap of closer relations."[75] They also expressed reservations that sudden efforts to improve relations might lead to projects that would soon turn into failures due to lack of interest on both sides, thereby damaging rather than helping British efforts. The CCG regarded as typical "the Army attitude that the Germans might well become suspicious, if a sudden, wholesale and too wide opening of doors became apparent."[76] Whereas a more gradual and planned opening of those doors over a period of time was considered to be the right answer by the BAOR, the British administration's view of the matter and also army attitudes differed considerably. The CCG considered that, apart from unsatisfactory army attitudes, regulations and a general lack of awareness of the problems in Germany prevented a quickening of the pace of reconciliation. At this point the CCG view of the British armed services warrants closer analysis.

The Control Commission View of the Army before 1949

As established above, the British civilian administration often took a critical view of the early army approach toward the Germans. Doubts about the value of the BAOR as a tool of rapprochement centered on army regulations, the fact the armed services had no time to spare due to their military duties, the language barrier, and lack of motivation as well as attitude. The attitude of army officers was, according to the CCG, one of "uncertainty in their 'off parade' relations with Germans."[77] It was evident that many officers had no interest in establishing contacts with Germans, and if this was to change, a considerable transformation of attitudes and the provision of facilities for informal contacts was required. Once again, the army had its own views here.

To a certain extent regulations rather than attitudes were to blame for the lack of contact. In order to ensure proper conduct, the only place where a British officer was permitted to entertain a German person was at a married couple's home. If an officer met "a German in the course of business he was not allowed to offer a drink, a meal or even a chair outside of the office."[78] As there was very little social contact in 1948, particularly between officers and Germans, all commanders now apparently agreed that a start had to be made. However, the army was rather selective in its approach. For military and security reasons all efforts had to be subject to initially being strictly formal, German guests "being 100% screened and informal parties in Messes being regarded as unsuitable at present."[79] The importance of ensuring that only "good Germans" were invited to officers and sergeants messes was considered vital because of the fear that "the respectable was mixed with the black market."[80] This strong emphasis by the army on "screening" guests certainly resulted in a few raised eyebrows at the CCG.[81] Nonetheless, the army continued to insist that married families were the best means to develop closer relations. Contacts between British servicemen and German families (or the increasing number of British families and German civilians) were to prevent morally questionable connections between troops and civilians. The result of the slow change of army attitude was the drawing up of very detailed plans by the CCG to encourage the British services to use all available means to improve relations, ranging from sports, youth clubs, voluntary teaching of English in German schools, cycling, and hiking to the lending of army equipment to Germans.

However, despite the BAOR's newfound willingness to cooperate, neither the plan to reeducate German civilians nor the use of the British armed services toward this aim was met with universal praise among CCG staff. The deputy regional commissioner of CCG Hamburg pointed out his abhorrence at the term "reeducation" with regard to the German population, saying, "It is patronising, and is one of the reasons for resentment on the German side."[82] He also emphasized that he believed it was most important to launch a program to thoroughly educate the army itself before even considering involving the military in projects to improve relations. The CCG had clearly made attempts to highlight the existing problems in Germany to the British armed services, "but I am sure we have not even scratched the surface."[83] Approaches to Germans also had to be developed slowly without applying pressure on individual units, as this would stand in the way of developing genuine and spontaneous contacts. Exchanges would therefore "inevitably be patchy, slow and with many failures." Above all, in the commissioner's opinion, "there still exists, far too generally, the view that in all spheres we can instruct the poor benighted Germans, a tendency to consider them as uncivilised Africans."[84]

Thus it was obvious to at least some Foreign Office staff that an immediate change of attitude of the BAOR toward the Germans would be difficult to achieve successfully. However, a significant reduction in the size of the CCG had to be anticipated after 1949, which meant that "in day to day business the Army will come into more direct contact with Germans."[85] The main problem for the CCG was therefore that it first had to convince the services to genuinely assist their efforts and then thoroughly brief them about their aims and the obstacles to overcome. "It really amounts to a re-education of the Army before you can start re-education of the Germans by the Army."[86] Even if the army was willing to help, the main problem was that it was already fully engaged in its military duties. The CCG was pessimistic with respect to both attitude and education of the BAOR considering "how little even Field Officers know of our aims and activities and how apathetic the troops are towards them."[87]

It is evident that before the establishment of the Federal Republic of Germany the Foreign Office saw much room for improvement not only of army attitudes toward the Germans but also of relations between the BAOR and the CCG, referred to by the BAOR as "Charlie Chaplin's Grenadiers" or "Complete Chaos Guaranteed."[88] The impending departure of the CCG therefore provided a potential opportunity for improving relations between the armed forces and the Germans. Although the CCG exercised a moderating influence on strategic errors by the BAOR, this was outweighed by the strained relations between the two organizations. The withdrawal of the

CCG, combined with the creation of the Federal Republic, fundamentally changed the military's relationship with both the British administration as well as the Germans.

In the light of army attitudes, the initial long-term aims of the first CCG-inspired efforts to utilize the BAOR developed in 1948 were modest. This was partly because of the early BAOR refusal to cooperate with the CCG and partly because of perceived German hostility toward British service personnel. First steps to establish contacts included, on the social side, formal mess parties; the acceptance of approved Germans, informally or as guests in British clubs; and the provision of facilities for mutual entertainment in restaurants, cinemas, and operas. Print material was also considered from an early stage. A daily newspaper, "delivered on the breakfast table, might be produced summarizing varying daily German political speeches and news, and 'united' with forthcoming British sport and entertainment, crossword puzzles, etc."[89] In order to overcome the language barrier between troops and civilians, the CCG envisaged financial rewards for passing tests on the German language. It was deemed unlikely that "the right kind of social progress would ever be made except in cases where a nucleus of the British taking part were prepared to do battle with the German language."[90]

From the outset the new CCG initiatives ran into difficulties. For instance, the army was fully employed and could not provide enough resources. Particularly the officers who would have to lead the move toward better understanding appeared unwilling or unable to make time, and therefore the CCG did not regard any forced measures as likely to succeed. Further-more, in almost all projects the obstacle of facilities cropped up—food, accommodation, transport, and, to a lesser extent, language. There was a reported lack of interest in Anglo-German discussion groups, and Germans often found it difficult to be admitted to British cinemas. German classes were generally not well attended. Initial army enthusiasm displayed at the highest levels, once the decision for cooperation with the CCG was made, was evidently still muted among the lower ranks. The envisaged solution to these problems was that the approaches to be used by the army should be planned on a two- or three-year basis in order to allow for long-term planning.

The CCG itself often stood in the way of promoting its own initiatives, as contacts that were considered too close with Germans could still have significant negative consequences for staff employed by the Foreign Office itself. In May 1948 the regional commissioner of Schleswig-Holstein voiced his disapproval of the way British officials who married German women were treated.[91] He quoted the case of one official who, as a consequence of marrying a German, "was threatened with transfer to another Region," only to be "refused by that Region." He also pointed out that officials married to Germans could not be transferred to Frankfurt owing to American attitudes about fraternization. The military governor replied that although "security was the only criterion for the treatment of an official who married a German," dependent on the position held by staff, "it might be necessary either to transfer him or to dispense with his services."[92] Clearly the CCG was not always leading by example when fostering closer Anglo-German relations.

The prospects for a rapid improvement of relations between the British armed services and the Germans in 1948 due to Foreign Office initiatives appeared bleak. A lack of resources, a lack of personnel, and a lack of motivation on the British side were difficult enough for the civilian administration to overcome. In addition, instead of being able to focus on these issues and improve Anglo-German relations, a number of more serious issues, such as requisitioning, maneuver damage, and incidents of misbehavior, threatened to cause a deterioration of relations rather than an improvement. Moreover, as will be discussed in chapter 2, the BAOR provided plenty of ammunition for communist anti-Western propaganda. An intensification of efforts was therefore inevitable if any improvements were to be achieved. Fostering an interest in German affairs among British soldiers was one such approach.

The British Administrative Presence in Germany after 1949

Anglo-German relations entered a new phase with the establishment of the Federal Republic in May 1949. This had significant consequences for the position and role of the BAOR. Negotiations with a semi-sovereign state now replaced orders, the armed services soon were the largest British presence in Germany, and the British Control Commission for Germany was now wound up with increasing speed. In its stead, the British representative at the level of the federal government was now the high commissioner, replacing the military governor. By 1950 the High Commission employed six thousand members of staff in Germany who were scattered across that country's entire British zone. It was made up of the "secretariat" as well as "the political, economic, financial, legal and manpower committees." Other notable divisions included the police division, the intelligence division, and the information and education services.[93] The functions and responsibilities of these various levels of the UK High Commission covered most aspects of life in Germany. One of many important functions of the High Commission was to negotiate between the British military and the German authorities and people and, at the same time, to "create and maintain the correct relations between them."[94]

The high commissioner was represented by *Land* commissioners (formerly regional commissioners) at the German state level who cooperated closely with the "four *Land* governments, resident officers in the garrison towns and observers in the French and American zones."[95] In the smallest German administrative units (*Kreis*), British resident officers were responsible for a group of Kreise. Since most of these officers had been in their position for a number of years, they had accumulated an extensive knowledge of local politics, conditions, and people as well as speaking fluent German.[96] Their value became evident by comparing the position with that of their predecessor, the Kreis detachment commander. In many cases both posts were filled by the same person, but the Kreis detachment officer in 1946 "was the local Military Governor with almost unlimited power, who was not permitted to have any official social relations with the Germans or the local government bodies within his district," whereas the resident officer of 1948 lived among the German communities "with little or no direct authority." Instead his role focused exclusively on the establishment and maintenance of close relations on both official and unofficial levels. According to the CCG, the value of the resident officers' status as accepted members of the German communities could not be exaggerated.[97] Apart from advising the British forces, they acted as negotiators in political and social matters arising between those forces and the German authorities and civilians at a local level.[98] British resident officers were now also at pains to distance themselves from former military government attitudes. From now on, Land commissioners and resident officers would no longer give orders to Germans. The question was how the army would adjust to this new attitude.

One effect of the introduction of the 1949 Occupation Statute of Germany was that many of the British services' requirements that were previously obtained by orders now became the subject of negotiation through the Allied High Commission. On all levels Foreign Office officials consistently dealt with the issue of relations between service personnel and the Germans and exercised their executive powers in the few fields still reserved for the Allies after 1949. Although the Occupation Statute had reserved some rights for the Allies "and there was even something resembling an Allied government," these were now matched by the constitutional rights of the Federal Republic.[99] Despite the supreme Allied authority, Federal German reality soon led to the transfer of further rights to the Germans.[100] This was clearly a potential source for misunderstanding and serious trouble, as everything the British armed services required or did in Germany had an impact on the German people or the German economy. Furthermore, the services were now by far the largest visible sign of the occupation of Germany at the time of a change of status from "an occupation to a non-occupation regime."[101] It was therefore extremely important to carefully convey to the German people and the German authorities the actions and requirements of the armed services, which, as will be shown in chapter 5, the British Foreign Office duly set out to achieve.

The BAOR as a Factor in British Policy toward Germany

Regardless of the British attempts to use the British armed services to improve Anglo-German relations, the presence of the BAOR was a constant factor in the political affairs between the two countries. At this point it is worth considering some of the political functions of the BAOR that were not necessarily aimed at the improvement of the dialogue between Britain and Germany but nonetheless had an impact. For instance, in 1949, the year of the establishment of the Federal Republic, the British high commissioner Sir Ivone Kirkpatrick argued that unpopular British measures, combined with the handing over of responsibilities to the Germans, made the presence of the BAOR crucial to the successful rebirth of Germany:

> The possibility of serious trouble such as a general strike is a real one. This would stretch the Army to its limits even under present strength. The Germans are cynical and increasingly nationalist and hopeless in their utterances. Our policy of making Western Germany an eventual partner in [the] Western Union is threatened by German lack of faith in this Union. The Germans are already alarmed by talk that the Western countries will "stand on the Rhine." They fear that Germany will be abandoned if war threatens and that therefore we are not sincere in our efforts to restore the German economy.[102]

Even before the establishment of the Federal Republic in September 1949, the military governor of the British zone in Germany, Brian Robertson, reacted rather unfavorably to a proposal by the chief of the Imperial General Staff, Field Marshal William Slim, to cut the strength of the BAOR to fifty thousand men. According to Robertson, doing so would undermine the armed forces' ability to perform their two main functions. In Robertson's view, the first function, "to support the prestige and authority of Military Government in the British Zone," was particularly important in 1949, when the establishment of a West German government would coincide with the implementation of a number of highly unpopular Allied policies that could potentially stretch the BAOR to its limits.[103] These included reparations, the creation of the International Ruhr Authority, and frontier rectifications. Such measures potentially allowed for "communist propaganda and nationalist tendencies" to inflame public opinion, and this danger of growing anti-British sentiment due to communist agitation was taken very seriously in both London and Bonn. Furthermore, a reduction of troop numbers would arouse suspicion among a pessimistic and hopeless western German population that fully expected war with the Soviet Union and knew that neither they themselves nor the Western Allies would be able to defend them. Robertson concluded with the somewhat pessimistic view that the Allied forces in Germany were too weak to carry out their second main function—namely, to prevent the Red Army from overrunning western Germany and to allow the military resources of the Western alliance to mobilize behind the front lines in the event of war. The reduction of British forces on the Continent would seriously undermine the aim of convincing France and the Low Countries to increase their troop contributions.[104] Although the BAOR was to act as a tool to improve Anglo-German relations, it was considered just as vital an instrument to police the British zone as well as guarantee British interests in Germany vis-à-vis both the Germans and the Soviets. These tasks led to the BAOR coming under increased scrutiny from the Germans.

In a report on his recent visit to Germany in January 1951, the parliamentary undersecretary, Ernest Davies, commented on the German "lack of confidence in the ability of NATO to hold the line of the Elbe in case of a Soviet attack." He encountered widespread suspicion that the Allies had no intention to fight the Red Army at the eastern border of the Federal Republic but instead would "immediately withdraw to the left bank of the Rhine, thus leaving German troops to cover their retreat." Therefore, the German participation in the Western alliance could only result in "great physical destruction with no purpose."[105] German mistrust was also sustained by the continuation of the occupation regime, the consequent lack of German equality, and the Allied refusal to lift restrictions on German industrial production. "Restrictions not significant in themselves had become symbolic of the contradictory nature of the policy of the occupying powers, who on the one hand asked for a German contribution to the defence of the West and on the other imposed restrictions which made this more difficult." On the one hand, there were frequent demands—for example, by the German Social Democratic Party (SPD) leader, Kurt Schumacher—to be given assurances and evidence that large numbers of Allied troops would be stationed in Germany to defend the country while Germany rebuilt its own military. On the other hand, the burgomaster of Hamburg, Max Brauer, complained that "the Occupation was unduly extravagant" and that the occupation authorities were "still occupying an undue proportion of accommodation and other facilities."[106] Ernest Davies therefore considered it necessary to convince the Germans of the Allied determination to achieve a number of aims. These included a growth in military strength and the ability to defend the Federal Republic on the Elbe rather than the Rhine; the removal of restrictions on industry that was useful for defense; an immediate end to dismantling; an end to the bombing of Heligoland; the transition from the Occupation Statute to a contractual agreement along with the production of evidence of cuts in occupation costs; and the cessation of any extravagant use of accommodation.[107]

This view was supported by Kirkpatrick, who in a letter to the Foreign Office demanded that the Allies "take stock of our position." As Kirkpatrick saw it, the Western Allies were encouraging western Germany "to join the community of western nations as soon as possible as a free and equal member" and were working hard to accelerate this process. Kirkpatrick urged the permanent undersecretary, Sir Donald Gainer, to reflect on whether this policy was realistic, considering the manner in which individual British aims and demands consistently undermined the overall aims of foreign policy:

> For example, I do not see—quite apart from any defence contribution which I do not believe is round the corner—how we can bind Germany effectively to the west if the Air Ministry insists on bombing Heligoland; [. . .] public opinion wishes to be tough over the war criminals; [. . .] industrial restrictions are maintained; supreme authority is expressly reserved to the Allies in Germany, etc. etc. We could get away in my view with one or more of the above blots on our general policy, but I do not believe that we could tie Germany to the West if we insist on all our desiderata, since the cumulative effect is to undermine confidence in the belief that we do intend in a measurable distance of time to accept Germany as a free and equal member of our community.[108]

Problems in relations between the British troops and the German population were compounded by the financial costs to Germany caused by the occupation. As Ernest Bevin pointed out to Labour Prime Minister Clement Attlee, these costs included "labour, accommodation, communications, travel within Germany, stores and supplies and the Deutschmark drawings of the Occupation Forces." The overall cost of the British occupation for the year 1948, all of which had been covered by the Germans, amounted to just under £120 million, and the figure for western Germany as a whole, including Berlin, stood at £290 million. These German funds supported "approximately 270,000 Allied troops and 10,000 Allied Control Commission personnel and their dependants." The "admittedly inadequate Occupation Forces and the High Commission absorb something like five per cent of the German national income."[109] This burden on the German taxpayer was to increase considerably in the near future due to the expansion of the occupation forces and the cost for the new German armed forces. Troop costs were therefore a significant factor in Anglo-German relations. (The impact of troop costs on German perceptions of the BAOR will be discussed in chapter 3.)

A Labour government had monitored the early postwar functions of the BAOR, but after the 1951 general election the new Conservative administration of Winston Churchill took up this task. The Churchill administration was very much aware of the delicate position of the BAOR with regard to Anglo-German relations, and at the highest level every effort was made to avoid any embarrassment to the Germans. This attitude was demonstrated by the controversy over the appointment of a new commander in chief of the BAOR in 1954. The candidate preferred by the chief of the Imperial General Staff (CIGS), Field Marshal Sir John Harding, was General Sir Gerald Templer. However, Templer had been the head of the military government in Germany in 1945 and had personally ordered the dismissal of Konrad Adenauer from his post as mayor of Cologne because of the slow-paced improvement of conditions in the devastated city. "Adenauer apparently bore him no grudge and although, when he became chancellor, he would never see Templer socially, he would send him a case of the best hock whenever he visited London."[110] Despite this, the then foreign secretary, Anthony Eden, refused Harding's request to make Templer commander in chief of the BAOR. The official explanation for Eden's objection was his opposition to "such a short tenure at a crucial period of German rearmament and not, as some suggested, because of Templer's brush with Adenauer."[111] Eden nonetheless made it clear in private that "our relations with Adenauer are so important that I do not want to take any chances with them, if I can possibly help it." He therefore asked Ambassador Hoyer-Millar "to mention the matter casually to Adenauer and see how he takes it." Although apparently not because of Templer's actions in 1945, Winston Churchill himself intervened and advised that General Sir Richard Gale, who had led the BAOR for only eighteen months, should not be moved from a command "which I understand he is filling with distinction. I think it is in the public interest that he should remain where he is for at least another year."[112] The case clearly demonstrated the transformation of the position of the BAOR in Germany since Adenauer's dismissal as mayor of Cologne in 1945. It also underlined the extent of British efforts to avoid any friction with the German chancellor, who was considered the driving force behind Germany's pro-Western policy and a "stabilising influence" by the Foreign Office.[113]

Despite the Conservative government's willingness to tie western Germany into the European defense against communism, Britain's own attitude toward Europe during this period was ambivalent. The view of Britain's position at the heart of Churchill's "three circles"—that is, the transatlantic alliance, the empire/commonwealth, and Europe—provided the rationale for Britain's claim to world power status after 1945.[114] The misguided perception of Britain's role as first and foremost the principal European partner of the Americans led to the decision to not join the drive leading toward European integration and the 1957 Treaty of Rome. The Churchill government saw a partnership with Germany as necessary "because NATO and the Atlantic Alliance were at the centre of British policy. Britain favoured loose forms of intergovernmental cooperation in Europe but rejected supranational integration."[115] British participation in European integration was considered detrimental for British transatlantic and Commonwealth ties. It was this attitude that increased the significance of eighty thousand British troops in the British Zone of Occupation as a means to exert influence over European allies outside the realm of the emerging EEC.

Controversies over the BAOR within the British Administration

The BAOR was not only controversial in an Anglo-German and European context; it also frequently caused disagreement within and between the various departments of the British government. The importance of the BAOR as a factor in British policy became particularly evident whenever the option of reducing the size of the BAOR was considered in order to relieve the British taxpayer. When the War Office considered a reduction of BAOR strength from fifty-three thousand to forty-six thousand in 1949 for financial reasons without consulting the Foreign Office, this led to protest from the highest political circles. Sir Brian Robertson, who found out about the War Office plans "by chance," complained to the Foreign Office. This resulted in a letter from Foreign Secretary Ernest Bevin to the minister of defense, Viscount A. V. (Albert Victor) Alexander, clearly expressing "some disappointment that when an overall reduction made necessary a reduction in the strength of Rhine Army [. . .], no consultation with the Foreign Office took place. I am sure you will agree that the strength of Rhine Army is a very important factor in our whole political position in Germany, not only vis-à-vis the Russians, but also vis-à-vis our French and American Allies and above all the German population."[116]A reduction of BAOR strength not only threatened to invite the Americans to act in a similar manner and thereby endanger the entire defense of Western Europe, but it also might create doubts among the Germans as to the Allied commitment to defend Germany against communism. The complete withdrawal of the British Air Forces of Occupation (BAFO) to air bases west of the Rhine for tactical reasons in 1950 was therefore implemented at the same time as the number of BAOR troops was significantly increased to prevent a negative reaction from the Germans.

An increase in BAOR strength, desirable as it may have appeared to the Germans for the purposes of the defense against communism, also caused friction within the British administration. In December 1950 Foreign Office figures stated that the Western Allies in Germany had a combined total of 186,000 troops, as against an estimated total of 320,000 Soviet troops in the Soviet zone.[117] When the decision was made to increase the strength of the BAOR from 44,000 in September 1950 to 65,000 by July 1951, High Commissioner Sir Ivone Kirkpatrick warned against doing so, as "we should have to ask for a supplementary appropriation of Occupation costs and [. . .] considerable inconvenience would have to be inflicted on the German population in the matter of housing and so on."[118] However, the chancellor of the exchequer dismissed his doubts, arguing that the increase of the occupation forces "would be good news and that the German population would simply have to put up with the resulting expense and inconvenience."[119]

Nonetheless, as chapter 3 explores, the issues of housing, occupation costs, maneuver damage, and land requisitioning for training grounds did cause considerable concern. The German population, while resenting the use of the BAOR as armed protection for workers carrying out dismantling work in factories, nonetheless expected to be defended by British rather than German troops. This was partly due to the genuine unwillingness of many young Germans to bear arms and partly for economic, political, and manpower reasons.[120] Those individual Germans who were affected by British housing needs, land acquisitions, and maneuver damage naturally resented the BAOR. Kirkpatrick's advice to "exercise the greatest care and the most rigid economy" was therefore rather pertinent.[121]

Conclusion

The analysis of British Cold War strategy and military organization reveals that in a number of ways the BAOR offered a unique opportunity to foster closer Anglo-German relations. The increasing physical presence of British troops, spread out all across the British zone, and frequent maneuver exercises provided ample opportunity for contacts with local communities. The

British troop commitment also demonstrated British determination to tie western Germany into the Western alliance against communism. At the same time, however, the BAOR also posed risks due to its role of implementing often unpopular British policies. The political position of the BAOR in the early Cold War climate was precarious. It was considered too weak to halt a Soviet attack, too expensive to maintain, and too much of a strain on the German economy. Yet it was a vital tool to convince the Germans, as well as the French and the Americans, of the British determination to protect western Germany. It was also an important means to prevent a West German policy of neutrality in the Cold War, the ultimate goal of British foreign policy in Germany.[122] The strategy to use the BAOR to improve intercultural discourse played a part in achieving this goal. Despite a plain refusal to cooperate immediately after the war, by 1948 the army's leadership was willing to support the Foreign Office strategy of improving Anglo-German relations. This plan was threatened by disagreements within the British administration itself. Financial constraints and the continued execution of unpopular policies agreed upon at Potsdam continuously caused friction within both the Labour and Conservative governments. The lack of faith in German democracy among the leading administrative staff in Germany, fueled by the experiences of two world wars, also played an important part when considering the perceived necessity for the BAOR to succeed in its new role.

The effectiveness of the BAOR as a tool for Anglo-German rapprochement not only depended on the changing attitudes of the services themselves. It also was closely connected to the acceleration of the process of accepting the Federal Republic as a free and equal member of the Western alliance as well as the ending of unpopular policies such as reparations and dismantling. The majority of these political steps would be completed by the time of the accession of the Federal Republic of Germany into NATO in 1955; therefore, the improving political relations between London and Bonn arguably made the BAOR's task easier. Nonetheless, in the prevailing opinion of the Foreign Office, Federal German sovereignty also made the task of incorporating Germany into the Western orbit of defense more urgent due to "a distinct trend [. . .] towards a more aggressive attitude in respect of German rights and Germany's proper place in the world."[123] It was this urgency that motivated much of the Foreign Office activity of the early 1950s, which is analyzed in chapter 5. It is now necessary to establish the impact of the attitudes of the British public on the effectiveness of the BAOR as a positive force for Anglo-German rapprochement. It is also important to go beyond the political context when considering attitudes toward Germany.

The following chapter therefore aims to provide a more nuanced analysis of the British public's view of Germany as, for example, expressed in popular culture and the press. A detailed picture of the perception of Germany is crucial to allow a better understanding of relations between British troops and Germans in the British Zone of Occupation.

CHAPTER 2

THE BRITISH

The Influence of Public Opinion on the Armed Forces

> It's puzzling. One part of me says remember Belsen, and such like. The other part says we'll have to forget and build up. Then one hears of Nazism not being dead. . . . I am all at sea about Germans.
> —"Attitudes to the German People," Mass Observation Archive, 23 August 1948

As established previously, a sizeable part of the British public found itself out of step with the policy of both the Labour and the Conservative administrations' policies toward Germany. The BAOR was to serve as a tool to implement these policies by developing cordial relations with the German population. However, the servicemen stationed in Germany naturally were subject to the same influences shaping British opinion on Germany as the rest of the public. An overwhelmingly negative public opinion would undoubtedly have affected the willingness of BAOR troops to engage with the German population and therefore undermined the BAOR's value as a means for a rapprochement with the former enemy. In order to establish how effectively the BAOR could be used to improve Anglo-German relations, it is necessary to establish a nuanced picture of public opinion on Germany in Britain. This allows drawing conclusions with regard to the attitudes of British troops in Germany.

As Patrick Major points out in his recent article on Anglo-German relations, most postwar historians dealing with Britain's view of Germany have generally focused on high politics in "response to the geopolitical pressures of the Cold War."[1] International political events did indeed have an influence on public opinion as highlighted by the desperate humanitarian situation in Germany immediately after the war and the Berlin blockade in 1948.[2]

The Korean War from 1950 to 1953, with its similarities to the situation in Europe, also changed perceptions: "The parallel between Korea divided and Germany divided was apparent to everyone."[3] The initial success of the North Korean attack on the South Korean and American defenders sparked fears that a similar scenario was about to be repeated much closer to home. Equally, the resulting debate about German rearmament had an impact on British mass public opinion, as recorded in various opinion polls.[4] The result was a more complex and less clear-cut view of Germany than two world wars and the revelation of Nazi atrocities would suggest. The realities of the Cold War led to a British policy toward Germany that attracted considerable amounts of hostile public sentiment in Britain.[5] It is important to stress, however, that there were also more positive views of the recent enemy.

The first essential task when considering British perceptions is to consider both the popular and the political debates on Germany in Britain at the time, by examining both the British press as well as Foreign Office attempts to influence views of Germany. The analysis here goes beyond the political sphere in order to establish a more nuanced picture of factors influencing those young Britons going to Germany with the British military in the late 1940s and 1950s. As the Gallup polls on attitudes toward Germany of the 1950s also revealed, the British public at large was increasingly less interested in foreign policy and therefore also in political developments on the Continent in general and Germany in particular. "Cross-section surveys in many parts of the world have shown that popular interest in foreign affairs nearly always takes a backseat to interest in domestic politics, which in turn, is of far less concern than personal problems."[6] The Labour Party Research Department, for instance, "reported in March 1950 that only eleven per cent of people polled had views that were at all influenced by foreign policy considerations."[7] Furthermore, there was some evidence that, in terms of politics and recent German history, many ordinary Britons deliberately turned away from "the German problem" and tended to simply not think about Germany: "I certainly do not hate them, yet I have no particular love for them. I should like to know what the significance of this is, because I am very interested in the situation in France and Italy and even in the Balkans, but I cannot work up much interest in Germany."[8] It is plausible that many young British servicemen sent to Germany did not loathe their former enemy but simply felt indifferent toward their new host country.

This argument is strengthened further by the fact that in 1954, at the height of the controversy over the European Defence Community (EDC) and the proposal for German rearmament in the context of a European army, only one in three Britons polled by Gallup "knew what EDC stood for," while only another one in three had even heard of it.[9] It therefore is apparent that it is not sufficient to pursue a strictly political angle in order to establish a comprehensive picture of British opinion of Germany from the late 1940s to the mid-1950s. As John Ramsden points out, due to the introduction of National Service in 1947, a considerable number of young British men spent months of their lives in Germany as never before or since, and in most cases this was the first time they had ever left the British Isles.[10] Many of these young men would have formed a view of Germany before they went there, based on factors other than Cold War politics. These views would have influenced their expectations of, and behavior toward, the German population they encountered. In order to gain insight into the attitudes of BAOR personnel toward the Germans, it is also important to consider how Germans were portrayed in Britain by popular culture. In this chapter, after an evaluation of the Foreign Office (FO) position toward Germany and the British press, an examination of the perception of Germany in the British press, and in cultural sources, notably nonfictional literature, novels, comics, and films about the Second World War, sheds further light on the influences of popular culture on servicemen. The BBC's attitude is also considered. As will be seen, these sources were crucial as vehicles for images and views of the Germans. The chapter also includes some more individual perspectives that were often based on encounters between writers and the German people. Finally, the impact of the reemergence of Germany as an economic competitor on perceptions of the former enemy is considered.

The British Press, the Foreign Office, and Germany

The effect of the major political events on British opinion of Germany after 1945 was outlined as early as 1965 by Donald Cameron Watt. The initially overwhelmingly negative attitude toward Germany by the elites and in mass public opinion was increasingly challenged by the humanitarian situation in Germany reported by the British press, which provided "an alternative image to counterbalance the one that presented Germans as evil and abnormal."[11] The surprising results of a Gallup poll of January 1947, which revealed that nearly half of those polled felt "friendly" toward the German people as a whole, can at least partly be attributed to this awareness of the conditions in Germany.[12] Despite Nazi atrocities, as George Weidenfeld suggests, German suffering did not find a similar level of sympathy anywhere else in the West as it did in some British circles.[13] This sympathy grew further due to the behavior of the people of Berlin during the 1948 blockade. "For the first time in a generation, the British were being presented with the sight of Germans behaving en masse in a way of which they could morally approve."[14]

Nonetheless, the economic and political revival of western Germany soon led to renewed hostility in Britain, often voiced by sections of the press. In particular, the issue of German rearmament and the danger of a resurgence of Nazism in Germany influenced the public perception of the Germans. By the early 1950s, opinion polls revealed a continuous and relatively even split into pro- and anti-German camps. Regardless of the attempts by parts of the press to convince Britons otherwise, a 1953 Gallup poll on the question of "whether there was much chance of the Nazis again becoming powerful in Germany," established that only 24 percent of those polled thought it likely.[15] However, this picture changed soon thereafter. As D. C. Watt points out, a sustained anti-German campaign by the popular press helped to push up this number by October 1954, prompting the *Observer* to comment that the reporting of papers like the *Daily Herald* or the *Daily Mirror* led "one to suppose that Hitler was still alive and the Nazis back in power."[16] At the height of the controversy over German rearmament in 1954, of those Britons asked by Gallup if there was "much chance that the Nazis would again become powerful in Germany," now 40 percent thought there was "much chance," 41 percent were of the opinion there was "not much chance," and 19 percent were undecided.[17] The idea of a rearmed Germany only ten years after the war clearly had an effect on public opinion that was not helpful to government policy. However, these figures also demonstrated that those British servicemen who did take an interest in politics were just as likely to be in the pro-German camp as in the anti-German one when considering rearmament and the resurgence of Nazism.

The policies of both the Labour and the Conservative governments were designed to integrate Germany into the Western defense against the Soviet Union. Considering this put Whitehall's politics at odds with parts of public opinion, it is not surprising that the Foreign Office closely monitored and, to an extent, explored means to influence the portrayal of Germany in the press: "I believe that the whole of Fleet Street is anti-German for the simple reason that the average reader in England is anti-German—and the newspapers in England pander to their readers. Unless they pander to their readers the street sales of a particular newspaper will fall."[18]

Although this statement by Sir C. Peter Hope, head of the Foreign Office News Department, partly contradicted the view of Germany expressed by the aforementioned opinion polls, it certainly rang true with regard to the attitudes of sections of the British press. The press in general played a major role in shaping Germany's image in Britain. Whereas most of the quality papers like the *Manchester Guardian* and the *Daily Telegraph* reported objectively on Germany, much of the popular press had "proved itself both unable and unwilling to free itself from the clutches of war-time propaganda."[19] The reporting of parts of the popular press on Germany was in fact a constant obstacle to improved relations between the two countries. The German section of the Foreign Office considered that the wider problem of anti-German tendencies in newspapers could arguably "be narrowed down to the Beaverbrook press, and perhaps *The Times*." On the other side of the political spectrum, "some of the more left-wing weekly publications were also not averse to printing anti-German material." The remainder of the British press did not appear to have particularly strong views on the subject.[20] Watt supported this view and argued that whereas news of crises and international friction was always reported, positive trends were often ignored. Particularly the British popular press distinguished only between the themes "foreigners are funny" and "foreigners are dangerous." Germany naturally always fell into the latter category, as neo-Nazism and the revival of anti-Semitism were what the press "thought their readers would expect to hear from Germany, so this [is] what they concentrated on providing."[21]

The *Daily Express* in particular was "the worst offender," but it was by no means alone in its tendency to "look for evil designs in anything the Germans do."[22] Coverage of Germany by the *Express* was indeed overwhelmingly hostile, and the paper even openly criticized German newspapers for retaliating against the negative *Express* coverage. Apparently the German press had complained "that a 'wave of hatred' was breaking over the English people" and that the *Daily Express* was among the leaders of those who hate the Germans. The tenor throughout the period in question was "that Germany must not be trusted, and that in the Federal Republic a new war-loving nationalism is at work."[23] The vast majority of *Express* articles either made references to British victories over the Nazis or, once Germany began to recover economically, accused the Germans of "paying the British soldier to defend them, freeing their own men to compete against Britain in the world's export markets."[24] Even *The Times* published "some pretty poisonous articles."[25] As late as 1957 the issue was regarded as so detrimental to Anglo-German relations by the British ambassador to Germany, Sir Christopher Steele, that he proposed "a personal appeal should be made to Lord Beaverbrook, the *enfant terrible* on this subject, to modify his attitude." One suggestion was even to ask Sir Winston Churchill to convince Beaverbrook "to stop rocking the boat quite so one-sidedly." The German section of the Foreign Office also considered arranging a private meeting between German Chancellor Konrad Adenauer and Beaverbrook in order to impress a more positive view of the Federal Republic on the latter.[26]

However, despite the negative attitude of the right-wing *Daily Express* and the Labour-leaning *Daily Mirror,* which had reflected the anti-German views of the Labour right since the Second World War, it must be pointed out that not everything said about Germany in these papers was negative. There were frequent examples of factual and neutral reporting on day-to-day Anglo-German relations that reflected a degree of normalization of relations between Britain and Germany. For instance, even the *Express* could not find anything negative in local German authorities inviting British military personnel to a champagne reception on opening the new British army headquarters at Mönchen Gladbach in 1954.[27] The *Daily Mirror* printed a letter to the editor that year from a sixteen-year-old Londoner who stated, "I have nothing against the Germans." The author did not want to be told about the crimes of the past war and wanted "there to be no grudge held against young German children."[28] Even in the most anti-German newspapers there were voices of reconciliation, although at times these came from the readers rather than the editors. After a reception at the German embassy in London in 1955, the *Daily Express* found itself reporting positively about the German ambassador to Britain and German efforts at improving Anglo-German relations.[29] Stories about British troops in Germany were repeatedly used for entertainment rather than criticism of Germany. This was demonstrated by the case of a young German who, after having posed as a Briton and served with the BAOR for two years, had been acquitted on charges of fraud, despite having "lectured to American soldiers, telling them British tanks in Korea were fitted with electrical tea machines and special plugs for razors."[30] Clearly such examples of "foreigners are funny" reporting provided a contrast to the dominating negative view of Germans.

Nonetheless, as late as 1957 the prevailing view in the Foreign Office was that "no British newspaper will ever say anything nice about Germany." Sir C. Peter Hope concluded, "They regard the subject as unpopular with their readers and their policy in this respect is firmly fixed."[31] The British correspondents in Germany were "largely anti-German by inclination," so not only the policy of the papers but also the character of the reporting of their foreign correspondents needed to change. This certainly was a "Herculean task."[32] The problem was further exacerbated by the fact that most of the German correspondents in England "write pretty poor accounts of this country in their own papers," so the unsatisfactory publicity worked both ways. Indeed, rather than solely blaming the British tabloids for providing a poor representation of Germany, the Foreign Office considered the German press to be just as negative about Britain: the German correspondents in London were considered to be "of rather poor quality and, politically, inclined to the left." Their reports appeared "often tendentious and unjustifiably critical, e.g., on colonial affairs, the economic situation, etc." If anything was to be done in Britain "to try to put our own house in order we ought at the same time to urge the Germans to deal with theirs." However, despite these views it appeared "doubtful whether the same widespread tendency to find something evil in everything the British do exists in the German press to the extent that it does, in reverse, here."[33] "What mystifies the Germans is the hostility of the Conservative press. They reckon with anything that comes from the Left but they cannot understand the attitude of Tory newspapers when compared with the consistently friendly attitude of H.M.'s recent governments."[34] The subject of the British press caused much concern, particularly as "a lot of our Press comment ran counter to the views of Her Majesty's Government on Anglo-German relations." According to the German Foreign Office, it was most noticeable that the press attitude in countries that had been subject to the harsh German wartime occupation such as France, the Benelux countries, Denmark, and Norway, was more positive and constructive than in Britain.[35]

According to Patrick Hancock, head of the Western Department of the Foreign Office, the reasons for this hostility were mainly the attitude of the British press and the quality of British correspondents in Germany. Foreign Office powers to address these issues were extremely limited, and in Hancock's view there was a real danger of doing more harm than good in attempting any improvement. This "may well be due [. . .] to the fact that, broadly speaking, the German alliance is accepted in England with the head rather than the heart. But, whatever the origins of this feeling, the fact is that it sells newspapers."[36]

Clearly also, as in the case of the *Daily Express*, the anti-German attitude was a matter of policy dictated from the highest level. Ultimately, "given the natural susceptibilities of the press to any suggestion of official direction," the main burden of improving the situation had to lie "in the first place with the Germans themselves." There was comparatively little the Western Department could contribute to this problem, but there was the hope that exchanges of visits and the experience of working together with the Germans as partners in organizations of all kinds, both official and nonofficial, would help to eliminate the anti-German legacy.[37] On the one hand, the BAOR was to be used as one means to this end. On the other hand, the negative press coverage of Germany threatened to undermine the BAOR's potential as a foreign policy tool by promulgating a negative view of the Germans.

Thus it was evident that the powers of the Foreign Office to influence the press were negligible and that alternative means to make Germany more popular had to be found. According to a 1957 Foreign Office note, unless some kind of powerful influence was brought to bear on Lord Beaverbrook himself, there seemed to be very little hope of changing the tone of his papers. *The Times* correspondent in Bonn, Louis Heren, was well known for his anti-German dispatches,[38] but the paper's headlines on Germany were often hostile in tone, and it appeared that this was due to editorial policy. *The Times* suffered from the additional handicap of having to avoid the impression of repeating its 1930s policy of keeping out of the paper "anything which might upset the Nazis."[39] Only top-level pressure could bring about a change here.[40] There was little point in trying to change the views of the *Express* or the *Evening Standard*, or indeed the *Daily Mirror*. "But the Germans would be well advised to work out a programme to cope with *The Times*, the *Manchester Guardian*, the *Herald*, the *News Chronicle*, the *Telegraph*, the *Birmingham Post*, the *Scotsman* and the *Yorkshire Post*."[41] There was also the view that a good deal could be done to popularize German culture, as opposed to German political thinking, in order to revive at least some of the sympathy it had enjoyed in Britain in the early nineteenth century: "Why don't [the Germans] do exhibitions of Nymphenburg china? They need a skilful showman to set all this up and it must be done discreetly. I think these ideas are practical but I rather despair of the German character, because I doubt if they have anyone who is imaginative enough to launch such a programme effectively."[42] Despite the Foreign Office attempts to achieve a more positive portrayal of Germany in the British press, the head of its Information Policy Department, Sir Paul H. G. Wright, expressed pessimistic views on both the press as well as the Germans: "I am afraid the problem is really deeper[. . . .] I think the British press will continue to tend to be anti-German for the simple reason that the Germans are going to become increasingly unpopular; and this is because they are probably going to become more and more successful and, as a result more and more German!"[43] Sir C. Peter Hope also entertained doubts about the idea of making Germany more popular by televising Konrad Adenauer's speech during his 1957 state visit to Britain: "The German voice is not yet sweet music to the English ear and I am afraid the *Daily Express* will have a heyday."[44] The negative press attitude and the Foreign Office's inability to change it make the search for alternative means to improve Anglo-German relations, including the BAOR, understandable. However, BAOR soldiers were themselves confronted with this hostile press attitude.

Moreover, at times the BAOR itself was used as a tool by the British press to highlight anti-German views. For instance, the *Sunday Pictorial* targeted the allegedly hostile German behavior toward British troops in 1957. In an article titled "Yellow Bellies—by Order," the journalist Audrey Whiting accused "small-time German politicians" of stirring up "as much trouble as they can for the boys of the Rhine Army," by orchestrating vicious press campaigns and deliberately exaggerating minor skirmishes between British soldiers and local youths—"skirmishes which are invariably started by the Germans themselves."[45] British readers were regaled with stories about BAOR soldiers who were merely going for a quiet drink being told, "Out with the dirty English," by German louts. Not only this, but apparently British soldiers were now under strict instructions "not to rise to this kind of baiting" in order to avoid trouble. Apparently a War Office spokesman blamed local German politicians for exaggerating small incidents, as they wanted British soldiers out of Germany. A National Serviceman from Booth, Lancashire, told Whiting: "What it amounts to is that we are being told to behave like a lot of yellow bellies."[46] For *Pictorial* the case was clear: "These whipper snapper German politicians must be told by their own leaders to stop their monkey business!"[47] This kind of press coverage certainly did not aid the cause of the Foreign Office. The article sufficiently unsettled at least one Briton enough to write a letter to the Chancellor Adenauer, asking him to make a public statement in order to preserve the "firm friendship and alliance with Britain."[48] The German response to this letter essentially dismissed the allegations, blaming the "irresponsible boulevard press" as well as the new and not exclusively German phenomenon of the rise of the so-called *Halbstarken*, or teenage hoodlums. The former portrayed false images by constantly exaggerating, and the latter were mostly looking for fights without having any motives, let alone political ones.[49]

It does not come as a surprise that the British working class, the class most often targeted by newspapers such as the *Express* and the *Mirror*, was made up of those Britons who were most hostile to Germany; "those least unfavourable to Germany were the professional classes and the rich."[50] This potentially had a significant impact on the BAOR. "From 1939 to 1960, the British Army's social structure, values, and way of life survived with surprisingly little change. The British officer corps was still dominated by the 'gentleman' and the Army remained essentially a working-class Army officered by the upper classes."[51] This would not bode well for British efforts to use young working-class service personnel to improve Anglo-German relations once stationed in the British zone.

The topic of Germany was not only frequently debated in the British press, as the BBC also regularly featured Germany in its programs. BBC Radio coverage of Germany, although frequently touching upon issues related to the Nazi regime and World War Two, very much focused on current political, social, economic, and cultural issues and trends. Political programs ranged from German reunification over rearmament to talks on German resistance against Hitler.[52] Cultural pieces on Germany were frequent, covering issues such as contemporary German poetry or "the dilemma of the German novel."[53] The picture emerging from the political BBC coverage of the Federal Republic was one of concern about the future position of Germany in Europe and direction of Anglo-German relations but not one of resentment of the former enemy.

There were also frequent cases of a thorough analysis of and positive attitude toward the new Germany. In 1955 BBC Television screened "A Special Enquiry on Germany," a documentary on the ordinary German's view of German sovereignty, unification, and rearmament. The aim was to "get a bit more behind the personality of the ordinary German man-in-the-street" and to portray Germans against the background of day-to-day life, including their views.[54] The program addressed questions such as German trade competition, alleged Nazi influence on the Bonn government, the progress of democracy, and whether or not Germany could be trusted as a rearmed ally. With regard to trade competition, the documentary provided a somewhat more rational view of the Federal Republic than the popular press in Britain. As Germany dominated Western European markets once more, Germany's position in Europe made her indispensable to Europe from an economic point of view. "Europe cannot be prosperous unless Germany is."[55] Considering the question of "are we re-arming the Nazis," the program provided a wide range of German views, including the official government line, the views of the opposition, and those of Germans at large. The very detailed analysis, which also made use of interviews with both British and German journalists, essentially arrived at the conclusion that the FRG "means too much to Europe's bread and butter to be treated as France would like to treat her."[56]

Not only was the documentary's coverage of Germany favorable, but British audience opinion of the program after its screening in April 1955 was also very positive. An estimated 17 percent of the British adult population saw the broadcast, which was equivalent to 51 percent of the adult television-viewing public. Questionnaires completed by a sample of the audience revealed that most viewers welcomed the opportunity to hear opinions firsthand from a cross-section of Germans. "The subject, viewers said, is much in peoples' minds at the present time and this programme presented up to date information in a most interesting way."[57] Although one or two viewers admitted they were not much interested in Germany, the majority were "most favourably impressed" by the information provided.

Not only did the BBC aim at a more balanced portrayal of Germany in its coverage, but it also actively cooperated with the Foreign Office in order to increase its number of German listeners. According to the FO Information Policy Department, a listening audience in West Germany would be of importance not only in the case of a deterioration of Anglo-German relations but also "to ensure a bearing for the British case in those matters where German public opinion takes an emotional view and about which the German press will not give the British position a fair hearing."[58] In order to increase the BBC audience in Germany, the Foreign Office decided to finance a listener competition. Around 120,000 deutschmarks (DM) was to be drawn from the budget for "special projects of political importance" and used to pay for publicity and competition prizes. The main prizes, aimed at increasing the popularity of Britain as well as the BBC's audience, included visits to Great Britain and radio sets. The visits to London were to coincide with the much anticipated 1953 coronation ceremonies for Queen Elizabeth II. Despite fears that other European countries might complain about the preferential treatment of Germans in this matter, and despite the difficulty in obtaining the required number of seats for the ceremony, the head of the FO Information Policy Department, Angus C. E. Malcolm, remarked that there really was only one potential problem: "It would be awkward, of course, if one of the German prize-winners turned out to be Hitler."[59]

The weekly BBC magazine *The Listener* featured fifteen articles on Germany between July and December 1948 alone. Once more the attitude toward Germany differed from that of the Beaverbrook press. German politics featured regularly, but so did cultural subjects such as architecture, history, and youth culture. With regard to politics, the fear of a resurgence of German nationalism was a recurring feature . This was evident in 1949, when readers were reminded that "experience has taught us how malignant a form German nationalism can take."[60] In 1955 the historian Geoffrey Barraclough still warned his audience that Germany "today is master of its own fate. The question now, before it is too late, is to ensure that it will not also be the master of Europe's fate, and of your fate and my fate."[61] However, despite the doubts expressed by *The Listener* that "there really has been a change at heart" in Germany, the subject was dealt with far more objectively and positively than in parts of the popular press. As early as 1948, there were encouraging reports on German students,[62] and in 1955 the author and journalist Terence Prittie argued that although the "German desire to 'be friends' with other peoples was almost embarrassingly ardent and evident,"

German youth was "the fairest [. . .] promise of a sound and settled German future."[63] The image of a reemerging Nazi Germany, as portrayed by the *Daily Express,* was therefore counterbalanced by a more positive, if cautious view of a country that, ten years after the war, had "rejected racial theories and shrunk away from anti-Semitism, from cracker-mottoes and distorted mythology."[64] It is likely that a considerable number of BAOR soldiers would have taken note of this.

The Battle for the British Public in Nonfictional Literature

Apart from day-to-day politics, nonfictional literature was an important means for the British press, and even Whitehall, to influence the public's view of Germany while simultaneously keeping the topic of Germany in the public domain over the rearmament question. Although, according to one eminent British publisher, the British public had "their heads well in the sand as far as Germany is concerned," and "they simply did not want to recognize that she's there again, let alone read a long book about her," Germany was a frequent and controversial literary subject.[65] One particular case of a "battle of the books" between pro- and anti-German factions in Britain was the notorious case of the alleged Foreign Office attempt to suppress the publication of *The Scourge of the Swastika* by Lord Russell of Liverpool, then the assistant judge advocate general. This case also demonstrated the struggle of the British administration to prevent damage caused to Anglo-German relations by members of its own ranks. Russell had been wounded in the trenches of the First World War and had been opposed to appeasement of Nazi Germany. At the end of the war, he had been "responsible for all courts martial, war crime trials, and questions of military law in the British-occupied zone of Germany." The horrors revealed during the war crime trials he presided over convinced him that "because of their war depravities, the German people existed on a different level from the rest of humanity."[66] In March 1951 he created a major diplomatic incident by forcing his car through a German crowd celebrating in the village of Vlotho, where a group of Germans subsequently assaulted him and his wife. He had ignored the orders of local police, frightened pedestrians, and was therefore immediately recalled to London.[67] The next three years (1951–1954), during which he worked in London as assistant judge advocate, "were the most frustrating of his career." He then went on to write a detailed account of Nazi war crimes, which was published as *The Scourge of the Swastika.*[68] It is worth considering the case of the alleged suppression of *The Scourge* here, as it not only provided a further example for the Foreign Office's struggle with the press, but it also highlighted the difficult position of the British administration when faced with the charge of suppressing freedom of expression in order to achieve its policy objectives toward Germany.

Certain sections of the popular press jumped at the opportunity provided by the alleged government attempt to suppress Russell's publication. In the summer of 1954, Lord Beaverbrook's right-wing and anti-German *Daily Express* accused the government of being "guilty of an intolerable interference with the rights of the citizen," as it had attempted to prevent a book on Nazi war crimes from seeing the light of day. "It has exerted all its available power to achieve this purpose. And it has done so in vain."[69] The paper argued that at the very moment when the government was planning to rearm the Germans, the assistant judge advocate general was publishing a document "recounting the deeds perpetrated by certain Germans when Nazi Germany was armed!" The article demanded to "offer to postpone German rearmament in return for real talks with Russia on the future of Germany," and the author hoped that "some rich man will send free copies to all members of the cabinet."[70] The Labour-supporting *Daily Mirror* demonstrated more restraint on the Lord Russell issue than the *Express*. In a more balanced article it provided explanations by the lord chancellor for attempting to prevent publication, Lord Russell's subsequent insistence on releasing the book, as well as a Foreign Office statement denying any involvement in the matter. Although the *Mirror* stated that it was possible to criticize the lord chancellor for the attempted suppression, "his action can be defended on the ground that he is a member of the government and as such must uphold government decisions."[71] Although the *Mirror* was by no means particularly friendly toward Germany, in many of its articles the difference in portraying the Russell case is striking. The *Express* published twenty-one articles about the issue between August and December as well as publishing extracts of the book itself. By contrast, the *Mirror* considered the case worthy of mentioning only four times over the same period. The *Daily Express* used the book controversy to add to the "consistent stream of news and cartoons designed to drive home the image of a Germany returning to the state of 1939," whereas the *Daily Mirror* downplayed the issue and thereby followed the Labour Party line, which was slowly accepting the inevitability of German rearmament.[72]

The details of the *Scourge of the Swastika* controversy clearly demonstrate how nonfictional literature was used as a means to influence public opinion. The official explanation for the lord chancellor's refusal to grant publication of the book was that, considering Russell's position, it was unacceptable for him to influence controversial contemporary politics. However,

Lord Russell rejected the lord chancellor's view. He resigned his post as assistant judge advocate general and went ahead with the publication of his book, thereby forfeiting his government pension in the process. The *Daily Express* alleged that Lord Russell had been refused permission to publish his work by the Foreign Office. However, the lord chancellor insisted that the responsibility for the decision was entirely his,[73] which is not entirely convincing, considering confidential FO correspondence of the time on "influencing the publication of certain books."[74] The lord chancellor had carefully considered "whether anything further could be done to prevent Lord Russell from publishing this book but concluded that it could not."[75] Sir Ivone Kirkpatrick expressed his view on Russell clearly in a handwritten note, saying simply, "He is not quite sane."[76]

The publication of what Lord Russell described as "a solely factual and historical" account of Nazi war crimes certainly caused controversy in Britain.[77] In the words of the *Observer*, the "most serious problem of our age is exploited with a tastelessness and sensationalism normally associated with the worst kind of journalism." The justification that Lord Russell had limited himself to extracts from the available published records struck the paper as not convincing, as "the same defence could be made by any hack serving up selected extracts from divorce or murder cases."[78] The "book title, wrapper and general presentation differed sharply" from hitherto published war crime accounts in their level of sensationalism.[79] According to a report by the Lord Chancellor's Office, much of the press comment on this affair had been undoubtedly favorable to Lord Russell. However, many of the more reputable papers "have thought it clear that the publication of such a book by a person in Lord Russell's position should not be countenanced."[80] Controversial or not, the book proved hugely popular with the British public. Prime Minister Winston Churchill, who considered the publication enormously damaging, personally thought it necessary to inform the Foreign Office in November that he had heard that Lord Russell of Liverpool's book had already sold sixty thousand copies "and is being reprinted as fast as possible as the demand is very great."[81]

Although Russell's intention may well have been to ensure that German atrocities were not forgotten, some evidence suggests that the British public was not reading it for that reason. Images shown in the book included shrunken heads found at Buchenwald concentration camp, and, according to Wendy Webster, schoolchildren in Britain "secretly passed the book around under their desks." There was a perception of the "pleasure of horror," and in fact the alleged effort to ban the book most likely led to the surge of interest and its popularity.[82]

Literary attempts to influence the British public's view on Germany did not end with *The Scourge of the Swastika*. In the midst of the controversy over Russell's book, the High Commission in Bonn informed the Foreign Office that the widow of a Berlin socialist executed after the failed July plot against Hitler had recently published a book on the plot, called *Das Gewissen steht auf* (*Conscience in Revolt*).[83] Apparently the book was very well written and gave an interesting account of the part played in the plot by various Germans from all walks of life. Apart from paying tribute to the memory of these people, it gave "a general impression of the better side of Germany under the surface."[84]

The German Federal Press Office decided on publishing an English version of the book, "particularly in view of the criticisms of Germany in some parts of the British press."[85] As Robert Birley pointed out in his introduction to *Conscience in Revolt*: "When Western Germany became a possible partner in an alliance, the character and traditions of the people could no longer be ignored. It is not surprising, therefore, that several books, widely publicised and widely read, should have appeared, reminding Englishmen of the atrocities of the Nazi regime. This book is in no sense an answer to them. But it is an essential part of the evidence, and one largely neglected in this country."[86] Moreover, in October 1954, Norman Wymer, a literary advisor to Odhams Press publishing company, sent a letter to Anthony Eden to inquire if the foreign secretary personally objected to encouraging Konrad Adenauer to write a book describing the position in Germany at the time and "telling of his efforts to stamp out Nazism and re-build the country into a peace-loving nation." He thought it was important to publish a book highlighting the qualities of the new Germany to counter the vast number of publications about Nazi atrocities and assist the cause of better understanding between Britain and Germany: "a book designed to remove public distrust and, instead, sow the seeds of confidence and friendship."[87] This book was considered "a good antidote to the Lord Russell type of publication," though it obviously could not appear for some time. However, Wymer expected the value of such a publication to be just as great in 1955 "when, as we hope, a beginning will be made on the new German defence contingent."[88] This request clearly demonstrated that although the tabloid press and parts of the publishing industry were mostly interested in portraying Germany as evil, this was not universally the case. Typically, though, the Foreign Office was careful to not promote its pro-German policy at home too much. A draft Foreign Office reply stated that Eden saw no reason why Wymer should not write to Adenauer personally, but, as "he regards this as a matter which does not concern him, he would not wish to be quoted as having expressed a view."[89] According to the head of the Central Department of the Foreign Office, Patrick Hancock, the whole proposal came close to being imprudent: "What would we think if a German wrote to the Secretary of State suggesting that Sir Anthony Eden should publish a book and adding that in that case Dr. Adenauer would not mind?"[90] The battle of the books continued throughout the 1950s. "Books on German resistance were usually reviewed as being much ado about nothing, while accounts of the Holocaust mainly ignored Hitler's Gentile victims."[91] Whitehall continuously aimed at halting this trend. According to F. A. Warner of the Western Department of the Foreign Office, there were at least two other books connected with Germany, "the publication of which H.M.G. are at present seeking to influence"—that is, to prevent. One of these, *The London Cage*,[92] by a retired colonel, revealed British methods of interrogating POWs in the Second World War and highlighted several instances of improper treatment of Germans that "might cause us some political embarrassment in Germany."[93] The second, as yet unnamed, book threatened to reveal "much accurate information about our Intelligence Service, together with the names of many officers who are still serving in it." These cases were brought up "because there may be growing accusations in the press that the Foreign Office are trying to suppress all freedom of speech about Germany." The argument that the decision in both cases would be taken on grounds completely unrelated to the current political situation in Germany "would of course be overlooked by the Beaverbrook press."[94] Even though opinion polls revealed a certain apathy with regard to the German question, there is certainly ample evidence that efforts were made to influence views through publications on both "good and bad Germans."

The Representation of Germans in British Novels

More so than in nonfictional literature, young British men about to join the BAOR would likely have come across Germany in novels. David Lodge, drawing on his own experience of National Service, pointed out in his *Ginger, You're Barmy* that "the favourite form of escape literature among soldiers of the modern Army was not pornography, not westerns but war-books."[95] This idea is certainly supported by the fact that, according to a Gallup poll, Nicholas Monsarrat's war novel *The Cruel Sea* topped the list of best-selling books in 1952, ahead of Winston Churchill's war memoirs.[96] The portrayal of Germans in Monsarrat's novel was rather stereotypical, if not shrill. The only Germans encountered in the book were sailors of a German submarine whom the main character, British corvette commander George Ericson, had just dispatched to the bottom of the sea. One German was portrayed as raising his right arm and roaring out "Heil Hitler" while he was still in the water swimming toward his rescuers.[97] The U-boat commander himself was "tall, dead-blond and young," with "pale and slightly mad eyes." In typical Nazi fashion, he was full of contempt "that twitched his lips and nostrils," due to the "hatred of his capture by an inferior."[98] The German officer's behavior was described as so appalling that Ericson had to restrain himself to not immediately execute him. Later the U-boat captain started crying during the sea burial of British and German sailors, having been "emotionally shocked out of the arrogant mould: he admitted bereavement[. . . .] It was probably the swastika, Ericson reflected: the dead sailor from his crew would not bother him, but the 'gesture of honour' implied by the burial party and the enemy ensign would knock him out."[99] The Germans in *The Cruel Sea* were all of the same type: "We can only shoot them, and hope for a better crop next time."[100]

The postwar popular book market was effectively dominated by war books and autobiographies.[101] *The Cruel Sea* was still at the top of Gallup's list in 1955, followed by two other war books, *Reach for the Sky* and *HMS Ulysses*.[102] However, when one compares the portrayal of Germans in the 1952 novel *The Cruel Sea* with that in the biography *Reach for the Sky* of 1954, striking differences become apparent. The Germans encountered by the biography's main character, Douglas Bader, an RAF pilot shot down over France, were often "types after his own heart and he would have liked to have had them in his wing. What a damn silly war it was."[103] The Germans went to great lengths trying to fix the pilot's prosthetic leg, leaving him "impressed and rather touched,"[104] and they even allowed him to climb into a German fighter plane when meeting a distinguished German fighter ace. Although a number of subsequent encounters with Germans in POW camps provoked much "goon-baiting" from the British POWs, many of the German officers portrayed in *Reach for the Sky* were "tolerant and sympathetic." Douglas Bader "had to admit that some of the Germans were incredibly decent and reasonable, and had a passable sense of humour."[105] Once the hostilities ended, Bader found it difficult to express his feelings toward some of his fellow comrades, as "the trouble was he did feel sorry for the Germans. Now there was nothing to fight, some of the hate seemed to have withered, but he felt it unwise to try and explain it to the others because they were still living in the war and would not understand."[106] It is difficult to imagine a more positive portrayal of the former enemy only nine years after the war's end.

The popularity of biographies and war novels certainly kept the issue of Germany in people's minds, but in some cases the portrayal of the former adversary marked a distinct contrast to the "goon baiting" still practiced by parts of the British press at the time. Military campaign histories such as *The Story of Dunkirk* (1955) "sold an impressive 150,000 copies in only a few months" and had to be reprinted.[107] As Penny Summerfield points out: "In contrast to the previous decade, when sensitivities towards the feelings of the bereaved may have held back publishers, in the 1950s Britain remembered the military campaigns of the Second World War in the rites and rituals of public commemoration, as well as in literature."[108] Many Britons looked to the past and "took comfort from the war as a period of British successes" when the present was dominated by austerity and imperial decline.[109] As, for example, John Ramsden remarks, young British readers were inundated with novels "about prisoner of war camps, combat and espionage" as well as boys' comic books constantly reinforcing the stereotype of the German Nazi soldier.[110] The mass market in Britain was indeed flooded with books such as *The Dam Busters,* the *Colditz Story,* and *Reach for the Sky.* "The latter not only appeared in hardback and in paperback, but also in its first three years in an abridged version, a special young people's edition, and a simplified English edition."[111] However, it is important to stress the portrayal of Germans by many of these books as "ordinary people." Douglas Bader "felt no rancour towards the soldiers who had winkled him out and as far as he could see they felt no rancour for him."[112] Prisoner-of-war books became so popular they created their own market niche.[113] It was these "railway bookstall titles" that young Britons, about to be dispatched to Germany in an army uniform, would have most likely encountered. The picture of Germans emerging from these novels was not always that of the goose-stepping Nazi shown in *The Cruel Sea.*

The Portrayal of Germans in Comics

Comics were another medium that possibly influenced the young soldier and his perception of the Germans. However, it is more difficult to emphasize the nature and cultural impact of comics than that of mainstream novels and films or the daily press. This is partly due to the nature of the content of the comics and partly due to the target audience being young boys rather than adults. It is questionable if the comics published in the 1950s would have been read by many servicemen. It is therefore necessary to briefly consider the portrayal of Germans in comics of the preceding decades. Writing during the "Phoney War" in early 1940, the phase of the conflict between the declaration of war in September 1939 and the Battle of Britain from spring 1940, George Orwell suggested that boys' weeklies were a source of patriotism and implicit conservatism, although their main aim was to amuse their adolescent and teenage readers. He also observed that although the characters, from schoolboys to authority figures, were mostly middle-class and upper-class, their readership was predominantly working-class. British staple comics such as the *Gem* and *Magnet* also played to racial and national stereotypes, although it is relevant to consider Orwell's list of European stereotypes. This included the Frenchman ("excitable, gesticulates wildly"), the Spaniard ("sinister, treacherous"), the Italian ("excitable, grinds barrel-organ"), and even the Swede and the Dane ("kind-hearted, stupid"), but did not include the German.[114]

Comics had been a source of mirth and comfort to young boys during the First World War, and Orwell implied that the same would be the case during the Second World War. However, he noted that Nazi Germany and Hitler had only just begun to creep into the stories in boys' weeklies during the late 1930s: "If a Spaniard appears, he is still a 'dago' or 'greaser'; no indication that things have been happening in Spain. Hitler and the Nazis have not yet appeared, or are barely making their appearance. There will be plenty about them in a little while, but it will be from a strictly patriotic angle (Britain *versus* Germany) with the real meaning of the struggle kept out of sight as much as possible."[115] Orwell was arguing that the patriotism of the comics was mostly assumed and promoted within nonpolitical narratives that played on the essential correctness and decency of the British versus the "foreign" enemy.

In fact, paper shortages permanently closed down some boys' publications, including the *Gem* and *Magnet*, both of which had ceased publication by 1940. During the postwar 1940s, one notable comic that continued from the interwar period was the *Hotspur*, begun as an extension to the D. C. Thomson publishing empire. The *Hotspur*, published from 1933 to 1959, was almost completely devoid of references to the Second World War. The content was mostly concerned with the adventures of public schoolboys and their headmasters, detective fiction, the Wild West, adventures in the great outdoors, and iconic examples of modern trains, boats, and planes. In general, adolescent and young teenage boys during the Second World War and its early aftermath, those who would become the conscripts of the postwar years, had less exposure to comics because of the paper shortage. And what they did read was rarely full-blooded patriotism, but instead serial escapism.[116]

In 1947 a number of populist weekly papers started, including *The Eagle,* a new title for the Hulton Press, which also published the *Picture Post* until it wound down in 1957. Edward Hulton was a conservative in politics, but he was no xenophobe, having been a supporter of Labour's reconstruction plans.[117] Yet his weekly magazine for boys remained essentially nonpolitical in terms of references to party politics or ideologies and non-nationalistic in relation to the Germans. *The Eagle* was more captivated by the Wild West of nineteenth-century North America than the recent war in Europe, and by science fiction, modern motor cars, trains, weapons, and rockets. "Dan Dare, the pilot of the future," rather than Adolf Hitler, characterized the content of *The Eagle*. The Reds were from Mars, not Russia. "*The Eagle* was a publishing phenomenon of the 1950s with a circulation, at its height, of over a million."[118]

Despite the lack of overt references to present political developments, Dan Dare was nonetheless informed by the cultural and political circumstances affecting Britain during the 1950s. James Chapman argues, "*The Eagle* can be read as a narrative of British power in the early period of the Cold War." It is doubtful, though, whether Dan Dare's young readers would have shown any interest in stories about the country's power at the time. The Cold War context of the Korean War was projected onto the first Dan Dare adventure, in which the planet Venus was divided into two opposing sides. However, after the enemy is defeated and the planet is reunited, the comic goes on to endorse Britain's policy toward her new German Cold War ally: "'You mean you are not going to enslave us or take our land?' [asks a defeated enemy.] 'And breed another war?' Dan replies. 'No, my friend, we of the Earth have learned our peace-making in a hard, bitter school. Now we have a one-word policy for both victor and vanquished—disarmament!'"[119] This reference clearly related to the Allied treatment of Germany at the end of the Second World War rather than endorsing stereotypes from the past conflict.

Nonetheless, as David Kynaston points out in his discussion of comics in austerity Britain, most of them were based more on British class caricatures than nationalistic stereotypes and dealt with familiar people in familiar landscapes. He does not mention the war, or the Germans, in his analysis of boys' weeklies after 1945.[120] Indeed it was not really until the later 1950s and early 1960s that the pictorial celebration of the Second World War took off. The War Picture Library, published by the Amalgamated Press/Fleetway from 1958 and the *Commando* picture books (D. C. Thomson) were all about the blood and guts of warfare. And from 1962, Captain Hurricane of the weekly *Valiant* (published by I.P.C. Magazines) made his appearance, to the trembling fear of his enemies—namely, the Japanese ("slant-eyed weevils") and the Italians ("ice-cream wallahs"). The Germans were rarely called names but were characterized as hard-faced men in uniform who said "*Himmel*" a lot.[121] Such depictions were stronger and undoubtedly more violent than were to be found in boys' weeklies during the war and came almost a generation after the war had ended and as conscription ceased. Despite their popularity, which increased considerably in the 1960, comics were less relevant in the context of public opinion on Germany than, for example, novels and war films.

British War Films and their Portrayal of Germans

If the topic of World War Two and Germany was popular among young British servicemen in literature, then the same certainly applied to films. Whereas novels appealed more to middle-class readers, war films certainly also attracted large working-class audiences. The 1950s were the final period in which "the cinema was still the principal medium of communication and attitude formation in Britain." In 1955 twenty-three million Britons attended the cinema at least once a week (down from thirty million five years earlier).[122] Movies about the Second World War and the Allied fight against Nazi Germany were produced at a fairly impressive rate, both in Britain and the United States, throughout the late 1940s and 1950s. British audiences were influenced by a large number of films in the 1950s. *The Wooden Horse* (UK 1950—"a standard, solid POW drama"), *The Colditz Story* (UK 1955—"probably the most convincing of the British accounts of POW life"), and the popular Hollywood production by Billy Wilder, *Stalag 17* (US 1953—"quite different from the understated British films on the subject"),[123] were typical examples of the frequently produced POW dramas.[124] Overall, the portrayal of Germans in British and American films between the 1930s and 1980s was overwhelmingly negative.[125] However, it must be considered whether this also applies for the time period under observation here.

Between 1948 and 1958 at least forty war films involving Germans arrived in British cinemas, at times at a rate of nearly one every month.[126] This points toward a much higher level of engagement with at least some, albeit not the most fruitful or productive, aspects of the "German question" than the political polls of the 1950s suggest. The disparity between critical acclaim and popularity with audiences is striking. Most of these war films were highly unpopular with critics: this was reflected by their absence from lists noting the best films of the year as well as film festivals abroad. In fact many film reviewers were frankly hostile toward the cliché-ridden portrayals of the "stiff upper lip." One review of *The Ship That Died of Shame* (UK 1955, "a thin and rather obvious melodramatic fable"[127]) complained that "British film stars may not be the best in the world, but they were certainly the most waterproof. 'Above us the waves' seems to be their motto."[128]

Despite being branded "old-fashioned," "socially conservative," and "irresponsible in regards to attitudes towards future warfare" by film critics, war films proved immensely popular with audiences.[129] A Gallup poll indicated that the most popular movie in 1955 was *The Dam Busters*.[130] The film told the story of the 1943 Royal Air Force attack on the German Möhne, Eder, and Sorpe dams with the so-called bouncing bomb, in the hope to cripple German industry. It mostly focused on the technicalities of destroying the German dams rather than on the enemy. Although the carnage resulting from the bombing was briefly shown and the high number of British casualties was evident, the film was above all a glorification of British ingenuity in the face of adversity.[131] The audience appeal of war films like *The Dam Busters* was reflected by the fact that they regularly held the top spot at the box office.[132] The idea of war films being particularly popular among British military personnel is supported by the 1952 account of one National Serviceman, produced shortly after his arrival in Germany. Although pointing out that *The Sands of Iwo Jima* (US 1949—a "celebrated star war comic, still quite hypnotic in its flagwaving way"[133]) had been the first war film he had seen in a while, it had reminded him of the summer exercises in which he took part that year in Germany. He thereafter frequently mentioned war books and films in his diary.[134] It is interesting that in this case the film *The Desert Fox* (US 1951—a "vivid but scrappy account of the last years of a contemporary hero"[135]) even motivated the conscript in question to learn more of the German language. He had read the book and wanted to see the film in a German cinema where it was shown in German. Despite all criticism of the genre, here was a curious case of war films bringing the German language closer to a young Briton.[136] As Patrick Major argues, the film paved the way for the cultural rehabilitation of the *Wehrmacht* on screen not only in English-speaking countries but in Germany too. There was also an increasing tendency to remove the German armed forces of World War Two from their political context and instead construct an image based on chivalry and honor in order to persuade British public opinion to accept the need of the Western anticommunist alliance and the rearming of the Federal Republic.[137] It appears that American and British filmmakers were aiding British efforts to improve relations between the BAOR and the German people by presenting the recent German past in a less controversial light. This tendency, strongly evident in *The Desert Fox*, led the historian Hugh Trevor-Roper to warn that "'our friend Rommel' is becoming not a magician or a bogy-man, but too much of a hero."[138] Apparently this was exactly the effect the film had on the aforementioned young British serviceman.

Overall the portrayal of Germans in war films of the late 1940s and 1950s presents a less one-sided and negative picture than one might anticipate. First, a number of films did not feature any Germans at all, as in the case of *The Dam Busters*. Second, films like *The Battle of the River Plate* (UK 1956) were criticized in reviews for their pro-German attitude and the fact that, "as the *Daily Herald* put it, the Germans get all the glory."[139] British productions were transformed in their portrayals of Germans from *The Wooden Horse* (1950) and *The Cruel Sea* (1953) to *The Dam Busters* (1955) and *The One That Got Away* (1957—a "true life biopic, [...] all very well done"[140]). The majority of these films were preoccupied with the depiction of Allied soldiers rather than Germans. They also were centrally concerned with "promulgating a selective myth of national identity and national cohesion" within British society.[141] Nonetheless, the change in the portrayal from the inhuman yelping and barking goons in *The Wooden Horse* to that of Hardy Kruger in *The One That Got Away,* only seven years later, is quite remarkable. In fact, it was probably in large part the at times even heroic portrayal of Germans in *The Battle of the River Plate* that led to its being the most successful imported film in West Germany that year.[142] However, it was also voted the third-best film of the year by people interviewed by Gallup in Britain.[143]

According to *The Times,* the reason for the positive portrayal of Germans was partly to be found in the "semi documentary tradition which has gained so great a reputation for British films of war. It is a fine tradition, a noble tradition," which properly presented Germans "as soldiers going about their jobs."[144] Despite the sometimes hostile reception of the British press, by the mid-1950s, at least in British (as opposed to American) films, more rounded characterizations of Germans emerged. Increasingly the German film characters accepted defeat "like a sportsman."[145] The fact that Germany by the 1950s was one of the most lucrative film markets in the world might partly explain the motives for this newfound affection. This was impressively demonstrated by the contrast between Monsarrat's novel *The Cruel Sea* and its film adaptation.[146] The grotesque Nazis of the novel were completely eliminated from the film, and the only comment by the British corvette captain about German U-boat crews was that "they look a lot like our boys." The opening narration of the film stated that "the only villain is the sea—the cruel sea—that man has made even more cruel."[147] The effect of the changing attitude toward Germans in British war films of the period on the average British conscript is likely to have been noticeable.

The armed services themselves regarded the heroic portrayal of British military efforts in the Second World War as highly desirable because of its likely impact on prestige and recruiting at a time of heightened Cold War tensions. Therefore it is not surprising that the services provided significant support to filmmakers, without which the high volume of war films of the 1950s could not have been achieved. The Royal Navy regularly invited actors and producers to its Royal Naval Film Corporation dinner, and "the RAF had a special trophy for 'the best interpretation of the RAF to the public' each year, unsurprisingly won in 1955 by *The Dam Busters*."[148] Support by the services ranged widely, from the training of actors to the provision of equipment, and went as far as the entire Mediterranean fleet staging a training exercise to facilitate the filming of *The Battle of the River Plate*. Naturally, in return for such efforts, the military was granted every opportunity to recruit young cinema-goers into its ranks. Measures included window displays in cinemas and military parades outside of theaters. In at least one case in 1955, when showing *The Dam Busters,* the RAF was granted permission to open a recruitment center inside a cinema in the town of Rugeley in the county of Staffordshire.[149] In this particular case there was also "a display of medals and photographs, and a gala opening with an RAF guard of honour, fanfare trumpeters and the local civic leaders; an RAF cake-making competition for local bakers was organized, with all proceeds going to the RAF Benevolent Fund."[150] Although this sort of practice may well have increased the number of volunteers to the British armed services, it is questionable whether they aided the government's policy to turn West Germany into a staunch ally by promoting understanding between British soldiers and German civilians, let alone the future German armed forces. Critics frequently pointed out that there existed "a public appetite for war-glorifying films" and that those films depicting the futility of war due to the horrors experienced by everyone involved, or those showing British war crimes, regularly flopped at the box office.[151]

The Impact of Individual Encounters with Germans on British Opinion

A point worth making with regard to public perception of Germany is that despite the revelations of Bergen-Belsen and other concentration camps, the scope and detail of the horrible crimes committed by Germans were not as much discussed in public during the 1950s as, for example, during the Auschwitz trials of the 1960s.[152] It is this background that partly explains the outrage caused by publications like Lord Russell of Liverpool's *The Scourge of the Swastika* in 1954. Although British perceptions of Germany had naturally been influenced by Nazi war crimes in 1945, there are individual accounts by Britons that portray a more nuanced picture about attitudes toward Germans. Geoffrey Gorer thought it worthy of attention that Germans, like foreigners in general, appeared frequently in nonmarital sexual relationships of English people interviewed for his 1955 work on the "English character": "I would suggest this is a cross-cultural phenomenon, rather than a reflection on the sexual habits of most peoples other than the English. The foreigner is 'less dangerous,' less likely to be censorious; and foreign techniques of courting and flirtation, with their greater apparent aggressiveness and confidence, may well be more successful with the 'exceptionally shy' English than they would be in their own countries." [153]

Whereas this phenomenon would certainly have affected the experiences of many young British servicemen spending their time in Germany, a considerable number of British women came into contact with German men too. Political views of Germany in the late 1940s and early 1950s therefore have to be considered in the example of a miner's wife from Essex whose "one real love affair outside marriage" had been with a married German prisoner of war.[154] Of course this did not always lead to a better view of Germans, as probably proven by a twenty-four-year-old working-class girl from Ilfracombe who had an affair with a German man "who, realizing we were getting serious, told me he had no room for marriage in his plans."[155] It is likely that for some Britons the personal became semipolitical. The lived experience of relationships between the English and the Germans went to the heart of popular perceptions of Germans, if only for a minority. The controversial issue of relationships between Britons and Germans so shortly after the war was taken up in films such as *Frieda* (UK 1947—a "stuffy and dated drama about how one English family learned to love one particular German"[156]), portraying the difficulties of married life of a British soldier and his German wife in Britain shortly after the war. Symptomatic of changed attitudes, more Londoners who were interviewed by Mass Observation in 1947 approved rather than disapproved of lifting the ban on marriages between German prisoners of war and English women. However, one interviewee said, "I think if an English girl goes so low she should be segregated. If there aren't enough Englishmen, heaven help us!"[157]

Despite this negative opinion, the encounters of individual Britons with Germans after the war must be taken into account when considering British views of Germany. Famous German individuals, such as the much-revered Manchester City soccer goalkeeper Bernd Trautmann, certainly helped to improve the view of ordinary Germans.[158] However, he was only one prominent example of a multitude of contacts between Britons and Germans after 1945. Contacts on a broader scale were also established soon after the ending of hostilities through a broad range of British initiatives. For instance, the twinning of German and British towns and cities began as early as 1947 as the example of Reading and Düsseldorf demonstrates. Lord Pakenham, the minister in charge of Occupation Affairs and the regional commissioner for North Rhine-Westphalia, warmly welcomed an initiative by the mayor of Reading. This initiative attempted to "establish friendly associations" with a German town and, as one local paper reported, "friendly correspondence [. . .] would go far towards breaking down the suspicion and antagonism that comes from suffering and despair."[159] The project had apparently been given "warm approval" by representative citizens of the town. The "attitudes of grassroots movers and shakers in politics, religion, academia, the arts, business and the unions" often expressed themselves in immediate practical action, and the need to "inculcate the young with principles of European co-operation and peace."[160] It is doubtful whether town-twinning programs had any mass appeal, but local initiatives such as this have to be added to the broader perception of Germany at the time.

The Impact of Germany's "Economic Miracle" on British Opinion

Finally, economic factors must be considered when discussing British views of Germany. The town-twinning programs mentioned above were initially often a means to assist the war-torn German towns and cities. However, the German economics minister Professor Ludwig Erhard's "social market economy" was transforming the Federal Republic quickly. With the aid of the European Recovery Program (ERP), German industries were recovering at an impressive rate, and the resulting improvement of living standards soon led to jealous comments in Britain. As early as 1948, *The Listener* commented on the fact that British officials in Germany could no longer afford to eat in German restaurants. One British official summed up his feelings by saying that the British in Germany were in danger of becoming "the poor relations of the Germans."[161] Britons were "compelled to eat dreary official rations" while some of the Germans "who used to be glad to accept a tin of corned beef [. . .] now eat roast goose."[162] Confronted with these changes and facing a general election in 1950, the Labour parliamentary secretary to the Minister for Food responded "that Germans were to be pitied, not envied for the fact that food-rationing in the FRG was being abolished." Her explanation was that this "allowed the wealthy to buy up available supplies," leaving ordinary Germans worse off than the British population.[163] However, in the same year, the leader of the West German Trade Union

Federation, having just returned from a UK visit, told the German press that "the British people today are living worse than the Germans. [. . .] The German delegation could hardly satisfy its hunger in Britain. [. . .] I was glad to get a square meal when I got back to Germany."[164] The growing discrepancy between Britain and Germany with regard to the quality and available amount of food even contributed to the failure of some British initiatives to foster Anglo-German understanding. When Sir Brian Robertson ordered the opening of British clubs in Germany in 1950, one British observer was told by a resident of Düsseldorf, "We don't want to go there anyway. The food is quite ghastly."[165]

As the impressive rate of West German economic growth continued throughout the early 1950s, British concerns increasingly focused on the resulting competition in traditional British export markets.[166] According to one British journalist, "The sharpness of the German export challenge in the first instance, coming as it did in markets where Britain had held undisputed sway since the end of the war, provoked apprehensions as exaggerated as they were uninformed."[167] In an international context the German economy indeed enjoyed a number of distinct advantages over the British. In an era of decolonization, many newly emerging states chose the Federal Republic as their trading partner, as, in contrast to London, Bonn was considered to be politically neutral. The Korean War provided a further boost to German exports, and apart from the occupation costs, the Federal Republic did not have to spend large amounts of its Gross Domestic Product on armed forces.[168] "Comments among British producers grew so acrimonious by 1954 that the Foreign Office became worried that a serious deterioration in Anglo-German relations might ensue."[169] Some British carmakers blamed their failure to sell their products in Germany "on the intensity of German nationalism which has been drummed into them over the past seventy years, and particularly by Dr. Goebbels."[170] Others adopted a more open-minded perspective while still finding fault with the Germans. The journalist Fyfe Robertson wrote to the *Picture Post* in 1955 claiming that the Germans had a "new secret weapon"—namely, "hard work": "The Germans are steadily taking over our markets. They've rebuilt their cities, re-equipped their industries, and achieved a remarkable degree of prosperity in a remarkably short time, *with scarcely any rise in prices.*"[171]

But as David Kynaston shows, Robertson went on to ask if the real problem was simply that the British were not working as hard as the Germans, "not giving 'a fair day's work for a fair day's pay.'"[172] The notion of a resurgent German nationalism was increasingly accompanied by the fear of German economic competition, which inevitably highlighted the economic problems facing Britain: "'After 1945' seems to have had the same effect on the Germans as 1940 had on us. [. . .] I can think of a gloomy list of signs ever since the war that all is not well with us."[173] Despite a certain degree of soul searching, many Britons found it easier to blame the Germans rather than themselves for the reversal of their countries' economic fortunes.

A less ambiguous hatred of the Germans and undoubted resentment of their economic recovery were evident at the very apex of British politics. As Peter Hennessey has pointed out, Conservative prime minister Harold Macmillan "simply could not stand the Germans," and he even shocked the Duke of Edinburgh with a rant against "the Huns." As chancellor of the exchequer in 1955–1956, when the German economic recovery was forging ahead, Macmillan became acutely aware that the economic balance of power was shifting away from Britain to Germany and other members of the European coal and steel community.[174] Or as the *Daily Mirror* put it in 1957: "The old Teuton, fatter than ever, sits in the best and most lavish counting-house outside the shores of the United States. Who really won [the war]?"[175] Many regular British soldiers and conscripts about to go to Germany would have been exposed frequently to such reports, as the *Daily Mirror* and its rival the *Daily Express* were the most popular daily newspapers in Britain, "each selling over four million copies by the early 1950s."[176]

Conclusion

The picture emerging of the influences in media on young British men and their views of Germany was not exactly positive, although it was not quite as negative as might be expected so shortly after the Second World War. Although public opinion on political issues regarding Germany appeared equally split into pro- and anti-German camps, large parts of the British press were clearly anti-German to an extent that caused concern in the Foreign Office. Whitehall's reluctance to impede freedom of expression effectively reduced the control it might have exerted on anti-German publications, thereby increasing the necessity to establish other means of improving Anglo-German relations.

Whereas Foreign Office influence on the press was very limited, more was achieved by influencing the publication of nonfictional literature, *The Scourge of the Swastika* being a notable exception. The constant reminders of the Nazi past and warnings of the reemergence of right-wing politics in Germany in the British press undoubtedly would have left an impression on young servicemen. There is also evidence, however, that some young Britons were unwilling to accept the negative view of Germany, and particularly German youth, that was being presented to them. Furthermore, it has to be stressed that despite the widespread hostility in the popular press, a normalization of relations was evident even in papers like the *Daily Express.* The BBC's attitude toward Germany, although not always friendly, was clearly more nuanced and positive. Equally, despite the fact that British victory in the Second World War was increasingly glorified during the years of austerity and slow economic recovery, the countless nonfictional books, novels, and war films did not always portray the Germans in a bad light. War movies and novels were becoming more and more popular and served to provide comfort by retelling stories of British glory and prestige. Nevertheless, it appears that, at least during the late 1940s and 1950s (and in marked contrast to the stereotypical Nazis emerging in the following decades), the Germans portrayed in a number of films and novels were ordinary people, not unlike the British, who happened to fight on the wrong side of the conflict and occasionally even "brought a breath of the chivalry lost from modern war."[177]

Despite stark and controversial reminders of the Nazi past, such as *The Scourge of the Swastika,* and widespread skepticism as to the future of the Federal Republic, the subject of Germany in British popular culture was more complex and less one-sided than might be expected. British servicemen going to Germany most likely would have absorbed both the image of the goose-stepping Nazi as well as that of the "ordinary people" who had already been encountered by a number of Britons in the form of German POWs. Despite the predominantly working-class composition of the British military, this made the prospects of using the BAOR as a tool for Anglo-German rapprochement more promising than the negative views of the popular press suggest. Having considered British views of Germany, it is now time to look across the channel and consider the German perspective by analyzing the view of the British occupation forces held in the Federal Republic. This also entails an analysis of the problems caused by the presence of up to eighty thousand Britons in the British Zone of Occupation, a picture that was equally complex and diverse.

CHAPTER 3

THE GERMANS
Complaints, Criticism, and Demands?

> There were two cases of English soldiers robbing and assaulting
> German youths in the town of Lueneburg in 1957. As the
> number of incidents in the area had increased significantly the
> local Free Democratic Party demanded a complete break of
> relations between the town and the British troops. Particularly
> the lack of an apology by the British officers caused anger.
> —[Landesarchiv Niedersachsen], NI, Nds. 50 Acc. 96/88 Nr 165/2
>   Pressebericht Pressestelle Hannover, 6 August 1957.

In October 1952 the German national newspaper *Die Welt* reported on
the curious case of the wife of a British soldier beating the owner of a pub
unconscious during a bar fight in the small town of Hameln. A German
disabled war veteran had blamed a group of ten BAOR soldiers and their
wives for his injury and subsequent fate, which led a soldier to attack the
man. The wife of the disabled German then used his crutches to knock out
the British soldier. In return the British wife accidentally beat the publican
with a bar stool when he tried to calm the argument. "When the police arrived all they found was the publican with a head wound."[1]

It was the projection onto a national stage of seemingly minor and at times
even comical incidents like this one that regularly influenced German perceptions of the British occupying forces. Local incidents commonly caused
controversy, first in the local press and then at the national level, as well
as leading to repeated political attacks by anti-Western political parties. As
the German journalist Paul Sethe wrote in 1951, "In the past six years the
number of anglophiles in Germany has dropped steadily" and bitter feeling
had grown up among Germans "against this island nation."[2] In order to
establish exactly how the problems created by the presence of the BAOR
affected Anglo-German relations from the local to the highest levels and

how both the British and German authorities worked on eliminating them, it is essential to understand the nature and causes of grievances perceived by the German civilian population. What were the German views and experiences of the presence of the BAOR in the British Zone of Occupation? Some of the German official and individual attempts at improving relations also require exploration to allow a comparison of the British and German perceptions of the BAOR and its role.

The grievances suffered by Germans at the hand of the BAOR can largely be divided into three major categories: economic, political, and personal issues. Although there was always a degree of overlap between the economic issues, the political processes, and the lived experiences of Germans and British servicemen, they are largely addressed separately here. The first category to be analyzed concerns the economic demands of the British armed forces to ensure the functioning and efficiency of the services. These demands regularly set off outrage among the civilian population. According to the German member of Parliament and leader of the Christian Social Union of Bavaria (CSU), Franz Josef Strauss, Germany paid the same amount of money toward the occupation as France was using to pay for its entire army, air force, and colonial troops as well as the war in Vietnam. According to Strauss, an occupation soldier in 1951 cost nearly ten times as much as that of 1918, and for every two occupation soldiers there were nine civilians employed in Germany.[3]

The financial impact of the occupation was frequently criticized by German politicians and the press. Nonetheless, the majority of West Germans in 1949 thought that the establishment of a German army in order to replace foreign troops was "not at present necessary or desirable." In addition to pacifist sentiments so soon after the war, there were also economic arguments in support of this view, "as a German army would attract young men from essential industries, which can ill afford such loss." A German army would also imply an increase in national expenditure and taxes. "They consider that the Allied policy during and since the war, carries with it the obligation on the part of the Allies, to defend Western Germany."[4] On the one hand, a strong presence of British troops in the FRG was a reassuring factor for the majority of the German population. On the other hand, the economic damage caused by British troops in Germany, in addition to the regular occupation costs, was under constant scrutiny. Maneuver damage; the requisitioning of training grounds, private houses, hotels, and public buildings; as well as noise pollution by aircraft prompted the most frequent complaints. These complaints regularly evolved around material issues at a time of economic hardship for most Germans, which often stood in stark contrast to the standard of living of the British armed services. In most cases the economic grievances stemming from the occupation subsequently generated social tensions between Britons and Germans, as will be seen in the case of the requisitioning of housing.

Secondly, in the political sphere a large number of problems arose from British official communications or, rather, the perceived lack thereof. On several occasions the Foreign Office or the British armed services themselves caused offense when implementing decisions in Germany, usually made in cooperation with the Bonn or Land governments, without sufficiently communicating these arrangements to local communities. This often led the press to criticize not only the perceived British arrogance toward local and national German government bodies but also the general lack of effort by senior British officers, unit commanders, and Foreign Office officials to publicize decisions. The increasing level of sovereignty of the Federal Republic after 1949 exacerbated this problem and led to the growth of German demands to be treated as equals rather than inhabitants of an occupied enemy territory.

The third and likely most difficult category for the British and German authorities to address was made up of the actions of individual soldiers and negative experiences by individual civilians. These often involved drunkenness, violence, theft, cultural issues, sexual jealousy, or the recent history of Anglo-German relations. An entirely independent problem that influenced all three of the categories was the issue of mishaps and errors by British personnel occurring on all levels. Furthermore, as seen above, a significant factor in turning minor complaints into threats to Anglo-German relations on a national level was the German press, both in the FRG as well as the German Democratic Republic.

It is important to analyze how these different categories developed and how they affected the various strands of Anglo-German relations. Of particular importance were the frequent cases of local discontent spreading into the highest circles in London and Bonn. Three specific examples of German discontent are particularly prominent in the available primary sources and highlight how the discontent aroused by troops was used by those political groups of the left and right in Germany (and Britain) that were against German cooperation with the Western Allies in the climate of the early Cold War. The most controversial examples are the requisitioning of housing, maneuver damage, and, curiously, fox hunting by British troops. Furthermore, the increase in German official concerns about damage caused by troops requires analysis. As the British armed services were not the only NATO troops in the British Zone of Occupation, a comparison to the behavior of Canadian troops sheds further light on the popularity of British troops. Finally, the quality and success of attempts by German nongovernmental organizations and the federal and Land governments at countering the dissatisfaction of the public with British troops is considered in detail. Although a wide variety of initiatives were taken, there is also some evidence demonstrating a lack of interest among some German ministries to fund projects.

Economic Causes of Discontent: Requisitioning of Housing and Land

For the German population the issue of requisitioning was mostly an economic problem during times of hardship. It nonetheless led to social tensions between occupiers and occupied in its wake. As a result, much of the activity of German authorities regarding this issue consisted of reacting to the anger caused by the British military. In order to function as a defense against the perceived Soviet threat, the British forces required large training grounds. According to a British report, the amount of land under requisition in North Rhine-Westphalia (NRW) in 1952 amounted to approximately 125 square miles, which was one percent of the entire Land. These figures excluded new British demands for "four new airfields, a large training area for Dutch troops, an air-to-ground firing range of large dimensions, extensions to installations allowing for the accommodation of an additional 10,000 Belgian troops and the requirements of a Canadian brigade," among others. The same report highlighted concerns that there was little coordination of further Allied demands for territory and predicted that the Germans would "oppose strenuously any further loss of agricultural land."[5] Particularly in larger cities the lack of housing due to bomb damage and requisitioning of accommodation by the army brought about severe resentment. Requisitioning of land also came at a high social and financial cost. For example, a planned airfield in the Niederrhein area in 1951 required the eviction of 151 farms at a cost of up to six million deutschmarks.[6]

Because of its large scale, the requisitioning of training grounds and accommodation was a potential and often real point of friction between the German civilian population and the British military. Most German cities and towns suffered from severe housing shortages resulting from Allied bombing during the war.[7] The most heavily populated areas of Germany lay in the British zone, and most of the major and many of the smaller towns had been severely affected by the strategic bombing campaign that was unleashed in order to undermine German morale during the war. In

1943 alone the city of Wuppertal, in the industrial heartland of the Ruhr, lost 153,000 homes; the nearby Krefeld lost over 40 percent of its housing that year with more than 70,000 people left homeless. Eighty-five percent of Cologne's housing was destroyed, and 90 percent of Hannover lay in ruins.[8] Nonetheless, in the FRG in 1951 the Allied forces had in their use thousands of requisitioned houses, rooms, flats, and plots of land, as well as hotels, restaurants, and numerous other installations.[9]

From the outset of the British occupation, one of the most publicized scandals, which greatly damaged relations with the local population, was the services' widespread practice of requisitioning large numbers of properties only to then either leave them unused or not derequisition them when they were no longer needed. At times the military refused to relinquish empty accommodation in case units arrived from abroad, and occasionally houses were simply forgotten about, but in many cases "the well-known Army principle of never giving up property once acquired" was applied.[10] It is important to go beyond the immediate postwar period and consider how German attitudes about requisitioning developed once the BAOR was transformed from an occupation force to an Allied force. Unsurprisingly, once the Federal Republic was established, German resentment of requisitioning grew. The German press carefully monitored the situation and reported that despite a considerable effort by the British to reduce these figures, according to the German finance ministry there were still sixty thousand requisitioned buildings in 1951.[11]

The lack of suitable accommodation in the British zone immediately after the end of the war due to bombing and the arrival of refugees is well documented.[12] In the British-occupied Land of Schleswig-Holstein nearly 3 million refugees had to be accommodated alongside the 1.6 million residents. The population of Lower Saxony had grown from 4.5 million in 1939 to 6.7 million in 1947. In the British-occupied Rhineland alone there were 200 camps with nearly 100,000 refugees.[13] By February 1947, approximately 906,000 refugees from the east had made their way to North Rhine-Westphalia.[14] The arrival of British families beginning to join service personnel in 1946 had naturally exacerbated the "unparalleled" housing situation in the zone.[15] Many Germans were evicted at short notice from their homes to make room for British families.[16]

What is less well documented is that despite the successful German efforts to build new homes on a large scale, the issue of requisitioning continued to threaten relations between BAOR and the Germans until at least the mid-1950s. The British Düsseldorf resident officer reported as late as September 1954 that the city's population still grew by five hundred a day and that "despite signs of new dwellings, the hard core of bunker inhabitants remains a constant figure."[17] In contrast, British soldiers and their families often found life in the British zone extremely comfortable. For example, the homes of the fifty families of the 15th/19th The King's Royal Hussars in the city of Lübeck on the Baltic coast were located "in what had been before the war the smartest area of town. It was not unusual for a senior NCO [noncommissioned officer], his wife and one child to live in a six-bedroom house surrounded by a vast garden and to receive the services of a nanny and a daily help, all free of charge."[18] Many of these benefits enjoyed by British troops in Germany were only slowly given up in 1956. This change of heart, however, did not occur in order to improve Anglo-German relations but, rather, because the Germans were no longer required to pay for the costs of the cheap German labor used for the provision of domestic servants for British officers. According to the chancellor of the exchequer, Harold Macmillan, "somebody else" had been paying for the privileges, and the military had to accept "that the situation is different when this heavy new burden falls on their own people in the United Kingdom."[19] In fact, the secretary of state for war very much regretted abolishing the benefits enjoyed particularly by British officers in Germany, as previously these had been beneficial for the recruitment of new officers. The "comfortable conditions" in Germany were to counterbalance the hardship endured in other stations around the world.[20] This luxury was obvious to the local population and shaped the German attitude toward the British forces' accommodation situation. The generally slow speed of derequisitioning of homes was a frequent point of complaint by Germans.[21]

The German press and many political parties constantly campaigned against requisitioning, thereby causing problems for the Bonn government. For example, in 1951 the *Frankfurter Allgemeine Zeitung* reported on the demand of the Social Democratic Party that the government ensure no more housing was to be requisitioned in case of any further increase of Allied troop strength in Germany. In addition, the restrictions that prohibited Germans from sharing accommodation with service personnel should be abolished.[22] Furthermore, in 1951 the SPD issued an official request to Parliament demanding the government reach an agreement with the Allied high commissioners to not remove victims of Nazi oppression, refugees, those affected by the war, and those displaced by the occupation regime from their current premises. The fulfillment of this demand would have left very few properties for the BAOR to requisition. The SPD also demanded that the necessary housing and installations for Allied troops be built immediately.[23] This put additional pressure on the Bonn government to spend more money and resources on housing at a time when the increase of BAOR troops itself heightened the occupation costs for the FRG. There was evidently a demand by the German population that the transformation of the BAOR from an occupation force to an ally should go hand in hand with a reduction in the often lavish accommodation of British troops. (The British attempts to accommodate these demands are analyzed in chapter 5 following an examination of German civilian attempts to wrestle the control of their homes from the British.)

German civilians who were displaced by and dissatisfied with the occupation regime (the so-called *Besatzungsverdrängte*) increasingly organized their protests and founded official organizations in North Rhine-Westphalia and Lower Saxony.[24] According to a 1951 German press report, the number of people with claims against the German government due to requisitioning was as high as 3.5 million. For six years these people had been waiting for the return of either their homes or other property, such as furniture, that had been requisitioned by the Allies.[25] The same newspaper estimated that the number of displaced persons as a result of requisitioning made up as much as 6.8 percent of the entire German population.[26]

The *Besatzungsverdrängte* organizations arranged frequent demonstrations throughout the British zone, and their demands continuously increased throughout the early 1950s. Postulations ranged from the return of the requisitioned properties and the exclusive housing of Allied troops in barracks to the repatriation of all Allied families to their home countries and a general end to the "colonial policies" ostensibly represented by the BAOR.[27] The *Besatzungsverdrängte* organization of North Rhine-Westphalia threatened to take legal action against the state of NRW after a man had been removed from his house by a force of "nearly fifty policemen." This incident had occurred even though the requisitioned property in question had stood empty for a long time. Apparently the return of the house had been promised repeatedly and this was only the latest in a series of cases in the area.[28] At least one protest march by the organization in the town of Detmold had to be dispersed by the police, as it threatened to turn violent.[29] In January 1952, desperate German families in the town of Herford moved back into their requisitioned homes without permission. The local German authorities issued stern warnings to the residents, as it would be impossible to protect the families should the BAOR forcefully remove them.[30] In 1953, despite the protests by displaced Germans, there were still British couples without children living in entire houses by themselves in Herford. An attempt by displaced homeowners to move into their empty but requisitioned houses ended with water and electricity supplies being cut off and German guards, employed by the BAOR, enforcing the strict isolation of the Germans in question.[31] The pressure of the *Besatzungsverdrängte* groups also contributed to the pressure on the German authorities.[32] These cases demonstrate not only how the unpopularity of British requisitioning affected German views of Allied troops but also how the image of the Land and federal governments suffered as they enforced unpopular measures previously agreed on with the British. Thus, the largely economic issue of requisitioning also had political implications for both Britain and Germany.

Cases of displaced persons illegally occupying their still requisitioned houses were reported by the press as late as 1955. Interestingly, there were some similarities here with the occupation of military accommodation by homeless squatters in Britain in 1946. In Britain as in Germany the military seemed indifferent to the problems of ordinary people, despite the possession of many unoccupied or partly occupied premises during a period of housing shortage.[33] The German authorities continually attempted to force the occupants to leave their properties by cutting off water and electricity supplies. The *Besatzungsverdrängte* organizations, on the other hand, keenly supported the individuals in question, much to the frustration of the British authorities.[34] In one case a local German court forbade neighbors of one particular property that was illegally occupied by their owners to install an alternative gas supply to the house. The court also ordered the owner to leave his home, which, after a lengthy court case, he did in January 1956, and the requisitioning continued until May of the same year.[35]

In several cases where homes had been requisitioned but subsequently left empty by the British, landlords and families in need of housing simply moved back in as a sign of protest. For example, in the small Westphalian town of Lübbecke, where 160 houses with fifteen hundred rooms had been requisitioned, seven families moved back into their requisitioned but empty homes and raised the European flag as a sign of protest.[36] Lübbecke had a population of approximately seven thousand people with an additional three thousand refugees when it became one of the key British administrative centers of the British zone in 1945. And the housing situation continued to be severe even after barracks for British troops were built in 1948.[37] Once more this situation led to the formation of local protest organizations that supported those Germans occupying their homes. The Lübbecker *Notgemeinschaft* telegraphed the minister president of North Rhine-Westphalia as well as the personal security advisor to the German chancellor, Dr. Theodor Blank, to advise them that the seven families had moved in, claiming their rights in accordance with the Basic Law for the FRG. The British, however, demanded the immediate evacuation of the flats, threatening to arrest the families in question, who then left without causing further disruption.[38] Events of this type occurred all over the British zone, particularly in those more rural areas that had been spared the worst of the Allied bombing and were now inhabited by a large number of refugees from bombed-out cities and the east. The establishment of friendly relations between troops and communities that had to make way for British families as late as ten years after the end of hostilities was undoubtedly going to be a difficult task.

The worst area of the British Zone of Occupation with regard to requisitioning was without doubt the area of Bad Oeynhausen, which housed the headquarters of the BAOR until 1954. The town had largely escaped bomb damage during the war, but an unwelcome surprise of a different kind affected the majority of inhabitants in 1945: "'Baddo' as it was called, was a very pleasant spa, about twice the size of Southwell in Nottinghamshire, with twice the population. Unfortunately the 10,000 'Deutschers' had been evicted from their nice little town to make way for 1,000 officers and 2,000 other ranks who acted as clerks, batmen, drivers, runners and every kind of dogsbody to the officers."[39] The town was substantially requisitioned until 1954. The railway station itself was requisitioned, and Germans using it were segregated to some extent. "I find it impossible to imagine a situation anywhere else parallel to that which still obtains in this town, seven years after the end of hostilities and on the eve of the Federal area resuming sovereignty."[40]

Barbed-wire fences separating the British from the Germans in Bad Oeynhausen were removed only in 1951, when seventy hectares of requisitioned land, including the spa gardens, were handed back to the Germans. Nonetheless, 40 percent of all available living space in the town continued to be requisitioned by the BAOR.[41] By the time the British headquarters at Bad Oeynhausen were finally closed, the physical and economic damage caused by the BAOR was considerable. The town had lost, "apart from [the damage caused by] the thirty-two minor and medium fires, the Protestant church, a 750,000 DM bathing house and four private residences," all of which had been requisitioned by the British. A local newspaper article outlined how under British "rule," the largest thermal spring in Europe had remained closed to anyone but the BAOR and how the only public building in town that was accessible to the German public had been a public lavatory. The entire train station, including all ticket offices and waiting rooms, was reserved for "the handful of British tourists," while "the last remaining church bells were not allowed to ring for German but only for English services."[42]

Requisitioning brought on more than economic grievances. For an increasing number of Germans, it stood in the way of achieving the reestablishment of German sovereignty. As diplomatic relations between Britain and

Germany on the highest levels increasingly normalized, it was economic questions such as requisitioning that threatened to turn the BAOR into a liability rather than an asset to Anglo-German relations. The ostensibly economic grievance of maneuver damage also clearly highlights how economic damage translated into political problems.

The BAOR and the KPD:
Maneuver Damage and Its Political Consequences

The requisitioning of land and property was not the only major source of complaint created by the BAOR. At least once every year the British services, together with their allied NATO forces, conducted large-scale maneuvers across wide parts of the British zone. These inevitably caused damage to property and distress to local inhabitants. Roads were ruined by tanks and armored vehicles, farmers lost their crops, damage to forests and even houses and farms frequently occurred. Furthermore, a number of areas were repeatedly affected by their proximity to training areas, which led to an increasing resentment of British troops and the fear of a rise of political extremism. Maneuver damage quickly developed into an economic problem with serious social ramifications. On a tour of damaged areas near the Reinsehlen training area in 1951, a British officer met with local German farmers and officials who had been affected. The officer concluded that all the locals "had a full understanding that considerable damage was to be expected and unavoidable and that they accept necessary damage with equanimity." However, they were "becoming increasingly bitter and resentful" over what appeared to be "unnecessary, avoidable and even wilful damage. [. . .] The Germans met had a genuine fear that extremism in political feeling is being engendered."[43]

British fear of providing political extremists in Germany with ammunition over the actions of the BAOR was not unfounded. West German communist groups in particular made good use of the issue of occupation forces. A 1953 British Information Services report highlighted the "increasingly frequent and more scurrilous" attacks on the Allied defense forces by the communist press in Germany. The campaign turned "every small incident involving an Allied soldier, even remotely, into an act of terrorism or drunken brutality"; damage caused by troops on maneuver was "pictured as wanton destruction which was ruining the farmers"; and protests against requisitioning of land "were published almost continuously under bold and provocative headings." In the run-up to the 1953 German general elections, "the same type of material was repeated ad nauseam in the Communist Press" in order to

Local inhabitants taking an interest in a British tank on maneuvers in Germany during BAOR exercise "Agility," 1949.

attract votes for the Communist Party of Germany (KPD). The communists specifically linked the federal government with the Allied troops and demanded, "Out with Adenauer, out with the Occupation troops. Vote KPD."[44] Communist agitators frequently used British plans to create new training areas or enlarge existing ones to claim that "in the interest of war preparation they will first take your land and then your sons shall be driven to the slaughter for the profiteering interests of the war-mongers in this country and abroad. The bombed cities are still lying destroyed, the tears of widows and orphans have not yet been dried, and *again the same hands—which are still smeared with the blood of the last war*—are grasping at your land, at your houses, at your lives."[45]

The communist press in Germany and in Moscow used every opportunity to campaign against the BAOR. In a number of cases this proved hugely damaging to the British military as well as Anglo-German relations. This damage took months of intense efforts from both Bonn and London to undo. Often these incidents were instigated by local communists. An article in the weekly national paper *Die Zeit* traced how one such incident had turned into the number-one news issue for a whole week throughout the entire country. It began with a typically brief British military press note, announcing the enlargement of the Teutoburg Forest training area. The local communist press and the Soviet news agency TASS then jumped at this and fueled speculations with rumors. A local communist newspaper article, headed "Warmongering in Teutoburg Forest Demands First Victims," called for protest after the alleged eviction of 266 people from the Teutoburg Forest region to make room for maneuver areas. The article repeatedly referred to Allied war preparations and highlighted the danger not only for the water supply but also for the lives of local inhabitants and called for mass protests to preserve the existence of communities as well as peace.[46] Local German opinion apparently had been affected by the behavior of a particularly insensitive British army officer who made it very clear he did not like Germans, and by the memory of British tanks in 1945 destroying twenty houses in the village despite there being no German soldiers left and white flags hanging out of the windows.[47] The issue was then picked up by the noncommunist press. According to the conservative newspaper *Westfalenpost*, the potential environmental impact of the decision to extend the British shooting range that had led to the evacuations had been brought to the attention of UNESCO. Environmental concerns now added to the economic problems that had resulted from the affair. The British allegedly had ordered the residents of several villages to evacuate their homes for three days per week when the BAOR planned to practice artillery and machine gun shooting.[48] The forested area to be destroyed by British troops was valued at 15 million DM and considered vital for the local tourism and logging industries.[49] GDR propaganda now also seized the opportunity to attack the BAOR. Radio Leipzig reported that many inhabitants of the area had protested in the name of the National Front of the Democratic Germany against the destruction and colonization of their home country, or *Heimat*, and for national and economic independence. It also referred to the rise in number of members of the National Front in North Rhine-Westphalia.[50]

Despite British attempts to calm the mood and explanations as to the real aims of the extension of the training area, the German press continued to doubt British promises and the plight of the local population received attention even in the nonaffiliated press.[51] Only at a later date did the West German press report that the evacuation was designed merely as a safety measure around the actual practice area that had been used since 1945; that only two families, who previously had been informed about this, had to leave their homes for three days per week; and that logging could continue on the days when no practice took place.[52] As a result of this negative publicity, the decision on the extension was referred back to the British high commissioner, General Robertson, and also became a matter for the federal government.[53] The subject dragged on for weeks and ended with a British announcement to reverse the decision to expand the training area.[54] On the same day, however, the British announced the requisitioning of a different area in the Sauerland region, which promptly led to renewed uproar in the press.[55] This example highlights only one of many cases receiving national attention due to a combination of factors: requisitioning and training exercises exacerbated by a perceived lack of communication by British authorities; alleged actions by British officers; and an at least partly hostile German press. The British military presence threatened to cause resentment not only because of economic grievances but also because German citizens were becoming subject to political agitation by the KPD.

It is evident from this type of propaganda that relations between British troops and the German population really were a potential source of problems for West German integration as well as European defense. Although Adenauer's Christian Democrats (CDU) comfortably won the 1953 election and the number of communist votes dropped below the 5 percent mark required to enter Parliament, the federal government feared that Germans at large had not yet been convinced by the idea of democracy.[56] Therefore, the threat to Anglo-German relations posed by the KPD was taken seriously by both the German and British administrations. The communists had entered the 1949 Federal Parliament with 5.7 percent, and the 1953 election still returned around six hundred thousand communist votes in the FRG. The poor performance of the KPD in 1953 was partly attributable to the brutal crushing of the June 1953 uprising in the GDR by Soviet tanks.[57] This decline of the KPD's popularity was certainly greeted with satisfaction by the British high commissioner Sir Frederick Hoyer-Millar.[58] The fear of potential consequences of anti-Western propaganda nonetheless increased over time. Only the banning of the KPD in 1956 finally alleviated the perceived threat posed by the extreme left to the newly established German democracy.

As with requisitioning, maneuver damage caused problems not only for Anglo-German relations but also for the German Land and federal governments. Once the occupation status had given way to that of equal partnership, the demands of the German population grew rapidly. These demands could then be taken up by the press. There was to be no military training and shooting on German public holidays. The damage to trees in requisitioned training areas was to be minimized, and, among other demands, there was to be no low-level flying of aircraft. Warnings by local German officials

British Centurion tanks with mounted platoons "causing traffic jam" in Haltern, Germany, 1955.

about the political consequences of maneuver damage steadily increased.[59] According to the trade minister of Niedersachsen, by 1953 the population's anger was mainly targeted at the Bonn government, which, considering the looming elections, was a problem. Furthermore, many of the claimants of previous years were still waiting on compensation for maneuver damage.[60] The number of disgruntled German voters was potentially growing year by year. Problems for Anglo-German reconciliation also arose from other unexpected problems as the case of fox hunting demonstrates.

Fox Hunting as a Cause of Intercultural Friction

Hunting impressively demonstrated the fragile nature of Anglo-German relations at the local level. It also highlighted the willingness of both the British armed services and the German citizenry to use the issue of "friendship" as a bargaining token. What was intended to promote intercultural communications was instead sometimes a significant hindrance. Tensions arose from the fact that the traditional British way of fox hunting had been outlawed in the Federal Republic, considered as being cruel to animals. After 1949 this ban also applied to Allied troops in Germany. In spite of the Bonn government banning the practice, in at least one case a local British unit had different ideas and strongly demanded an exemption from the ban.[61] The British desire to use dogs for fox hunting in the town of Wolfenbüttel even led to the British resident officer in the area, a Colonel Day, who was responsible for liaising between troops and German civilians, using his influence with local German politicians. Apparently Day and Captain Lord Blandford of the British Life Guards put considerable pressure on the German official who was responsible for hunting in the town of Wolfenbüttel. A letter by Lord Blandford to the German official used drastic language to highlight the potential damage of the hunting issue for Anglo-German relations in general. Apparently fox hunting was taking place in a large number of European countries, and "the only reason it was outlawed in Germany was due to Hermann Goering's decision in 1937."[62] It is doubtful, however, that this letter would have swayed the German official's view in favor of the British request. The British government had informed BAOR units that, in the interest of Anglo-German friendship, hunting was now allowed for troops but only with the permission of the local German owners. In the eyes of some officers, these owners had endangered British-German friendship by their refusal to "leave a few hares, which was really not much to ask." After all, British officers had spent considerable amounts of time and money to buy and train their dogs and would, "due to this unfriendly and short-sighted action of yours, receive preciously little joy and amusement in return."[63] Lord Blandford stressed that the Germans had to be aware that Anglo-German relations in the area would suffer considerably unless the Germans were willing to compromise.[64] This thinly veiled threat, however, was only the beginning of the conflict over fox hunting in Wolfenbüttel.

The German official Herr Lieberkuehn subsequently complained to the Lower Saxony Land government. Apparently British troops had harassed him after he refused to grant the desired exemption for British fox hunting in the area. According to Herr Lieberkuehn, such decisions could be made only in Bonn or Wahnerheide, and local Germans were very upset about the British practice of employing dogs for the chase. To make matters worse, the night after the refusal of an exemption, Herr Lieberkuehn's house was attacked by "heavy and very heavy" British pyrotechnic devices, and it appeared obvious that this was a response to the refusal.[65] The excuse given by the British for launching three "attacks" during that evening was that apparently the soldiers who had launched the flares meant to deliver an ovation to their commanding officer to celebrate "Battle of Hastings Day" and that they had accidentally picked the wrong house![66] The German police report concluded that the fire from the flares that were used easily could have led to the entire house burning down and that the home of the commanding officer was located in a completely different part of the town.[67] Naturally, the incident, which caused considerable damage to the house as a number of small fires were started, was gratefully taken up by the communist press in the GDR.

This was a remarkable case of the problems incurred by the attempts of individual officers to circumvent British orders from high levels on the ground. The consequences in return had to be dealt with by the minister president of the Land government and the British Land commissioner. The issue was finally resolved with a British apology to Herr Lieberkuehn and the end of fox hunting in the area. The British hunting dogs "were returned to England."[68] It is questionable, however, whether after this incident the local BAOR unit or the German population had much interest in improving Anglo-German relations. Incidentally, a British Information Services report for 1952 highlighted the emergence of "a violent and obviously organised Press campaign in Lower Saxony against hunting by Allied troops."[69]

Individual Officers and Social Causes of Anti-BAOR Sentiment

There is further evidence demonstrating the damage done to the British image in Germany by individual officers. At times, apparently insignificant episodes led to enormous problems. It is worth considering some examples here in order to understand the varied nature of German grievances against the BAOR. In September 1952, the senior head of the Lüneburg City Council was denied access to the tennis court of his requisitioned estate by a British officer. Claiming the borders of the requisitioned area were unclear, the German official went on to openly attack the British officer in a public council meeting. The incident led to a formal protest by the city council and naturally attracted the attention of the press. One parliamentarian stated that the Lüneburg public was aghast that seven years after the war a single British officer could still remove the first representative of a large city council from his own private property using military police: "Incidents which may still be possible on the Fiji Islands should belong to the past in Europe."[70] This in return prompted a letter of protest from the British Land commissioner of Lower Saxony and a lengthy argument between German and British officials aiming to establish whether or not the tennis court had in fact been requisitioned. British officers in command in 1945, when the requisitioning took place, had to be consulted, and detailed plans of the property were produced in order to establish the exact boundaries of the requisitioned premises. Both the British and German authorities once again had to spend considerable amounts of time and effort to minimize the damage and propaganda value for both left- and right-wing political factions in Germany. Another noteworthy case of this kind occurred in 1952 when an officer purposely drove his tank into the garden of a restaurant in Lower Saxony because he had been refused a drink. Having caused "some thousand pounds worth of damage," the officer was officially "severely reprimanded"—"unconfirmed reports however had it at the time that he had been subsequently congratulated by his commanding officer for show- ing 'initiative.'"[71] Similar grounds for complaints were provided by one British major who had to be dealt with by the military police in Hamburg after crashing his car into a German taxi and subsequently kicking the driver in the stomach while "under the influence of drink."[72] This type of incident provided ample ammunition for the German press to ridicule Brit- ish attempts to use the BAOR to display the values of Western democracy. However, German complaints about British behavior were by no means limited to the actions of individual officers.

Incidents Caused by British Troops

The relations between troops and civilians were frequently overshadowed by minor as well as major incidents created by British troops in Germany. The frequent reports of clashes between soldiers and Germans gave an indication that things did not always progress as smoothly as planned. British resident officers generally produced positive reports about relations between Brit- ish troops and German civilians, but the monthly newsletters issued by the Public Safety Department of the British High Commission shed a different light on the situation on the ground. For example, the April 1954 Public Safety Report for the Westphalia area alone listed two serious late-night incidents between soldiers and civilians. One German civilian died from his injuries, and one British soldier was stabbed in the back and seriously wounded.[73] The same report for July 1954 listed nine cases of malicious damage by British personnel, ten common and four indecent assaults, and one case of rape by servicemen, not to mention seven brawls involving ser- vice personnel and four thefts.[74] In Hamburg one typical incident occurred in May 1954 when "a soldier grabbed a German woman by the breast and hip and offered her five DM for permission to have sexual relations with her."[75] Local incidents such as these brought frequent complaints, but par- ticularly during the mid-1950s the behavior of British troops in some parts of Germany deteriorated and caused major reasons for concern.

Incidents Caused by Canadian Troops

Despite the threat to Anglo-German relations arising from certain British actions, it is noteworthy that Canadian troops were often regarded as far worse than the British, and German authorities recorded widespread complaints about their drunkenness, violence, prostitution, and black market activities.[76] One example involved twenty-five Canadian soldiers who had organized the raid and destruction of a bar in the town of Bergen and injured guests because the publican had called a Canadian officer to calm an argument between Germans and Canadians a week before.[77] As a result, three Canadian soldiers were sentenced to one and a half years in prison with hard labor. In another incident in December 1951, two Canadian officers were set upon by a group of twenty German youths armed with sticks and chains. Further reports of unprovoked attacks in the town by German youths had led up to the incident in the pub.[78]

As in Britain, relations between troops and civilians led to comments in the Canadian press. The fact that the Federal Archive in Koblenz holds records of Canadian press reports on relations between troops and Germans demonstrates the considerable level of concern among the German authorities. The *Vancouver Sun* reported in 1956 that Germans "resented the presence of Canadian troops in their country" and that although there was little open hostility, there was "continual sniping at Canadian soldiers in the German press." Going further, the article claimed that "the effort at good community relations appears to be all one-sided—on the part of the Canadians." According to the *Sun* article, the German attitude toward Canadian soldiers was hardly surprising inasmuch as many Germans who were opposed to rearmament resented their own soldiers, and it was therefore likely that Canadian and German troops would get along much better than Canadian troops and German civilians.[79] One Canadian reporter claimed he had not found a single man who did not want to go home as soon as his tour of duty was completed. One frequently heard Canadian reaction was that "the Germans like our money but not us."[80] However, according to the German embassy in Vancouver, the *Vancouver Sun* itself consistently demonstrated a hostile, subjective, and tendentious attitude toward Germany.[81] Clearly it was not only Anglo-German relations that posed a potential threat to the German commitment to Western defense in the British Zone of Occupation. However, the fact that Canadian behavior was rated worse by many Germans arguably worked in favor of the British.

German Official Concerns over British and Other Allied Troops

As the above examples demonstrate, the presence of British troops in particular and Allied troops in general was not universally welcomed by the German population. In 1952 a survey by the German political opinion polling company Emnid Institute attempted to gauge how successful the Allied attempt to transform occupation troops into protective forces had been. Only 14 percent of those polled throughout the three Western zones saw the troops as "welcome protection." Sixty-seven percent regarded them as either unavoidable or even as an unwelcome nuisance. This view was spread equally across all zones.[82] Despite these negative attitudes, a poll conducted by the American High Commission revealed that 75 percent of respondents were against a withdrawal of Allied forces from Germany for fear of a Soviet attack. Seventy-four percent thought it unwise to engage with the Soviet suggestion to withdraw all Allied troops from Germany. This constituted an improvement, as at the end of the Berlin blockade in 1949, only 46 percent had declared support for a continuation of the occupation.[83] These figures suggest a fairly widespread and increasing German willingness to accept the presence of Allied soldiers for reasons of anticommunist expediency. However, the statistics do not demonstrate a particularly friendly attitude toward the occupation troops.

Despite this, the behavior of the soldiers in Germany was rated better than their role as "welcome protectors." Forty-one percent of those polled by Emnid thought the behavior was "very good" or "good," 34 percent answered "average" or "bad." In fact the British fared the best, with 48 percent "very good" or "good" and only 22 percent "average" or "bad."[84] German sources suggest that the unpopularity of French and American troops was at least partly due to German resentment of the allegedly poor behavior of black American and French Moroccan troops. According to a report by local German officials on relations in the southern German Land of Baden Württemberg, Moroccan troops had committed "countless cases of rape" in 1945.[85] French Moroccan soldiers were frequently the subject of complaints to German authorities. The American troops not only demonstrated appalling, "rowdy-like" behavior, but particularly black American soldiers were blamed for continuous sexual assaults of German women.[86] Statistics compiled by German authorities in areas occupied by French and American troops revealed a long list of crimes, including several cases of children (both girls and boys) and pregnant women being raped, as well as murder and assault, among others.[87] Compared to the severity of these cases, the behavior of British troops indeed appeared better, and the issue of racial prejudice was largely nonexistent in the British Zone of Occupation. These statistics reflect the findings of this chapter, as the unpopularity of British troops did not necessarily stem from their behavior but rather from the economic disadvantages, political resentment, and inconvenience caused by their presence.

It is nonetheless surprising that the highly rated British behavior deteriorated in the mid-1950s and gave rise to increasing concern by German federal and Land governments. Particularly after the admission of the FRG as a full member into NATO, German official concerns and attempts to improve relations and minimize crimes committed by soldiers grew. Apparently the behavior of at least some British troops markedly deteriorated, particularly from 1955 to 1957. At the very moment when London and Bonn considered relations between the BAOR and Germans crucial to ensure West German integration into the Western orbit, local incidents in Germany indicated a turn for the worse in several areas. By 1955 the frequent occurrence of incidents as a result of the actions of individual servicemen became a serious concern to the federal government. In particular, serious crimes like theft, rape, and even murder gave constant rise to complaints by the German press.

The growth of British crime did not go unnoticed by the German public and in fact coincided with a decrease in popularity of Allied troops recorded by opinion polls. A poll published in *Die Welt* in July 1956 on German views on the behavior of Allied troops in the FRG revealed that now only 3 percent of those questioned thought the behavior of Allied troops was "very good." Thirty-one percent rated it as "good," 40 percent as "fair," and 17 percent as "bad," with 9 percent not having any views on the subject. Further questioning revealed that 45 percent of those polled considered the presence of Allied troops "an unavoidable necessity," and 38 percent "an undesirable burden." Despite this decline in popularity, the chancery of the British embassy in Bonn considered the reaction of the public "quite reasonable," as there was little doubt that the results had been influenced by "recent press publicity given to incidents in which troops were involved."[88] In July 1956 this significant rise in the number of incidents led the Bonn government to send requests for statistics on the numbers of incidents and cases of prosecution to the Land governments. Furthermore, the Federal Ministry of the Interior (*Bundesinnenministerium*) inquired about the quality and truthfulness of local German press articles. These steps were taken in order to consider whether or not to take diplomatic actions.[89]

As a consequence of the increasing number of press reports on crime committed by Allied soldiers, the NRW interior ministry had already compiled
a list of all crimes perpetrated by Allied soldiers during the second half of
1955 and the first half of 1956. The statistics clearly revealed an increase
in the number of crimes by British soldiers.[90] Particularly incidents involving drunkenness in bars and restaurants showed a rise for the British (from
eighteen to twenty-eight). Burglaries rose from thirty-one to forty-eight.
According to the interior ministry of NRW, the level of crime had decreased
slightly among the Canadians, whereas it had risen significantly among
the British. There had been no change in troop numbers among any of the
forces. The interior minister demanded that the minister president point
out the rise in crime to the British authorities and suggest measures to deal
with them, such as an increase in military police, the eviction of criminal
elements, and sharper punishment.[91] The demand even included a template
for a letter of complaint to the British Land liaison officer.

Moreover, German officials raised concerns over perceived damage to
Anglo-German relations the BAOR's behavior was causing in Britain. In
September 1956 one observer highlighted the negative publicity the rise
in crime had caused abroad. Particularly the Beaverbrook press reporting—which, unsurprisingly, had blamed the rise in crime on a resurgence
of German nationalism—was viewed with concern, as it insisted that the
best solution to this problem was the complete withdrawal of Allied troops
from Germany. In light of such reports, it appeared wiser to deal with the
issue informally with the British Land liaison officer rather than file an
official complaint.[92] Nonetheless, the interior ministry did send an official
letter to the Land liaison officer and pointed out that in some garrison
towns—mainly Minden, Detmold, and Münster—the number of crimes
had risen alarmingly. The letter asked to prevent crimes specifically over the
Christmas period, as in January 1957 a large number of civilian properties
in these areas was due to be requisitioned by British troops.[93] Despite this
plea at least one German newspaper reported that over Christmas numerous
incidents had occurred in eastern Westphalia, the very area in question.[94]

Not all Land governments chose to complain formally to the British as
in the case of NRW. In fact, the interior minister of Lower Saxony decided
against reporting individual cases to the federal government as requested,
because he simply did not want to draw further attention to the issue,
reasoning that "relations were rather better than those in the American
zone."[95] The minister also pointed out that many cases reported in the German press turned out to be false and he was against any diplomatic steps
as a result of recent cases.[96] Nonetheless, between July 1955 and July 1956,

302 British soldiers committed crimes in Lower Saxony, including 2 cases of manslaughter, 17 cases of rape, and 130 cases of theft.[97]

Despite the attitude of the Lower Saxony interior ministry, the federal government was so concerned about the behavior of Allied troops that a meeting with members of the military police of all three allies was organized at the British headquarters in Lower Saxony in November 1957 to come up with solutions to the most pressing concerns. A federal interior ministry consultant outlined some of the main German apprehensions.[98] The problem of relations involving soldiers had long been a concern of the federal government, and German statistics showed that in some areas relations had deteriorated significantly since the spring of 1955. The timing of this deterioration of relations was important, as it occurred at exactly the time the Federal Republic was to be treated as an equal ally against communism. The federal government had begun to collect data in 1955 when reports of incidents increased. The nationality of troops was an important factor, and figures for American troops in Bavaria and Baden Württemberg were "alarmingly high." Conditions in the northern states with British troops were significantly better despite a number of serious incidents. According to the Germans, the main reasons for misbehavior were the attitude of "being in occupied enemy territory" and the fact that most soldiers were young and unmarried, had too much money, and in some cases wished to import "cowboy manners" from their homeland.[99] The interior ministry stressed the view that no army stationed abroad could afford to accept attacks on the civilian population, as this undermined morale and discipline and thus endangered fighting power and capability of the troops. The federal government clearly regarded the issue as a real threat to the defense of Western Europe.

In order to improve relations, the German interior ministry suggested soldiers engage socially with Germans—for example, in sports clubs. This was considered more productive than having sports events with teams from each country, because such competitive interaction potentially proved counterproductive. These measures, however, were considered to be feasible only when they involved "the older, more reasonable, intellectually interested soldiers." In many cases all efforts with "the young, inexperienced, intellectually close-minded, primitive soldiers" would be doomed to failure.[100] In the view of the Germans, this type of soldier often had left home for the first time and was "confronted with problems he then failed to deal with." Apparently such people naturally tended to spend their free time consuming alcohol and consorting with the local fräuleins. It was felt that these soldiers did not use their time in Germany for their own more ostensibly rational personal development. The ministry advised that if all efforts failed to bring this type of soldier into the fold of civilian life, the only thing left was strict disciplinary supervision. Finally, the Germans urged the Allies to be more careful in their selection of troops sent to Germany in the first place and to consider if it was possible "in the interest of good relations to only send soldiers to Germany who could be expected to behave and send those home who did not."[101]

Despite the federal government's concern over the situation in some parts of the country, German crime statistics of 1957 revealed just how favorably the behavior of British troops compared to that of the Americans. Between July 1956 and September 1957, US troops in Bavaria committed 8 murders, 319 cases of grievous bodily harm, 136 robberies, and 207 rapes. The corresponding figures for the British area of Lower Saxony were 0 murders, 27 cases of grievous bodily harm, 9 robberies, and 23 rapes. Corresponding figures for North Rhine-Westphalia, which was also predominantly under British control, were 0 murders, 64 cases of grievous bodily harm, 26 robberies, and 36 rapes. The overall number of offenders in Bavaria during this period was 714, whereas in Lower Saxony this figure was remarkably low, with only 26 British offenders. In North Rhine-Westphalia there had been 195 delinquents during the period in question.[102] The collection of data by the federal government continued, and in March 1957 the German Ministry of Foreign Affairs produced a list, compiled by the Länder, of incidents between the Allied forces and the local population for the eighteen months ending December 1956. For Baden-Württemberg, Bavaria, Hesse, and Rhineland-Palatinate (the areas where French and American troops were stationed), the total number of criminal incidents was 1,051; in contrast to this, North Rhine-Westphalia, Lower Saxony, Hamburg, and Schleswig-Holstein (the British and Belgian area) totaled a mere 137 incidents. The British Foreign Office commented that "even after making allowances for the greater number of the American forces, we had every reason to feel satisfied with the general behaviour of our troops."[103]

Although the statistics provided by the German authorities do not indicate an overall rise or fall of crimes committed by the BAOR, they certainly demonstrate the restraint exercised by British troops compared to the other Allies. Overall, the British forces were relatively well-behaved. According to the British embassy, most disturbances were of very recent occurrence and should be seen against the background of the generally acceptable behavior of the British services in Germany.[104] Therefore, German official attempts at reconciliation, analyzed in the next section, were not terminally undermined by the articulated disquiet about the excesses of some members of the BAOR.

German Efforts at Conciliation

The attitudes of the German civilian population toward British troops varied considerably depending on the geographical location, proximity to the Soviet Zone of Occupation, and whether garrisons were in urban or rural locations. The changing economic and political situation of the FRG also had an impact here; as a result, attitudes in 1957 often differed significantly from those expressed in 1948. Some of the views held during the early period of occupation are outlined in the official history of the 15th/19th The King's Royal Hussars, who arrived in the northern German city of Lübeck in October 1949. According to this source, the initial attitude of the 250,000 inhabitants was ambivalent at best. In the eyes of the author (who wrote his account in 1981), this "depended mainly on just how much the Germans needed to get on with the military authorities in order to make a living." This meant that the majority of Germans avoided the British altogether, but, unsurprisingly, those civilians who were employed to work in British garrisons and those who hoped to engage in black market activities were very friendly. The German "shopkeeper would almost literally roll out the red carpet when a soldier or his wife entered the shop," and "these were still the days when a pretty German girl would somehow manage to swallow her pride when a bar of chocolate or a packet of cigarettes were on offer."[105] The citizens of the Westphalian town of Münster apparently developed "a somewhat stolid, almost off-hand attitude" to the British presence, which some Britons considered to be a result of the traditional Westphalian hostility to any military presence, regardless of nationality. However, "if one is to indulge in generalizations it is probably best to record that the further away from the East German border the less spontaneous Anglo-German relations tend to become and the faults do not all lie on one side."[106]

German attitudes recorded by British observers in smaller towns were often more favorable, and there is evidence of German attempts at cooperation and genuine interest in the occupation troops on local levels. The local policeman of the small town of Wesendorf, for instance, defused a potentially embarrassing situation when the military band of the 15th/19th The King's Royal Hussars gave a concert to entertain the villagers. When the German and British national anthems were played at the end, the spectators "stood firm" to the playing of the German anthem "but began to wander off during 'God Save the Queen,' presumably from ignorance rather than bad manners. One loud grunt of disapproval from the policeman and the crowd stopped in its tracks where it remained until dismissed."[107] At times during exercises in the German countryside, troops found they even had to fend off curious local Germans visiting from neighboring villages "in the hope of picking up the odd treat such as a bar of chocolate or 'finding' some useful spare bits and pieces with which to mend their cars." Fencing off the entire area to keep out civilians was not considered an option, as "we're supposed to keep good relationships with the locals."[108]

Despite the hostility in parts of the German press and public, there also were large-scale concerted efforts by German authorities and also by non-governmental organizations to improve relations between Allied soldiers and civilians. The Anglo-German Association (*Deutsch-Britische Gesellschaft*), founded in May 1949 in Düsseldorf, quickly became the most prominent organization fostering understanding between the British and German people. Its privately arranged bilateral Königswinter conferences aimed at planning meetings to "discuss matters of particular substance and moment [*sic*]."[109] Although nongovernmental organizations largely focused on Anglo-German relations in general rather than the BAOR in particular, the annual appeal for "Christmas in peace and freedom—union of hearts" by the Anglo-German Association, which was widely advertised in the German national press, stood out as a prominent example to include service personnel.[110] This appeal called for Germans to invite Allied soldiers into their homes for Christmas. In particular, troops who spent their first year in Germany were to be shown a traditional German Christmas. Noteworthy was the nonmilitary character of the appeal, as the invitations were designed as a thank-you to those Allied soldiers who themselves had provided many German children and elderly people with gifts in the past. The invitations by German families were to be sent to local unit commanders and contain special requests based on age, profession, religious affiliation, and language skills of the soldiers.[111] To further emphasize the nonmilitary character, the appeal was continuously widened so that by 1954 the program also included foreign students and refugees from the Eastern Bloc. In order to tempt more people to join the appeal, the organizers constantly pointed out the value of the invitations to the Germans, who could improve their language skills and learn about other cultures.

German official efforts also continuously increased on all levels. German politicians made regular appeals to both the German population and British troops to improve relations. For instance, as early as May 1951 the minister president of NRW, Karl Arnold, called for an improvement of relations between the British and the German civilian population when visiting BAOR headquarters at Bad Oeynhausen. He suggested transforming the BAOR from an occupation force to a protection force and asked for the British officials to work toward this aim.[112]

In a similar vein the state-run northern German radio station (*Norddeutscher Rundfunk,* or NDR) broadcast a program in December 1956 on the relations between the civilian population and Allied troops. This included a two-minute address by the German chancellor Konrad Adenauer, thanking those who worked to create friendly and cordial relations. Adenauer stressed the willingness on both sides—from the grass roots of local people up to federal authorities and Allied headquarters—to foster better relations. He also reminded his German audience of the many benefits they had gained from the presence of Allied troops, ranging from sports grounds built by soldiers to support of children in need to employment opportunities. Furthermore, he stressed the considerable economic benefits presented to the Germans by the presence of the troops.[113]

Efforts by the various German ministries affected by relations with the British services varied in scope and success. The German Foreign Office compiled a directory for Allied soldiers with suggestions on how to improve relations between themselves and German civilians. This effort came at the height of the debate about misbehavior of Allied troops in November 1956. The means toward this goal was to foster the personal and professional interests of the soldiers stationed in Germany. The directory aimed to provide an overview of cultural and professional bodies in Germany that could be of interest to the soldiers in order to encourage the development of contacts with the local population. Copies were initially sent to the American and French headquarters, but British and Belgian troops were also supplied with them. The compendium was divided into trades, industries, agriculture and forestry, sports, music and arts, technology (engineering), universities, and tourism. Essentially it provided a detailed list of a wide range of trades and leisure activities, ranging from subjects as diverse as agriculture and boxing to dog training.[114] When compiling the directory, the German Foreign Office sought advice from all minister presidents asking for additional suggestions to be made by the ministries involved. The trade and transport minister of NRW reported that companies and factories had already offered guided tours for Allied soldiers and their wives, which had been a success.[115] The Ministry for Food, Agriculture, and Forestry suggested that a useful addition would be to include youth organizations in Germany, as most young soldiers had expressed the desire to establish contacts with organizations related to those in the home country of the soldier.[116]

Despite good intentions, the compilation of the directory above all provided an example of a lack of cooperation between the German and British authorities and demonstrated the complexity of such a task in the FRG. The publication of this expensive brochure was significantly delayed due to a legal battle with the German printing company, as large numbers had been printed before important amendments had been made, essentially rendering them worthless.[117] When it was finally available, it proved less popular with the British than had been anticipated. The reason for this was simple: although the directory demonstrated the willingness of German authorities to improve relations, the British response to the directory, which was essentially a very long list of addresses and phone numbers, was reserved at best, because it was written in German. The German Press and Information Bureau offered three thousand free copies of the directory to the British embassy, but the reply to the "generous offer" stated that, "due to the very particular nature of this guide book," it was of very limited use to the simple soldier: "If in the future you should again consider producing brochures *in English* for Allied Service personnel I would be most grateful for an opportunity to see a draft as we or the military authorities surely would be able to make some useful suggestions *before* the brochure is actually printed."[118]

Other promising German initiatives failed to materialize altogether. For instance, a member of the German Lower House (*Bundestag*) suggested the German-wide establishment of meeting places for Allied soldiers and German youths, based on one successful example in the American Zone of Occupation. The idea was to organize coach tours, dances, movie screenings, and talks, aimed at both Allied soldiers and Germans.[119] The plan envisaged three such meeting places in the British zone (as well as eight American and three French) and was in principle approved by all German ministries involved. However, when it came to funding the project, the idea was axed after a lengthy debate. The defense ministry refused to contribute the 300,000 DM necessary for 1957. Because the project involved only German civilians, the defense ministry did not consider itself responsible. The interior ministry refused to pay on similar grounds, as the impact of the project was mainly related to foreign policy. When the foreign ministry disagreed with this assessment, the member of Parliament was duly informed that there were no federal funds available for the project.[120] The apparent lack of interest on the part of the federal ministries involved raises the question of how seriously at least some German ministers were taking the issue of relations between Allied soldiers and German civilians.

Despite the varying attitude of German ministries, it was the concern about crimes committed by Allied troops that led the German foreign ministry to establish an inter-allied commission involving the embassies of the FRG and those of the Allies. Its overall aim was to examine incidents between troops and Germans. The German interior minister, defense minister, and federal press office were also involved. Depending on the subject of the meetings, commanders of Allied headquarters and local German officials were also in attendance.[121] The findings of this group again stressed that in general the British efforts to bring troops and civilians together compared favorably to those of the United States. The statistics of negative incidents also put the British into a positive light. According to the German Foreign Office, the comparatively low number of incidents involving British soldiers stemmed partly from successful British measures such as the establishment of local Anglo-German committees; jointly organized events; the distribution of English books on Germany; and the showing of films about Germany. Further measures included discounted travel in Germany for BAOR soldiers and encouragement to join activities of the Anglo-German Society.[122]

Despite the aforementioned concerns from Land governments about crime levels among Allied troops, by November 1957 the German foreign ministry decided that the situation had sufficiently improved and postponed a planned meeting of the Allied working party, due to "the lack of specific concerns."[123] It is apparent that despite a temporary rise in crimes committed by British troops between 1955 and 1957, in the view of the German foreign ministry the situation had improved by the end of that year. It was not until the 1960s that the behavior of British troops became the focus of federal concern and the German Foreign Office suggested a renewal of the talks between Germans and the BAOR.[124]

Conclusion

It is evident that from a German perspective the presence of the BAOR in the Federal Republic increasingly threatened Anglo-German relations precisely because of the improvement of diplomatic relations between Bonn and its new Western partners in the defense against communism. The requisitioning of housing and land that was imposed on German communities in 1945 continued into the late 1950s and attracted increasing hostility from the significant number of civilians affected. Added to this was the regular negative attention troops attracted because of maneuver damage, which was frequently used by the German press to stir up anti-British sentiment and even invited communist propaganda. During election campaigns, the presence of British troops was a potential problem to be exploited. It was used in attempts to damage the reputation of the Christian Democrats under Konrad Adenauer. Even when acting within the boundaries of policies agreed upon between London and Bonn, the BAOR often attracted widespread criticism based on the lack of communication with the German press and local German officials. This in particular was harmful to relations and frequently led to lengthy arguments and complex attempts at minimizing damage at the highest levels.

When considering German efforts to improve relations, it is apparent that, compared with French and American troops, the British were regarded as very civilized and willing to facilitate more harmonious relations between servicemen and civilians. Many of the official German efforts—such as the directory for Allied soldiers—were well-intended, yet, through a lack of consultation with the British, severely flawed and often not effective. Whereas many nongovernmental organizations successfully brought British troops and German civilians together, there was a notable reluctance in the German interior and defense ministries to fund initiatives, even when these clearly had been proven to be successful. It is also apparent, however, that, according to the German administration, the rise of incidents caused by British soldiers noted after 1955 had been sufficiently brought under control by 1957. Efforts to use the BAOR as a tool to improve Anglo-German relations were regarded as less urgent in Bonn, as might be expected, considering the view of the British Foreign Office on the matter. However, before analyzing the British administration's concerns about the impact of the changing relationship between Britain and Germany brought about by federal sovereignty in 1955 and its attempts to change the behavior of the British armed services, it is necessary to consider the position of the services themselves. In order to fully understand the relations between the BAOR and the Germans, the situation in Germany as seen by British troops requires investigation. This allows for an evaluation of the efforts made on all levels by the armed forces themselves to work toward better Anglo-German relations.

CHAPTER 4

THE SOLDIERS, THE AIRMEN, AND THE GERMANS

Military Strategies to Improve Relations with the German Population

> During the time we are in camp it is hard to believe we are in
> Germany. All the chaps naturally speak English, and the German
> workers here also speak English. We have German women
> cooks, and lovely meals.
> —National Serviceman Corporal Malcolm Barker, Queen's Royal
> Regiment, in a letter to his mother, 6 July 1952

The *Westdeutsches Tageblatt*, a local German newspaper, reported in 1952 that attempts to improve Anglo-German relations by both British troops and Germans showed some signs of success. However, a number of difficulties still had to be overcome, including "the typical Anglo-Saxon lethargy which prevents the English from actively looking for new friends and learning new languages" as well as the German tendency to "come across as too friendly and therefore give the impression of ingratiation."[1] As the previous chapter has demonstrated, any absence of contact between the British armed services and Germans was not necessarily due to an overly friendly attitude on the side of the Germans. However, many observers commented on the perceived lack of effort by British troops to overcome their "Anglo-Saxon lethargy." Having analyzed the view of the British and German media along with those of the administration in Bonn of the services' efforts to improve relations, the focus here is on the BAOR itself and its efforts, both on the official level and more individual levels. On the one hand, this chapter considers the changes made by the armed services before 1955, when the Federal Republic's sovereignty fundamentally changed relations between Bonn and London. On the other hand, some of the measures taken by the services in 1956 and

1957 in order to demonstrate to what extent they could be used to bring about an improvement in relations are explored. As the analysis of German responses to occupation has shown, a number of incidents caused by British soldiers threatened to seriously undermine Anglo-German relations. It is important to highlight some of the underlying reasons for these incidents from the perspective of occupying military forces. Operational difficulties encountered by many British regiments in Germany often made organized efforts to improve relations with Germans difficult. The life of BAOR officers and ranks in Germany as well as the more personal contacts with the local population also had an impact on the value of the BAOR as a tool for rapprochement. As will be seen, a change of attitude toward Germany was evident and reflected, for example, in regimental magazines. It is the aim of this chapter to investigate the attitudes and behavior of the services in the run-up to Federal German sovereignty in 1955 and to highlight some of the problems and attempted solutions by the British armed services once Germany was a fully established member of the Western community. There is ample evidence of thorough and successful attempts by British forces—incidentally, RAF units—that require investigation. The measures introduced by the RAF are also compared to those of the army. The analysis of service attitudes and efforts allows for conclusions to be drawn with regard to the value of the BAOR in the context of the improvement of Anglo-German relations envisaged by the British Foreign Office.

Operational Difficulties

The British armed forces in Germany faced considerable pressures in fulfilling their military role in the early Cold War period. As a consequence, the improvement of relations with the local population was not necessarily a priority for the military leadership. As established in chapter 1, General Brian Robertson himself considered the role of the BAOR to be largely political. He was gravely concerned about the strength and condition of the forces in Germany: "It was not, properly speaking, a trained army and to put it in the field if a crisis arose would present very great difficulties indeed."[2] It is important to consider the consequences of this weakness for the troops involved. The commanders in chief of the British forces in Germany had serious concerns about the ability of the BAOR to successfully repulse or even slow down a Soviet attack. According to a report on the perceived lack of reinforcement for the operational plans of the British forces in Germany, the efficiency of the troops varied "considerably between the various arms of the Services." British military planning for a potential Soviet attack assumed

there would be "no warning period which will enable any preparatory mo-
bilisation measures to be taken."[3] However, there were considerable shortages of manpower, and the BAOR relied on the arrival of reinforcements
from Britain in case of an emergency in order to become fully operational.
These vital reinforcements were unavailable at unit locations until at least
six days after an initial attack.[4] The Commanders-in-Chief Committee for
the British forces in Germany pointed out that the Royal Armored Corps
had only enough men to crew 50 percent of their tanks, field regiments
of Royal Artillery could man only 75 percent of their weapons, whereas
light antiaircraft regiments could man only half of their guns. Royal Artillery headquarters was able to operate only "by withdrawing officers from
regiments."[5] Royal Engineer units were only able to "produce fifty percent
of their 'working numbers.'"[6] This situation was regarded as particularly
grave in view of "extensive demolition programmes" to be carried out in
order to slow the Soviet advance and "the fact that seventy per cent of the
engineer effort is German Service Organisation, regarding whose loyalty
we have grave doubts."[7]

As early as 1948 the potentially dangerous position of BAOR in relation
to its dependence on German labor for administrative support had become
evident. If those 150,000 Germans employed by the BAOR should prove
unreliable due to communist action, "our forces there would ultimately
be greatly handicapped and movement on any substantial scale would be
difficult."[8] The Royal Signals fared little better, as "the present strengths
[. . .] would make the provision of adequate communications forward of
Headquarters Northern Army Group very difficult." Rear of Headquarters
Northern Army Group the situation was "deplorable. Even if existing units
are made up to Higher Establishment, the barest essential communications
cannot be provided." The position of the infantry varied considerably among
battalions, but all battalions were short of men, and support companies had
been "pared to the bone."[9]

The Royal Air Force in Germany apparently was in no better condition.
In case of an emergency, it would not be possible for the army to take over
aviation fuel from its Antwerp storage facilities and transport it to RAF
airfields unless more trained personnel were made available. The Royal
Air Force was "at the moment in danger of a breakdown in the command
organisation due to deficiencies of Signals personnel" and because of having its operations seriously curtailed due to shortages of personnel and
resources.[10] The commanders in chief demanded as essential that reinforcements were "trained men, in every way qualified and fit to undertake the
operational tasks required of them." The report concluded that in order

to be operationally effective, the British armed forces in Germany needed "considerable reinforcement of men who are ready immediately to carry out their operational tasks between Simple Alert and D-Day and sufficiently in advance of D-Day, to enable them to be absorbed into their units." It was considered "impossible under present arrangements to ensure that these reinforcements would start arriving at unit locations before D-Day plus six."[11]

The outlook in case of a Soviet attack was indeed bleak. Despite the desire to assure the Germans that the Allies would hold the river Elbe in case of a Russian attack, there was no mention of any plan other than to fall back to the Rhine in British COS reports on the subject. The effect on the army of manpower shortages during the withdrawal phase following a Soviet attack was considered to be grave: "The delay imposed on the Russians will be reduced because the covering forces as at present constituted will be too weak. [. . .] The danger of successful airborne 'coup de main' action against both the Rhine and Maas bridges will be greatly increased. [. . .] During the initial phase of the Rhine battle, the inability of all arms and services to deploy a reasonable fighting potential will cause unacceptable delay in the preparation of the Rhine position."[12] The success or failure of the British forces in Germany was therefore "gravely prejudiced by the lack of a comparatively small number of trained men."[13] This lack of resources might partly explain why many personal recollections by unit commanders of their time in Germany focus very little on relations with the Germans. For example, one regimental commander in his account of a three-year period in Germany mentioned Anglo-German relations only once, when he met an officer of the new German army in 1957, whom he found a "sound, level-headed and practical officer," despite having spent eleven years in Soviet captivity.[14] Therefore the absence of any major initiatives by the British army can be at least partially explained by the military situation and the lack of personnel.

The military preparedness and performance during maneuvers did not boost either British or German confidence in the BAOR's ability to stop a Soviet attack. According to the *Westdeutsche Allgemeine* newspaper, the 7th Armored Division had performed abysmally in a maneuver in 1950. Apparently, the commander of the BAOR, General Charles Keightley, had accused the division of being "slow, lacking any element of surprise and generally not being what it was in 1945." According to the article, much of the equipment was outdated, and nine out of ten vehicles were "scrap."[15] The serious situation in Germany did not affect only the higher echelons of the British forces and their ability to spend much thought on Anglo-German relations. For many British soldiers stationed with BAOR, the international situation, combined with the perceived unpreparedness of the BAOR, proved rather unnerving: "Korea was on and communist domination was feared in the West. The Armoured Corps was on forty-eight hour standby, looking at the Russian tanks looking at them and knowing that war was the squeezing of a trigger away. We didn't have Centurion [tanks] then, we had obsolete Valentine Archers designed in 1939, and we got numerous calls to arms in the middle of the night, with rumours of Russian attacks. Truthfully there were occasions when we thought we would never see another dawn."[16] Glyn Jones, a wireless operator at Royal Artillery Battery HQ in Düsseldorf, felt bemused when his sergeant told him that he "was an essential cog in the wheel that would roll back the Russian hordes." Jones himself was less confident, as "in two years I [had] fired ten rounds from a rifle, ten from a Sten, five from a revolver and I'd never been on the field guns."[17] Considering this situation, it may not come as a surprise that many units as well as individual soldiers stationed in Germany considered Anglo-German relations to be a comparatively minor issue. Nonetheless, there is some evidence that particularly in the early 1950s, several unit commanders noted that relations with the Germans returned "back to normal" and that British regiments had organized an increasing number of Anglo-German social events.[18] Apart from the impact of the Cold War, issues such as the nature of the accommodation of troops in Germany also had an impact on relations between the British armed services and the Germans.

BAOR Accommodation and Its Impact on Community Relations

Although some wives of service personnel stationed in Germany felt guilty about living in comfortable houses in the United Kingdom while their husbands were "probably in some horrid slum," the barracks in Germany that housed British troops were in most cases a pleasant surprise for British soldiers.[19] Most had been built in the 1930s by the German armed forces and were equipped with central heating as well as double glazing and "had constant hot water—and men slept two to six to a room." One National Serviceman commented on the camp cinema "the size of the Odeon, Leicester Square, an indoor sports complex that included a full-size hockey pitch, and an officer's mess like the Taj Mahal." These barracks also had "a gymnasium that could have been a venue for the Olympic Games, swimming pools and acres of playing fields."[20] All British garrisons in Germany "were self-contained units." Leisure facilities were often provided within the barracks;

Privates of The Buffs (Royal East Kent Regiment) picking a tune on a German wall jukebox in the NAAFI in Dortmund.

as a result, contact with the local population was to a certain extent limited. "The Army Kinema Corporation provided recent releases of popular films and the British Forces Broadcasting Services [. . .] provided a cosy mixture of record request programmes and military gossip."[21]

Off-duty activities for troops were often limited. A soldier could spend his spare time in the Navy, Army, and Air Force Institutes (NAAFI) canteen, or "with a pass and in uniform, he could go into the town and spend the evening until midnight in a 'Gaststube.'"[22] However, in more remote garrisons this proved difficult. For example, the 15th/19th Hussars at Wesendorf were stationed in a small village with little entertainment on offer, and larger towns were too far away from the garrison. Particularly in the early postwar period, the lack of available transport discouraged soldiers from traveling, as "one moves about by the rule of thumb method." Not all soldiers had "sufficient courage to face a refusal" and walked quite long distances at times.[23] The increasingly unfavorable exchange rate between the British pound and the deutschmark also made it "almost impossible for a British soldier to go to a German restaurant or attend German entertainment."[24] It is not surprising, then, that many soldiers spent their free time in "the camp NAAFI and the squadron clubs which held the occasional dance."[25]

These conditions did not necessarily make Germany a popular posting for young Britons. An article in one regimental magazine lamented the lack of the friendly and homey atmosphere of the local public house back in Britain. The pub was not the only institution absent in Germany. Possibly most of all "the soldier out here misses the fish and chips after a cinema show or what have you. Open fish and chips shops in Germany and many more, I'm sure, would soldier on."[26] Nevertheless, many young British men did visit the local German towns during off-duty hours. Some found that from the early 1950s onward, conditions in Germany seemed better than back at home: "The streets and buildings in Germany [. . .] were clean and in good repair, the people were well-dressed and confident and the food seemed plentiful and of high quality. The first thing that struck me after only three weeks away was the drabness of austerity Britain."[27]

The nature of British military accommodation remained a regular obstacle in the way of using the BAOR as a tool for improving Anglo-German relations. This was due to the physical separation of many bases from their local surroundings and the self-contained nature of at least the larger barracks. Thus it was often easier for service personnel to spend their time completely separated from their host country. In many cases only the routine and boredom associated with army life inspired young Britons to explore the surrounding areas. Some soldiers found that life outside the camp was more interesting. Groups of young British men explored the country by train, tram, and Rhine River cruises on weekend leaves.[28] Some, like the National Serviceman Malcolm Barker, even traveled by themselves, as "strangely enough, I cannot find anyone else with the same lust for travel."[29]

Despite the limitations described above, contacts between German civilians and British soldiers were—depending on the location, size, and amenities on offer within the garrisons—a frequent occurrence. When it comes to overcoming language barriers, "young soldiers make little effort to learn adequate German and thus find new pleasures in being stationed in Europe."[30] However, a considerable number of young Britons did make an effort to at least get by. Malcolm Barker asked his mother to send a German-language book, as he was "picking up the language in bits and pieces" and was determined to find out "how to put those pieces together." He was hopeful that "with the book and the help from the Germans on the staff here I should be able to pick up the language before we go home."[31]

Those soldiers who did overcome the language barrier frequently encountered and reported on the many cultural differences between the British and Germans on those occasions when contacts did take place. As discussed in the previous chapter, British attitudes and behavior frequently upset the feelings of local Germans. One young Briton commented on the apparent

German lack of humor at a Christmas party the German staff working in the barracks had been invited to. At one point the party nearly broke up when someone suggested they sing "the old German hate song (the song the Nazis sang during the war and going something like this: Today we rule the world, tomorrow we rule England). They all rose in disgust that an English soldier should even suggest it and became rather offended."[32] The German guests "vowed to never fight against England again," and the young soldier thought "they were very sincere. At least I hope so." The party was not helped by a drunken corporal shouting "Vive Stalin," which apparently led to more German guests walking out. "It proved one thing—that the Germans have a very little, if any, sense of humour." Furthermore, the incident demonstrated to the young Briton that the Germans were "rather despondent and helpless, fully expecting another war very soon."[33]

Differences in Attitudes of British Officers and Other Ranks

From a British perspective, personal relations between soldiers and Germans varied significantly, depending on a number of factors. These included the preconceived ideas of Germans (discussed in chapter 2); the memory of Nazism and its impact on the view of individual troops as well as garrison commanders; and personal attitudes of service personnel. During the immediate postwar period, attitudes of at least some British troops toward Germans were quite clearly negative. As one serviceman recalled in 1948, "We did our 'Army of Occupation' duties. It was called 'showing the German population who won the war.'" Former SS soldiers were scrubbing the billet floor and "the German workers in the camp were usually badly treated."[34] It is useful to distinguish between officers and other ranks when considering personal relations between British soldiers and German civilians, as a difference in behavior between the two groups was often apparent. For example, the more distant and reserved behavior of officers is made evident by the recollections of a young British serviceman who noted after six months in Germany when one officer left his regiment and "came round and said goodbye to us all. [. . .] He even said goodbye and shook hands with the German staff—a thing I have never seen any officer doing before."[35] The diary of another British officer in Germany revealed a curious mix of sympathy, humor, and disdain that shaped the attitudes of some Britons during this period: "Dinner in Tyrol: Not too bad. Two star. Sat with two Krauts and their child. Made child aeroplanes out of table napkins. Child pleased. Obviously a future Messerschmidt."[36] The same officer's impression of Hamburg in 1951 was dominated by the "drab" Hotel Four Seasons, the "vaguely dreary" country club, and the "frightful" people, all of which rendered the place "like any other European city."[37] He nevertheless cut short a holiday into Luxembourg and France to spend time in the "clean, well-run Germany."[38] Frequent visits to a German friend in Cologne demonstrated the "economic miracle," or *Wirtschaftswunder*, to him when he saw "the huge place he has built since we knocked it down in the last war—and the country house and so on."[39]

Asked how he got along with the Germans during his time there, one former British staff officer replied that although he had had "the most interesting time" there, it was "quite close, six years after the war." He thought it unfortunate that there "was still a barrier between fraternising with the Germans. You were not supposed to do too much of this and it was a pity because I could have improved my German a bit."[40] Another British officer was impressed with how the German people worked and their efficiency: "I'd come through Germany from Italy when it was all blitzed—every city was flat and when I went back and saw the way they'd built these towns—you had to take your hat off to them."[41] A British unit commander commented on the good relations with his German civil labor teams and his admiration of "the way they stuck into clearing the bomb damage and rebuilding everywhere."[42]

David Findlay Clark, an RAF officer on his way to Germany in 1953, encountered other British soldiers on their way to their units in Germany and reported: "It was encouraging that most of them seemed to have enjoyed their postings in Germany."[43] The soldiers he met appeared to show very little interest in "the present social or political conditions" in the Federal Republic. "Some had learned a little German but few mixed to any significant extent with local German people."[44] The same young NCO "still felt strangely exposed in this land of our former enemies" when he crossed the border into Germany.[45] This initial response, however, was slowly replaced by the "attitudes of a member of an Occupying Force." Nonetheless, having seen the extensive bomb damage to German cities, he was concerned as to "how the indigenous population might react to RAF personnel, especially in uniform."[46] When spending some free time in a beer garden in Münster, it occurred to Clark that "our Luftwaffe predecessors must have lounged at these self-same café tables with their beers some years before." He was told by the proprietor that "we were disarmingly like our former Teuton equivalents both in style and habits."[47] The majority of the inhabitants of Münster, which had suffered severe bomb damage during the war, apparently were "polite and helpful" to British airmen, although "there were several people of both sexes who would turn away very deliberately and spit as I passed."[48] This kind of experience of being sworn or spat at was shared by other British officers, but as one aptly summarized: "In general, we were accepted, and after all, we weren't the Russians."[49]

The experiences of soldiers of other ranks in Germany often differed from those of officers. Asked how British soldiers regarded serving in Germany, one regular soldier hesitated before replying: "I was a little against Germans in general and I think that the whole,—at least the majority of squaddies were with me,—had this sort of thing about Germans because of what they did during the war. I don't think it would be a long, long time before they were really forgiven for this. Nevertheless, we had a job to do and we done it to the best of our abilities I think."[50] Despite this he claimed he "got on alright" with the Germans. Nonetheless, he said, "I still think that, looking back on my time in Germany there that, although the British had this thing about the Germans, I still think there was a lot of conflict there you know." It apparently did not take long, then, for an argument to develop "if you were that way inclined." But having learned his lessons about "what happens when you're in the wrong I decided very much to turn the other cheek you might say."[51]

Once the Korean War was over and the death of Stalin led to a temporary improvement of East-West relations, being posted to Germany constituted a considerable change from other postings for many British soldiers, as "in Northern Ireland we had been on semi-active service dealing with urban guerrillas. In Germany we were part of an Army of Occupation in peacetime conditions: the heat was off." This brought problems as "sex (the absence of) and boredom soon began to preoccupy the minds of all ranks and alcohol consumption rose enormously."[52] Soldiers were "herded together in barbaric conditions, surrounded by wire fences and guards in a foreign country whose language they know nothing of." Not surprisingly, these conditions led to a rise of "drunkenness, inefficiency, and absence without leave."[53] This "pronounced sense of apathy and boredom" was also remembered later by some of the National Servicemen who had been in units "directly on the front line"—that is, on the border to the Soviet Zone of Occupation.[54] Despite Cold War tensions, a busy daily routine, and countless maneuvers, "there were lengthy periods of inactivity and boredom."[55] Such boredom often led to disruptive incidents. According to one National Serviceman who served in Brunswick in 1957, one particular recreational activity was highly popular among soldiers: they would "simply go down to the railway station and start a tremendous brawl with the locals." These "Goodwill Missions" tended to "frequently involve hundreds at a time and sometimes last all night."[56] Recollections of this kind of event were common among British soldiers, often with the justification that "these same Germans had caused us all a great deal of inconvenience" in the last war. These stories of "anonymous" mass attacks and German "counter-attacks," however, were often accompanied by positive memories of encounters with individual Germans.[57]

The experience of first entering Germany left a lasting impression with many British servicemen. One noticed the change once he crossed the German border on a train to his unit, as "all along the railway line there were the remains of warehouses and other buildings bombed by the RAF during the war. And what a pitiful sight it was, too!"[58] Troops were nonetheless received warmly by Germans, who often waved and cheered at passing army trucks and, in some cases, even provided British soldiers on exercise with bottles of ice-cold beer.[59] One National Serviceman recalled how a German family took him into their home to dress his wounds after he had fallen off his motorcycle. Relations became so cordial that he even tried "to get a date with their daughter."[60]

British Wives in Germany

For many of the BAOR officers and regular soldiers, life in Germany was made more enjoyable by having their wives and children living with them. Despite initial German resentment, the presence of British families had a positive effect on Anglo-German relations due to the growing contacts between women and children. "Operation Union," the accommodation of British married families in married quarters in Germany, had received cabinet approval in 1946, and the first families arrived in Germany in August of that year.[61] As established in chapter 2, the necessary requisitioning of dwellings to house British families was not looked upon favorably by the German population and also created controversy in Britain. Immediately after the war the attitudes of some BAOR wives, who considered that "requisitioning a few houses from the German people" was necessary "to make up for the injustice of having been separated by war," did not help to alleviate tensions.[62] However, other wives were "examples of all that an ambassador should be."[63] According to a report by British women's organizations, the strain on the German housing situation resulting from British requirements for married families was so great "that the living space allowed to each German after British requirements had been met would be four square meters—'the floor space of two ordinary beds.'"[64] Operation Union was subsequently adjusted to take into account the housing situation in Germany.

Despite the increased tensions over housing, the arrival of British mothers and children quickly brought down barriers between occupiers and occupied. For young children the past war and nationalities did not matter when looking for new playmates; as a result, their mothers also began to develop contacts. Although Germans often found themselves evicted from their homes, many friendships still developed between the new British inhabitants and those Germans who were now employed as maids, nannies, cooks, or gardeners. Those Britons who found themselves "in the lap of luxury after a tour in the UK" or abroad were provided with plenty of information on how to spend their time while also exploring German customs and meeting the local population.[65] Regimental magazines painted increasingly inviting pictures of German fairgrounds, festivities, and travel opportunities for British families. Some wives of servicemen in Germany wrote letters to these magazines, highlighting the positive aspects of British family life in Germany: "If all the holiday centres in this country are the same—so well run, with civility and no worry for the wife with a baby, however young—then I am staying until my husband has to leave this country through no fault of his own."[66] In a similar vein, as early as 1949 the Royal Signals magazine, *The Wire*, described the pleasant life in the town of Bückeburg, where "in the morning the German nursemaids can be seen wheeling their English charges about, and in the evening the park becomes the playground of all the local children."[67]

However, British and German children did not always get on well. One local German government report highlighted a case of a German child of elementary school age being set upon by a group of English children between the ages of ten and fourteen: "The children stole his purse, tied his hands and feet together and threw him into a pond where he was saved from drowning by a passer-by."[68] It was now the task of local resident officers to cope with spontaneous and sometimes potentially dangerous events like this. Nonetheless, although initially controversial, the arrival of British families to Germany undoubtedly had a positive effect on relations at least between married servicemen and the German population encountered by their families.

British Soldiers and German Women

For those young Britons without families in Germany life was somewhat different. Fraternization with German girls occurred very early after the end of hostilities and by January 1946 was considered so normal that it was frequently mentioned in regimental magazines: "'Ladies' night is held once a week, one man may accompany one 'lady' to an evening in the club. Up to the present it has proved successful. The 'Non-Fratters' generally occupy their time in one corner playing darts, whilst the others are quite content dancing with the frauleins."[69] The same magazine later commented that "we do not take too seriously the Sapper, who in a recent essay on 'Life in BAOR' alleged 'there is plenty of sport here besides frauleins.'"[70] One soldier commented on how much was written in Britain about the low moral standards in Germany and said that "little more than a low standard can be expected amongst the poverty and the ruin of Germany at the moment." Official attitudes toward relations with "the better type of German girls" had clearly relaxed at least in some regiments, as an article in *The Wire* in 1949 revealed. The author wished those soldiers married to German girls "the best of luck" and urged them to accept this as "a normal outcome of close contact by occupation."[71] Figures collated by the War Office in 1950 showed 717 marriages by BAOR soldiers to German women, 12 of those by British officers. In 1951, 7 officers married Germans and so did 390 of other ranks.[72] Some RAF officers were nonetheless warned as late as 1953 to be cautious about fraternizing with German women, due to anxiety of classified information being passed on to Soviet spies. However, this attitude did not exist in all units; the Royal Signals magazine published a photo of one of its officers and his new German bride as early as 1949.[73] Whereas some servicemen stationed in Germany for a longer term formed firm relationships with German girls, others seemed to enjoy a colorful sex life instead. However, as many of the National Servicemen had girlfriends waiting for them in Britain, often nothing more than "pleasant little episodes" developed, which were "simply part and parcel of the adventure of being abroad in the comfortable warmth of a Westphalian summer."[74]

Those British soldiers who were willing to pay for sex were served by numerous brothels in Germany. In Hannover the whorehouses were located next to the train station and referred to as "Platform Six." Hamburg, with parts of its notorious red-light district "turnstiled at either end, was described as the biggest brothel in the world." Those who made use of the services offered by prostitutes saw prices rising steeply, from "a tin of Nescafe, a bar of chocolate or perfumed soap," and sometimes "as little as two cigarettes," to twenty cigarettes by the middle of the decade. By the mid-sixties "it was strictly cash only."[75] The changing status of the BAOR, combined with the growing purchasing power of the German population, led to significant inflation for the soldier who paid for sex.

It appears that contacts with German girls among British officers were less common than those among other ranks. British women in Germany appeared to be more popular. Some officers of the Royal Northumberland Fusiliers stationed in Münster "managed to achieve pleasant relationships with teachers at a local British school" whose parties were "famed for the kind of satisfaction they afforded. But on the whole, Germany, for an unmarried officer, was fairly barren sexually."[76] The other ranks in Münster appeared more willing to engage with German girls. As one signalman recalled, "Troops always seem to respond to a nation's ladies as opposed to its men," and it was not uncommon for young Britons to "simply cut holes into the perimeter fence" in order to invite German girls to have sex within the grounds of the barracks.[77] The patrolling officer often "had to make short detours to avoid the writhing bodies."[78]

Efforts by Army Units to Improve Relations

The preceding pages have outlined some of the conditions encountered by British troops in Germany. Having explained some of the factors preventing closer Anglo-German relations on the more individual level, as well as pointing toward a slow improvement, the analysis now turns to the efforts made on the level of army units and garrisons. Records show that the efforts of the British army generally lacked both the scope and the long-term commitment to produce significant results in this regard. In fact, as late as 1955 the British civilian administration in Germany commented on the view shared widely among members of the BAOR "that something like Hitler will emerge more or less inevitably in the Federal Republic in the course of time."[79] But a general change of attitude was nonetheless increasingly apparent. The satisfaction with the efforts of the armed services that was expressed by the British ambassador in 1956 demonstrated the willingness of at least all senior BAOR officers to improve relations. A brief for the ambassador concluded that negative German press reports had fallen from 112 in July and August 1956 to only 15 in October of the same year and that the number of positive reports had risen from 19 to 23. This was largely the result of the work of the army's public relations officers, and much of the remaining criticism of troops had come from remote areas "where there is neither an Army Public Relations Officer nor a British Consular Officer."[80] The commander in chief of the BAOR, General Richard Gale, commented that "the Germans were noticeably more friendly to the Forces since the end of the Occupation."[81]

Some army units did actively work on relations with the German population from an early stage of the British occupation. Attempts to engage with the local German population were made by inviting German children to Christmas parties at British camps.[82] A particular effort, which in some areas began as early as 1945, was made by the British armed services to improve Anglo-German relations by hosting or participating in sports events. As Tony Mason points out, sport was of high importance to the British military, and many unit commanders in the BAOR displayed a "ferocious commitment to sport of every kind."[83] Perhaps it is no surprise, then, that BAOR sports teams who were eager to play soon invited German teams to compete against them despite the hostile attitudes of the army leadership about fraternization in the immediate postwar period (see chapter 1). Once again the CCG jumped at the early opportunity to improve relations and soon decided that "the playing of matches between British and German teams can contribute to the democratic re-education of the Germans."[84] National Servicemen proved particularly keen participants in BAOR sporting events such as the BAOR football cup. Sports had proven a valuable factor in encouraging the mixing of regiments and civilians in Britain itself, as well as increasing "the pleasure and prestige to be had when service sportsmen reached the highest levels of a particular sport."[85] This tactic was also to be applied in Germany. Despite being involved in a large number of sports events within their units, several units increasingly tried to improve local relations with Germans by organizing Anglo-German matches. Attempts to promote good relations through sports were often met with an immediate positive response—for example, "the entry of an RAF team into the Geilenkirchen *Kreis* football league" or the participation of troops in local town anniversary celebrations.[86] Soccer matches were organized in large capacity stadiums in Münster,[87] and "although feelings are bound to run high," a "most successful international boxing match" had been organized in Münster between the Twenty-third Armored Brigade and the local boxing club.[88]

However, occasionally the BAOR strategy to use sports to build bridges failed without the armed forces themselves being to blame. According to the local resident officer, a soccer match held in the town of Wuppertal between the Wuppertal and Manchester City teams "did a very great deal to destroy the reputation for sportsmanship and fair play which had been established and consistently maintained" by British service units. The incident in question involved an English player who was "sent off the field for foul play, refused to go for a little while, and finally left giving the crowd a short, sharp series of gestures which may conceivably have been mistaken by the shorter sighted for the 'V' sign."[89] It is evident that occasionally the efforts made by the forces were undermined by British civilians, who were under no instructions to improve relations with the Germans. Nonetheless, the

strategy to organize sporting events with local German teams, to offer the
service bands to play at German festivities, and to generally demonstrate a
high standard of discipline to local communities largely paid off, as pointed
out by the Recklinghausen resident officer, who claimed the withdrawal of
British troops from Wuppertal was "genuinely regretted" by the German
population.[90]

Drag hunt meets, a form of hunting with hounds where a scent is laid over
a course of around ten miles, provide another particularly well documented
example when it comes to using sports as a means to foster Anglo-German
understanding. The motivation for the British units in question was not
necessarily to improve Anglo-German relations when approaching German
landowners for permission to use their land for hunting; it was simply the
need for facilities that brought this about. Nonetheless, the results were
noteworthy and a contrast to frictions over fox hunting (see chapter 3). In
typical military fashion, some units drew up detailed lists of various hunting lines, including comments on the German owners, their willingness to
cooperate with the services, and their willingness to allow further hunts.
Comments ranged from "Herr Heidmann is useless and there is little support" to others demonstrating genuinely friendly relations between British
and German hunting enthusiasts.[91] In the case of the Royal Engineers, this
led to several Anglo-German drag hunts being favorably reported on by
the local German press.[92] It is worth mentioning at this point that army
reports on drag hunting provide a typical example of BAOR documentation
of records. Regimental records dealing with German issues are rare, and
those that exist often focus on obscure details. For example, the minutes of
the Second Battalion Durham Light Infantry officers' mess discuss in great
detail the planned purchase of German coffee cups for the officers' mess.
This plan included the establishment of a mess committee to examine various German cups and make recommendations at a subsequent meeting.
However, very little material on dealings with the German population that
supplied the cups has been preserved.[93]

Nonetheless, records that demonstrate changes in attitudes also exist
outside the field of sports. Regimental publications for British service personnel revealed that within army regiments attitudes toward the Germans
were slowly changing. Regimental magazines transformed from being entirely focused on the regiments themselves to providing information about
German culture and customs. Whereas the Royal Engineers magazine, *The
Sapper*, only ever mentioned German fräuleins or children very briefly in
the 1940s, the publication began to take more interest in the host country
from around August 1949 onward.[94] By 1952 the magazine reported signs

that "barriers are collapsing," as quite a number of privates, or "Sappers," were enjoying attractive invitations by the local Germans. "One Sapper was seen being driven away in a motor car which was strangely reminiscent of a Rolls Royce."[95] By 1956 the magazine printed full-length feature articles such as "Life in the BAOR—you may be posted here," to inform soldiers stationed abroad and overseas. One feature, split over two separate issues, stressed the excellent travel and sports facilities as well as luxurious accommodations for troops in Germany. Although these articles were factual rather than entertaining, a detailed overview was provided of German festivities and traditions.[96] Even German language classes were highlighted for soldiers and their wives. A later edition featured an organized visit to the Volkswagen factory, essentially completing the transformation from an inward-looking regimental magazine to a tourist-style guide to Germany.[97] The change in focus and content of this particular magazine constituted a significant change toward normalization of relations between the British and Germans and was evident in a number of other army publications.

Efforts by RAF Units to Improve Relations

Despite manpower shortages, parts of the British forces went to surprising lengths to improve relations with the German population. However, it appears these organized, long-term efforts were largely confined to the Royal Air Force and not the British army. Because of the need to practice low-level flying for training purposes, the RAF had to contend with the additional problem of aircraft noise in terms of relations with local populations compared to the army. As RAF records at the British National Archives reveal, the results of initiatives to address German grievances were impressive. For example, a "Review of Press Liaison Officer Organisation," produced by the Command Information Office Headquarters of the Second Tactical Air Force (TAF) for July to December 1956, outlined the great lengths to which the RAF in Germany went to improve "community relations" and outlined the considerable success that had been achieved.[98]

Station commanders in the Second TAF had appointed press liaison officers (PLOs) at twenty-nine units within Western Germany, with a further two units in Holland and one in Belgium by December 1956. "Under authority of the Air Ministry, the Commander-in-Chief laid down for all units in 2nd TAF a programme of public relations work, the main tasks of which were community relations, [. . .] news supply, [. . .] press visits and inquiries." The aim was "to stimulate community relations activity" between British units and Germans under the guidance of the station commander and to maximize publicity by achieving "coverage on a national level and by keeping the local press informed by providing them with facilities to report the activity."[99]

The review of these initiatives showed "most encouraging" results. It demonstrated that particularly on the level of station commanders continuous efforts were made to develop closer ties with German communities and that "positive policies" helped maintain existing relations. According to the review, "the RAF in Europe had several tasks apart from its operational role" and was keenly aware that "support of the local population in order to safeguard its ability to carry out its operational role" was vital. This task was considered "particularly onerous in Germany where the military foreigner was bound to be a major target in the Election battle." With 1957 being an election year in the FRG, the paper was keen to stress that "we would, of course, have no justification whatever for interfering in internal affairs. But we have a perfect right to watch that we are not drawn into German politics to our own, or NATO's, disadvantage."[100] The review also indicated that in terms of developing strategies, "most progress was made in the field of community relations and least advancement in press activity." It was clear to RAF Headquarters, however, that relations with both the local and the national press were key to the success of British efforts, as "doing the good deed is only half-completing the job. It must be seen to be done, in other words publicised."[101]

The RAF scheme to improve relations continued for a year and was reviewed twice. The conclusions of the first review highlighted that "for a scheme which had never before been operated in Germany, the results had been encouraging." All units that actively participated in the program had reported significant improvements in their relations with local communities. However, the problem was that only just over half of the units in the area had carried out any initiatives, "and only six of those had seriously tried to achieve publicity for their efforts." Internal communications also were distinctly lacking, as "only seven out of twenty-two units had made any effort to inform Command Information Office regularly of their activities." With regard to the relations with the press so highly valued by RAF Headquarters, a similar picture emerged, as "seventeen units had established a drill for handling press visits and local inquiries and nine of them had earned the praise of the press for these arrangements." Based on the mixed result of the first review, "the efficiency of the scheme could not be assessed at higher than forty per cent." The main conclusion drawn was that the success of the scheme was entirely dependent on the attitude and ability of the commanders of local units and that of their PLOs. Failure to improve relations was often due to a lack of "energy and enthusiasm" on the part of the PLO. "If the aim was to be improvement the units would clearly have to appraise their own performances, where necessary re-orientate their views and change their PLO's."[102]

The second report assessing the scheme was compiled six months later, again evaluating all twenty-nine RAF units in West Germany. The overall result was considered an improvement over the first report, as this time "twenty-eight units conducted some form of community relations activity and sixteen of them informed Command Information Office of special events so that publicity on a national scale could be achieved." The performance of every unit taking part in the scheme was graded, and whereas the first report had found that not a single unit had delivered "outstanding" performance, the second report listed nine "outstanding" performances. Twenty units had now "established a drill for handling press visits" and "the scheme was now working at sixty per cent efficiency," a 20 percent improvement over the previous period. As in the previous report, the main lesson drawn was that of the value of press relations, as "there is a much wider market for news of local activity than units realise." Also, the British themselves could then "utilise local news of unit activity on the national scale to help bolster up the general picture of Anglo-German relations." The scheme demonstrated that a transformation of Anglo-German relations on a local level was indeed possible by using the British services, that this was also beneficial for relations on a national level, and that it was unit commanders and PLOs who were responsible for either the success or failure of initiatives organized by RAF Headquarters.

Unit commanders provided illuminating comments in the reports giving reasons for the lack of contacts with the Germans in some barracks. Sometimes this was simply based on the distance of the camp from the nearest large town, where in fact this distance also "accounted for the absence of friction over the noise problem." Whereas some commanders noted signs of improvement due to "a modest beginning in press work," other responses blamed the German population's unwillingness to improve relations. The station commander at Bückeburg commented that "individually, at officer and airman level, there are good local relationships. But the unit effort as a whole to get response from the population has had an apathetic reception."[103] At times the RAF unit commanders' main problem was indeed the British army because of the "tendency of [the] population to include RAF personnel among those responsible for isolated incidents of misbehaviour by Soldiers or Americans." There were also reports of failed efforts regarding press activity "after experience of distortion of material," referring to a bombing range used as a political issue in local elections. The majority of comments, however, did report an improvement of relations stemming from personal social contacts as well as sporting fixtures. Comments ranged from there being "no real problems other than the difference of language" to "hitherto official contacts have been on a formal if not frigid basis. There are now encouraging signs that certain institutions [. . .] are showing an increased interest in the station." A member of one unit commented that relations "have improved materially during the last twelve months, principally because RAF authorities have made every endeavour to understand local difficulties over land requisitioning and to ease them."[104]

Comments by the station commandant of the coastal town of Jever, consistently the best-performing throughout the initiative, were also very encouraging. Apparently relations with the local press were quite cordial, as journalists had been "invited to cover some of the main happenings on the station and, at other times, were supplied with material." This resulted in considerable publicity of British efforts. There also had been a marked improvement of relations between unit and local population. "One has the comfortable feeling that for peacetime routine one can rely on the co-operation of local inhabitants to the same degree as one can in the UK." Apparently the value of the scheme was obvious to the unit commander, as in his view "the station has aroused some feeling of local pride in their local NATO base." It was "the NATO angle which should be pressed as the German population appeared "to get immense satisfaction from learning that the base was a NATO rather than a British one."[105] Despite this local preference of NATO over the British services, the example of Jever demonstrated that a concerted and persistent effort on the part of the British units could lead to a significant improvement of relations with the local population, even if the Germans had to contend with aircraft noise.

Not all aspects of the scheme were a success, and many of the unit commanders involved also highlighted the problems they encountered. The task of developing good relations "should have more official recognition," as the time-consuming efforts of "preparing translations from local papers, dealing with reports, handling press visitors and answering numerous queries" were too demanding to be a part-time job. The workload of the station PLO was constantly growing, and "it should not be viewed in isolation from the many secondary duties existing for officers."[106] The role of the PLO was indeed a part-time one carried out by an already fully employed officer. Sometimes PLOs had more than one part-time role, and in some cases the PLO doubled as the unit commander. "One PLO was acting at the time as Commanding Officer, Adjutant and Accountant Officer. Another was Education Officer,

Official Interpreter, Station Translator and had several other secondary duties to perform."[107] According to the Laarbruch RAF unit commander, more encouragement was also needed for personnel to learn German. The language barrier constituted a significant obstacle, and the relative success of the scheme is somewhat surprising, as out of twenty-eight participating PLOs, "thirteen had a smattering of German, three others speak the language well, another two are of interpreter standard, one deputy PLO is a qualified interpreter and nine have no knowledge of the language at all." The report estimated that of all officers and airmen in West Germany at the time, only 12 percent of officers and 5 percent of airmen spoke some German. Improving on these figures proved difficult, as officers and airmen were reluctant to "learn without an incentive." Small units were in a more promising position here, as the men were "forced on to the German market for their entertainment." The percentage of German speakers in small RAF units was significantly higher than in large stations.[108]

In order to further improve relations, ease the workload of PLOs, and overcome the language barrier, unit PLOs were to be assisted by twenty-five joint services liaison officers (JSLOs). These officers spoke fluent German, had many German contacts in the local areas of RAF units, and were tasked to "assist RAF public relations in every way possible." To the dismay of the JSLOs, their services were not used by all units and the frequency of contact varied significantly. "One unit said their contact was 'daily,' two said it was 'weekly,' five replied 'fortnightly,' ten said 'monthly,' four 'quarterly,' one 'annually' and two units said they had never met their JSLO."[109] Apparently the lack of contact was often due to the remoteness of bases from the location of the JSLO.[110]

The comments of unit commanders provide useful insight into the very varied initiatives and activities developed by at least some local RAF units. These ranged from soccer or rugby matches between English and German teams, the joining of local sports clubs by service personnel, to the activities of "the Wives Club" in Schleswigland, which organized "the adoption of orphans and collections for local elderly and needy people."[111] The participating units generally tended to concentrate their efforts on regular local activities, such as sports, religious services, Anglo-German club meetings, school visits, and organized tours, because it was believed that such recurring events made the continued upkeep of contacts less challenging. PLOs and commanding officers also increasingly invited the local press to cover functions that might be of interest and shed a positive light on the RAF.

In the important field of RAF relations with the press, the initiative also resulted in improvements. In the six-month period observed by the second review, "German local newspapers printed a total of 157 articles and news stories, many of them illustrated, as a result of the facilities and information material offered by the PLO's." This material about local unit activities was then also used by the British armed services' own Command Information Office in their publicity campaign, which resulted "in sixty mentions in the larger German papers."[112] The plan to use local efforts by units to boost Anglo-German relations on a national level therefore yielded tangible results. When asked "to report frankly on the success or otherwise of their activity" as part of the scheme, ten PLOs reported "an improvement in relations with the local press." Twelve PLOs rated local relations as "good," and six of these "said that regular contact was being maintained in both directions." Out of the remaining officers, six assured that relations were "fair" and "eleven confessed they were 'indifferent.'" When asked the same questions, thirteen station commanders had "noticed an improvement in relations with the local population in the last year." Fourteen unit commanders thought relations were "good," six rated relations as "fair," and only six as "indifferent."[113]

With regard to future challenges for the relations between the British forces and Germans, the review highlighted the fact that "certain political groups will endeavour, in the months leading up to the 1957 General Election in Germany, to make the Forces as unpopular as possible." It was considered a vital task for the RAF to prevent this and ensure "the support and acceptance of the local population," because otherwise the entire "NATO programme in general, and the task which 2nd TAF was seeking to carry out, could not be effective." Therefore it was essential "to continue to strive for the best relationship with the population and counter every attempt to undermine it." The scheme had produced a significant overall improvement in "the community relations aspect of the PLO scheme," but more effort was needed to achieve a more positive portrayal of the RAF in the German press.[114] The main obstacle to be overcome in this respect was considered to be ineffective communication between the units themselves and the British Information Services and JSLOs. The British embassy in Bonn and the JSLOs had already developed a strategy to respond to negative German press reports by providing accurate information and evidence to counter false accusations. "This was, however, not something they could often do on their own as they required access to the facts." If units were slow to respond to requests about details of incidents from the British Information Services or JSLOs, "it was often ineffective trying to correct something which had been printed days or weeks before."[115] In order to stress this point, the report provided an example of successful cooperation between RAF units and Information Services that had prevented damage to local relations and negative publicity on a national level: the German press agency (Deutsche Presse Agentur) broadcast an evening news report in January 1957 claiming a British aircraft "from the airfield at Weeze-Laarbruch had flown into high tension cables near a farm at Wesel at 1541 hours with the result that the towns of Emmerich, Kleve, Bocholt and Rees-Geldern had been completely blacked out." This news report "was picked up at 2nd TAF within an hour of its broadcast and two hours later, after a check round the command, it was possible to issue a denial that the aircraft was British or from Laarbruch or in fact any other unit in Germany." As a result of this denial, "*Deutsche Presse Agentur* then amended their report and referred to an unidentified aircraft from outside Germany." Crucially, as a result of British intervention, all local and national German newspapers reporting the incident on 12 January "carried the correct story." Local discontent had been avoided, and "the politicians of four towns were not able to say their night of discomfort was the penalty of harbouring 2nd TAF."[116]

It was only the immediate response of all RAF units in the area that had enabled the Information Services to prevent negative publicity, and therefore "the burden falls entirely on the Services, which had the great advantage of being able to guarantee action at all times of the day and night." British Information Services and the JSLO were tasked with scanning German newspapers and had "been charged with the duty of hunting out adverse comment and notifying those concerned." However, unless individual RAF units participated in this exercise by searching those local newspapers that were not available to JSLOs and Information Services, it was impossible to prevent national papers from picking up negative reports issues by local papers. Commanding officers and PLOs also were in a position to keep in touch with local journalists in order to comment on negative reports before they were printed, in order "to ensure accuracy of facts."[117]

The effective improvement of Anglo-German relations required a complex system of cooperation between all British services, including local units. Only if local RAF bases informed their PLO of efforts to improve relations or negative incidents could the PLO forward this information to the Command Information Office, "which transferred material over the German national networks and through British Information Services, and via agencies to Holland and Belgium and if the story was good enough via Air Ministry to the press all over the UK."[118] One vital task of the PLO in this operation was to advertise British unit efforts by delivering written reports to the local German press about events that "would probably not bring a pressman up to the unit," such as "visits of local schools and any routine activity." These reports were translated into German by the PLO and essentially ready for publication and consequently considered "almost certain of inclusion." Crucially, these reports had the potential to present to "the whole population what otherwise only those in the visiting party experienced."[119] This proactive RAF initiative proved that a systematic and long-term strategy was capable of providing a significant improvement in Anglo-German relations in the short period of twelve months. The considerable efforts employed furthermore underlined the importance of the issue of Anglo-German relations in the Cold War context.

It is important to note at this point that British officers regularly expressed the view to German authorities that their efforts at improving Anglo-German relations were somewhat one-sided. The British Information Services in Bonn pointed out to the Federal Press Agency in Bonn that unit commanders had "given a great deal of thought to the question of Anglo-German relations as well as the formation of Anglo-German committees between military authorities and prominent personalities." At least in the Iserlohn area it appeared that it was now up to the local German authorities to "help a bit more from their side" and provide a lead.[120]

Conclusion

The conditions encountered by the British services in Germany were a crucial factor for Anglo-German relations in the towns and cities with British garrisons. The total management of the everyday social activities and social relations of the British servicemen with the locals was impossible, and every so often tensions came to the fore. For many servicemen Anglo-German relations were not a high priority. Isolated and self-contained garrisons, the language barrier, and reluctance to interact with the former enemy were some of the reasons for this. The tension of the Cold War, boredom, and alcohol also often prevented more cordial relations. However, this reluctance to explore Germany and meet its inhabitants was not universal, and over time at least a small change in attitude among some troops was apparent. However, this was not enough in the eyes of the British Foreign Office as the next chapter shows.

By 1957 the German authorities were not unduly concerned about the impact of troop behavior on Anglo-German relations (see chapter 3). In stark contrast to this view, there was ample reason for concern from the perspective of the British administration. As a result of this concern, the British services made some efforts to improve relations with the Germans. Particularly the RAF demonstrated that organized long-term initiatives could have a significant impact on community relations, once the Federal Republic had regained its sovereignty. A combination of frequent contacts with the local communities and press relations led to the desired outcome in a number of cases. Several of the RAF units examined managed to strengthen Anglo-German relations and foster the sentiment in local communities that Germany was a part of the NATO defense against communism. However, there were also rather more negative examples, and a number of constraints meant that army units generally did not make the necessary efforts to improve relations before 1955. Naturally this lack of initiative did not escape the Foreign Office in London, where the strengthening of Anglo-German ties was considered vital. The BAOR was to play a part in this, particularly after 1955. The next chapter sheds light on the British administration's view of the problems involved, beginning with the view of the British Foreign Office of the BAOR and its relations with the Germans.

CHAPTER 5

"HOW THE ARMY OF A DEMOCRATIC NATION SHOULD BEHAVE"
The British Administration and the BAOR

> The basic fact [is] that most British officers and soldiers just do not like Germans.
> —J. M. Fisher to Mr. Chaput de Saintonge, 16 March 1956

This statement by a British official employed in the Information Services Department of the British Foreign Office in Bonn, made as late as March 1956, is in many respects exemplary for the views on the British army by members of the civilian British administrative staff in Germany as well as London. However, the assumption made here also raises further questions with regard to the relationship between the British Foreign Office and the BAOR.

Having explored the obstacles in the way of better relations from the perspective of the BAOR, an evaluation of the efforts of the BAOR as seen from Whitehall is required. It is this perspective that lies at the heart of this book, as the Foreign Office was the driving force behind the attempts to change BAOR attitudes. As established in chapter 1, the potential opportunities for reeducation of the Germans, along with better Anglo-German relations offered by the stationing of British troops in Germany, had been realized in London very early on after the war and certainly in the run-up to the establishment of the Federal Republic. The potential threat that the BAOR posed to a better understanding with an increasingly independent Federal Republic became evident by the time the Paris Agreements, or *Deutschlandvertrag,* regarding German sovereignty were signed in 1952. Hence, it is important to analyze how the Foreign Office, using, for example, its Information Services Division, attempted to influence both the BAOR and the Germans during this period.

The near-complete restoration of German sovereignty and the acceptance of Germany as a full NATO member in 1955 again had a substantial
impact on Anglo-German affairs on all levels. It was this transformation
that the Foreign Office was most concerned about when considering the
British armed services. Relations between the civilian and military sides of
the British presence also require scrutiny, as these were not always without
frictions. Consequently, this chapter examines the view of the BAOR as seen
from the various levels of the British administration in the run-up to and
immediately after the restoration of German sovereignty. This involves the
Foreign Office in London, the military government and High Commission
in Germany, the staff at Land commissioners' offices, and the judgment of
the BAOR by British resident officers in local German communities. Because
of its liaising role between the BAOR and the German authorities, a close
inspection of the relationship between the civilian British administration and
its German counterpart is also essential. Similar to its German equivalent,
the British Foreign Office initiated a wide range of measures designed to aid
the transformation of the BAOR from an occupation presence to an allied
force and made large-scale efforts on all levels to improve the standing of
the services with the German population. This chapter assesses those measures and addresses the essential question of whether by 1957 the Foreign
Office deemed the BAOR able to effectively adapt its rationale to serve its
new policy purposes.

The Information Services Division and the BAOR

The various Foreign Office departments involved in liaising between the
BAOR and the Germans rigorously monitored developments in Germany
for fear of negative incidents and publicity causing a widespread anti-British
mood in Germany. The British armed services in Germany were even provided with what could be described as their own "public relations department"—the Information Services Division of the Foreign Office (ISD). The
ISD of the British High Commission for Germany had developed from
the former Public Relations and Information Services Control division of
the British Control Commission. Among other tasks, this department was
increasingly responsible for monitoring and improving the standing of the
British services in Germany and influencing the German media in order to
avoid negative publicity. As one ISD memorandum of 1952 stated, "Her
Majesty's Government maintain in Western Germany the cream of the British Army as well as a large contingent of Royal Air Force and some naval
forces." The ability of these forces to carry out their duties "depended upon
a friendly and co-operative German population." The ISD was very much

aware that "whatever the label placed on these forces," their considerable size on the ground "inevitably provided plenty of opportunities for friction with the local population."[1] One of the main tasks of the ISD was to monitor and influence the attitude of the German press because of its impact on the opinion of German citizens. "Hardly a day passed but some local newspaper printed a story of damage to crops, motor accidents, requisitioning and the like." Although most of the incidents reported were themselves insignificant, the considerable number of negative press reports "contribute[d] to a growing feeling of asperity on the part of the local Germans."[2]

The importance of the ISD increased as the reputation of the BAOR in Germany became ever more important after the conclusion of contractual relations and the end of the occupation in 1955. The Federal Republic regained most of the rights of sovereign states, and direct British influence was therefore significantly reduced at the very moment when communist propaganda in Germany intensified and concentrated on the presence of foreign troops on German soil. The ISD effectively anticipated a deterioration of Anglo-German relations after 1955 due to the presence of the BAOR in a Federal Republic with renewed confidence.

As discussed in chapter 3, there were a number of German grievances against the BAOR that had the potential to sour Anglo-German relations. However, the ISD predicted further trouble as British troops themselves posed a potential threat to relations if "economic measures affect seriously the amenities of the British troops," because the loss of privileges and luxurious lifestyle could lead to a hostile attitude of troops toward their hosts.[3] In the eyes of the ISD, the economic recovery of the Federal Republic, while aiding the incorporation of West Germany into the Western alliance system, posed a significant risk to relations on the ground. While the public relations officers dealt "with local matters affecting the fighting services," the ISD themselves took on "the important task of explaining the general policy requiring the presence of troops, maintaining German morale and preventing local friction from turning into widespread hostility."[4] The Foreign Office in London, as well as the staff on the ground in Germany, had clearly identified a significant number of potential threats to contain in order to avoid conflict between Germans and British servicemen and the potentially disastrous consequences for Anglo-German relations and European defense. The ISD was to play a significant role here.

Although the tasks of the Information Services Division in Germany were largely the same as those of other British information offices in other overseas missions, in many respects the situation in Germany differed from that in other countries with a British diplomatic presence. Once again, pessimistic British predictions of future attitudes of a sovereign German state permeated views on all levels of the Foreign Office. This led to increasing demands to change the attitude of the BAOR. This interpretation was held to be of relevance at the highest levels, as demonstrated by a dispatch from the British high commissioner Sir Ivone Kirkpatrick to Foreign Secretary Anthony Eden, dated 9 June 1952. This paper pointed out the special conditions the ISD had to deal with as far as the BAOR and the Germans. Anglo-German relations "in the political and commercial spheres, and in the sphere of defence co-operation, had obviously been of a special character," and Kirkpatrick did not expect this to change in the immediate future. One of the main reasons for the special nature of relations was "the presence in Western Germany of very large British Forces."[5] Moreover, the increased sovereignty of Germany resulting from the Paris Agreements brought with it a decrease in British administrative staff in the British zone. This reduction applied to both the staffs of Land commissioners as well as resident officers. As a consequence, the "duties of the British officials remaining in Germany," including the ISD, "are likely to remain respectively greater and more specialised (especially in the sense that they entail more involvement in internal German matters) than those of the Consular staffs subordinate to the normal diplomatic mission." Furthermore, the value of the ISD was highlighted, as the German Education and Information Department constituted a "more flexible and specialised source of material than is available to the equivalent staff at other missions." The ISD, therefore, was a crucial element in the British strategy to improve Anglo-German relations at a time when the size of the British administrative presence in Germany had decreased significantly.[6]

The ISD was confronted with a number of obstacles in their attempts to improve relationships with Germans. First, the actions of the British administrative presence had to be coordinated with those of the French and the Americans. Second, British initiatives to influence German opinion were dwarfed by those of the United States, as Washington's efforts "in the information and cultural fields are greater in Germany than in any other country."[7] Third, the complete absence "of anything resembling a centralised national press in Germany with some 1,000 newspapers of varying size and importance" made the task of influencing opinion much more difficult in Germany than in other countries. British efforts in the FRG were also under permanent scrutiny by "a large number of foreign, especially of British journalists, permanently assigned to Western Germany," which added to the complexity of the task. The combination of these factors had forced the British administration to develop the ISD in Germany into a body that was capable of "carry[ing] out the common objective of extending the range of diplomatic action by direct stimulation of the responsible public opinion of the country concerned."[8] This "stimulation" was partly to be achieved by relying on the BAOR.

The Foreign Office considered the ISD valuable due to its successful efforts to create "greater understanding and acceptance of the aims of British policy," its efforts to minimize press criticism of these aims in Germany, and its ability to utilize its extensive personal contacts to all British personnel effectively, including resident officers and army officers. "Information Services division makes as much use as possible of this indirect means of approach."[9]

The ISD itself considered its goals in Germany to be both short-term as well as long-term. In the short run, the department aimed at "discovering the points of tension in the relationships between Great Britain and Germany and, by judicious projection and influence on important people, aimed to decrease that tension."[10] In the long run, the ISD task was to "build up the prestige of British policy so as to create for Britain a position of respect." The means to achieve this goal were increasingly limited due to the Cold War context and Britain's changing world position. The use of British military might was not an option when dealing with the Federal Republic, and economic pressure could no longer be applied "due to the weakened economic position of Britain."[11] Because of these changes, the ISD frankly admitted, as early as 1952, that British diplomacy toward Germany "depended to a very large extent upon the sympathy and understanding for British policy which could be built up in Germany and the general prestige in which Britain and British institutions are held." The de facto independence of the Federal Republic in 1955 and the loss of Allied privileges would make this German "sympathy and understanding" regarding British aims particularly important.[12] Once German rearmament was under way after 1955, the ISD planned to use the BAOR to prevent a resurgence of the German militarism of the past: "The more we can influence the German Army the more likely we shall be to succeed. In Rhine Army we have the perfect instrument to hand. [. . .] Perhaps the most important peace-time task of Rhine Army is the cultivation of close relations with the new German forces."[13]

There was an acute awareness that British powers to influence German opinion were waning at the same time as the largest British presence in Germany was that of the BAOR, whose attitudes were considered ambivalent at best. British administrative staff and the ISD were useful in furthering unofficial contacts and influencing the German press, but, particularly after 1955, it undoubtedly appeared easier, to at least certain sections of the Foreign Office, to influence the BAOR rather than the Germans. It is in this light that many of the initiatives examined here have to be considered.

Foreign Office Initiatives to Improve Relations

Just like its German counterpart, the Foreign Office regularly aimed print publications at British service personnel in order to further British soldiers' understanding of German culture and customs. In common with so many other efforts, this practice began when it became clear that the western zones of Germany would soon merge into a semi-sovereign state. The CCG *Background Letter*, initially aimed only at Control Commission for Germany officials, was the first of this kind. The *Background Letter* was produced by the Information Services Division to inform members of the CCG about current trends and events in Germany "and in order to enable them to speak with one voice in their contacts with Germans." Published three times a week, it aimed at "providing a comprehensive picture of British and Allied policy in Germany against the background of the changing political scene." Although the publication was intended for use by the CCG only, it proved more and more popular with members of the armed services, "and by 1952 half of the total circulation of 2,500 copies was taken by the BAOR," thereby increasing its significance as a means to influence the views of soldiers once the CCG was wound down. The fact that British journalists in Germany made progressively more use of the publication added to its usefulness with regard to the Foreign Office effort "to influence press comment on British policy.[14]

Rather than merely changing army attitudes, the Foreign Office also aimed at eradicating the main German grievances, if necessary, against the will of the BAOR. As highlighted in chapter 3, the issue of requisitioning housing was hugely unpopular among the German population. The changing nature of the status of the FRG had a considerable impact on this issue, and because of the extensive use of German housing and land, the services were often required to go to astonishing lengths in order to minimize German ill-will. For example, a project in the town of Herford in 1951 forced a British garrison to share its requisitioned houses with German families—a measure that would have been unthinkable in 1945, and certainly one that was not popular with all officers in 1951.

In terms of housing shortages, Herford was a typical example of a German town. From November 1944 onward, Herford had suffered heavy air raid damage. The town had a shunting yard and a bridge and garrisoned two thousand German soldiers to defend the nearby autobahn, making it a "defended city," according to Nazi propaganda.[15] The marshalling yards at Herford were targeted by the US Eighth Air Force in November 1944 during a raid involving more than eighteen hundred bombers.[16] Despite the heavy bomb damage, a considerable number of refugees from the east arrived in Herford after the war. However, this did not stop the CCG from requisitioning a substantial number of properties in order to establish its own administration. When the local CCG unit disbanded in 1951, the army took over 257 requisitioned houses in Herford to accommodate an armored car regiment. However, due to German pressure, as well as the consent of the British Land commissioner in Düsseldorf, "the great moment had arrived for the carrying out of the Herford Plan."[17]

Sixty properties in Herford were being used as shared accommodation between German civilians and British officers with their families. The German conservative daily newspaper *Die Welt* reported on the mixed results of the Anglo-German project designed to alleviate some of the housing shortages. Each party had one story of a house; only the front door and garden were shared. According to the report, "They get on wonderfully together. They say 'good morning' and 'good evening' to each other."[18] However, there were another thirty houses that had been lived in by their former German inhabitants for several months while the story reserved for the officers' families stood empty. This, according to one German originator of the Herford Plan, was due to the unwillingness of the officers to live under the same roof with Germans: "The act of goodwill is in danger."[19] The scheme itself was proof of the intense efforts undertaken by the High Commission to improve housing conditions for the Germans and therefore improve Anglo-German relations, whereas the refusal of officers pointed to the difficulties of implementing these measures. The fact that about thirty officers simply refused to move in also suggests this was a class issue rather than only a nationalistic one.[20]

The army unit involved refused to take the blame for the partial failure of the scheme and negative press comments. According to a British colonel in charge, the cooperation between the British and local German officials on the Herford Plan was rather difficult and frustrating for the British side: "The trouble with these Germans is that they never give any credit for concessions we have made. The word 'compromise' does not exist in the German language. They expect that we should give way to every request they make on compassionate grounds quite regardless of our own needs, and, whenever we do settle any compassionate cases, a couple more come out of the bag as a matter of routine."[21] According to the report, the services, as a result of the Herford Plan, were also now in control of only 75 percent of the living quarters required for other ranks. The Herford Plan, envisaged as an opportunity for the BAOR to demonstrate its willingness to improve Anglo-German relations, instead highlighted the anti-German attitudes of a significant minority of British officers expressed in the report. Despite a partial success in eradicating some of the worst housing problems in the town, the anti-British elements of the German press evidently made use of this issue.

Requisitioned property remained a difficult problem for the British civilian authorities: many army officers were accused not only by the Germans but also by the British civilian administration of not caring "about property rights, or ever remembering that the accommodation they occupied belongs to someone." The apparent solution to all problems related to requisitioning, as proclaimed by the British high commissioner, appeared simple: "Behave in Germany the same as you would behave anywhere else. If this could be drummed into the Service mind, and they would develop a common standard at all levels of behaving here exactly as they would behave in their own country, ninety-nine per cent of the frictions that are constantly breaking out would be done away with."[22]

It is evident that as negotiators between the British military and the German population, some of the resident officers and commissioners were exasperated about British rather than German attitudes. In the eyes of the deputy commissioner, German resistance to the demands of the occupying armed services was likely to increase significantly due to the attitude of the BAOR, "and the atmosphere in which those demands would be negotiated is capable of being greatly improved," particularly once the civilian element of the British administration returned to Britain.[23]

Because of the continuously unsatisfactory army attitude toward the Germans, the office of the British services' relations adviser in Bonn produced a "basic brief" on the object and role of the British armed forces in Germany in February 1954.[24] Once more the main reason provided for this was the concern of the British high commissioner and the British commander in chief in Germany that commanders of service units did not fully grasp the nature of the political changes taking place in Germany and their impact on the relationship of the BAOR with the Germans.[25] This again referred to the almost complete emancipation of the FRG from Allied control based on the Bonn Treaty. In March 1954 a pamphlet was printed and copies were distributed to all British unit commanders and British resident officers as well as Canadian troops to use for the "process of indoctrination" of newly arrived unit commanders.[26] The pamphlet, simply named "Anglo-German Relations," briefly explained the political developments in Germany since 1945. It went on to highlight the fundamental change of role and status of the armed forces in Germany away from that of an occupation army and instrument of military government toward that of an army "stationed by agreement with the government of an ally." According to the pamphlet, "The Germans are well aware of the benefits which the new situation [. . .]

will bring them"; they were naturally "eager to enjoy these benefits"; and, as a consequence, "there is at the present time, therefore, a special need for both sides to exercise patience and forbearance in order to avoid prejudicing future relationships."[27]

The document also pointed out the increasing importance of relations between the British services and the German population at the time of the rapidly growing independence of the FRG. Being "welcomed by the German people" was considered an important factor for the morale of the troops as well as enabling the services to effectively carry out their duties in an emergency. According to "Anglo-German Relations," "the preservation of good relations depends largely on the avoidance of incidents which can lead to misunderstanding or resentment on either side." Although no specific cases were mentioned, most of these incidents apparently occurred due to a "lack of appreciation of the true conditions in Germany." The pamphlet described British and Germans as "two different people who have different viewpoints, especially with regard to the war and events during the Occupation, and who do not think or act on precisely the same lines."[28] For these reasons the pamphlet stressed the importance to avoid even minor incidents between troops and civilians, as "comparatively small happenings can be magnified beyond reason and cause repercussions out of all proportion to their real importance." The main responsibility for the avoidance of such problems lay with unit commanders, whose duty it was to explain to officers and soldiers what the principles of British policy were and what constituted appropriate behavior.[29] Furthermore, soldiers should be instructed not only on how to avoid incidents but also about "the repercussion they potentially cause, as the fact remained that the Services stationed in Germany have to live and work side by side with the German people."[30] Commanding officers were also expected to liaise with resident officers and Land commissioners to avoid friction with locals and to keep abreast of developments themselves.

The services in general and unit commanders in particular, armed with advice from the High Commission, took on the sole responsibility for ensuring good relations with the Germans throughout the British zone. The question remained how willing and well-suited the unit commanders were to carry out this duty. The pamphlet made it very clear that as late as 1954 the Foreign Office considered relations between the BAOR and the Germans to be unsatisfactory and in need of improvement. With less than a year until German sovereignty, the Foreign Office clearly held the view that further measures were needed to prevent the BAOR from turning into a major liability.

The Foreign Office assessment of the behavior of the services was at times quite negative, and a significant effort was considered necessary to prevent the army from destroying those improvements in relations that had already been achieved through diplomacy once Germany had regained its status as a sovereign state. Despite an overall improvement in Anglo-German relations, when it came to attitudes toward Germans in North Rhine-Westphalia in particular, there was apparently ample evidence that some members of the services "have got their ideas all wrong about being in Germany."[31] Even British resident officers frequently mentioned instances of this character, in which a British soldier or a British family behaved differently from how they would behave anywhere else. This apparently gave Germans ample opportunity to accuse the British of preaching democracy and equality without adhering to their own principles. "The root of this problem," according to the deputy Land commissioner of North Rhine-Westphalia, was "that from top to bottom in the Services' structure one continually comes up against the feeling that in dealing with Germany and the Germans ordinary considerations do not apply."[32] A Foreign Office minute dated 16 December 1954 still judged "the attitude of the forces in general and the Army in particular towards the German population" as disappointing. Apparently there had been "remarkably little contact with German civilians," and the significance of Anglo-German relations in the Cold War context aroused "little interest." The civilian administration maintained that "the trouble seems to lie mainly with the Unit Commanders and the senior officers in the smaller formations."[33]

Furthermore, as German rearmament had been agreed on in 1955, the BAOR was expected to provide "the best possible demonstration of how the army of a democratic nation should behave." It was therefore "desirable to make one more effort to try to get the Army to co-operate fully in establishing better and more constructive relations with the German population."[34]

The Foreign Office was acutely aware of the German dissatisfaction over maneuver damage (see chapter 3). Once again the BAOR had to readjust to the change in diplomatic relations between London and Bonn. After the FRG was established, the issue of damage to German roads and property caused by BAOR maneuvers led to far more concern in London than one might expect. The resulting changes required of British troops when training in Germany were drastic and undoubtedly unpopular with military personnel. Servicemen now had to behave in a courteous manner and avoid any unnecessary damage when driving their armored vehicles through German towns. The damage compensation procedure for victims of maneuver damage was continuously improved in order to prevent anger. Kreis resident officers and Land commissioners in Germany constantly dealt with claims made by German civilians, ranging from illegal hunting by British troops in private forests to entire houses being burnt down by British Verey flares.[35]

As was noted previously, there was a distinct fear among "responsible and reasonable" Germans, as well as British resident officers, that "extremism in political feeling is engendered" by maneuver damage. Evidence of willful damage being caused by the services threatened to exacerbate the situation.[36] It is important to note, however, that this fear was certainly shared in much higher political circles in London. This was demonstrated by a lengthy correspondence between the Office of the British High Commissioner, the War Office, and the Foreign Office with regard to maneuver damage caused in Lower Saxony in August 1953. As this had occurred during harvest time, the result had been an outcry by farmers and the German press. Mr. W.M.F. Vane, a Conservative member of Parliament and member of the Anglo-German Association, had become aware of the Lower Saxony Land government's concern about "unnecessary damage to crops" by Allied troops and the "fear that representations through normal channels will move too slowly to bring useful results." In his view this was "a strange business," and he decided to take up the matter with the Foreign Office directly in order to avoid German hostility. His request caused a considerable stir and led to a flurry of activity at both the Foreign Office and the War Office. The explanations provided by the High Commission in Bonn focused on two points: the growing size of the BAOR in Germany required the training of additional numbers of troops, and therefore maneuvers were likely to cause more damage than in the past. "To this natural factor for increased agitation must also be added the political factor of the forthcoming Federal Elections."[37]

There was an underlying fear that the BAOR could severely damage the prospects of the pro-Western Adenauer government to stay in power and strengthen both the KPD as well as right-wing splinter parties in the FRG. The British cabinet was worried about the instability of the German government due to CDU losses in local elections and the growth in popularity of the Refugee Party, considered "a focus for unhealthy nationalist and irredentist tendencies." Furthermore, there was the brief but unsettling rise of the "semi-Nazi Socialist Reich Party."[38] These organizations found fertile ground for anti-British agitation, as the compensation for damage was not paid by the British government, but came out of occupation costs; in other words, it was paid for by the German taxpayer. The amount of compensation paid for training damages on only one major training area "for the financial year ending March, 31, 1953" amounted to around 3.7 million DM.[39]

Unsurprisingly, the fear of creating any unnecessary antagonism before the elections led to a concerned letter from the War Office to British troops in Germany, photographic evidence being examined by the Ministry of

Defense,[40] as well as an explanatory letter from the High Commissioner's Office to the Foreign Office in order to provide adequate material "with which to reply to [. . .] any other Members of Parliament who may make similar enquiries."[41] In addition, new strategies to minimize or at least localize discontent were developed. For instance, by limiting maneuvers to "one general training area, the agitation, though intensive in that area, is localised, whereas otherwise it would be widespread and therefore embarrassing."[42]

A number of approaches were now employed in order to minimize German resentment of the British military. Tensions over maneuver damage between the services and the local German inhabitants in some areas ran so high that press conferences were now held before the beginning of maneuvers in order to assure the population that all measures were taken by the BAOR to avoid any unnecessary damage. A memorandum of 1952 about a press conference concerning the Reinsehlen area of Niedersachsen stated that if the assurances were "carried out by all formations it is possible that there may be considerable easing of the tension [. . .]; if not, there will be adverse comments and accusations of bad faith."[43] Once more it was the responsibility of the BAOR to avoid friction between Britons and Germans in the FRG. Emotions on the plains of northern Germany ran high, and the issue was frequently dealt with by the highest political circles in Bonn and London. By 1953 the Foreign Office considered that maneuver damage caused by the BAOR had been "exaggerated and made the subject of political propaganda by the irresponsible local press and by agitators of the extreme left and right." It had also been used for "electioneering statements by Federal Ministers and a personal approach by the Chancellor to the High Commissioner."[44] Nonetheless, in the view of the High Commission, the British military had done everything in their power to avoid any willful damage. A quick system of repayment had been introduced, and even positive measures like "the employment of special mobile repair teams equipped with road mending machinery" had been taken. The introduction of all of these precautionary measures led the High Commission to conclude that "the point has now been reached at which any further restrictions imposed on the troops would largely destroy the training value of the exercises they were required to carry out."[45] It was also expected that with the elections being held in Germany less than a month later, the volume of protest was bound to increase, "but we do not think that too much importance should be attached to it."[46]

Despite this dismissive view of German protests, measures to prevent German anger were strengthened even further in some areas of Lower Saxony. Apart from the complete avoidance of fire and the protection of trees and fences, the armed forces were now also barred from driving across fields and from dropping litter, as this might endanger livestock. They were required to refill any trenches and allowed to use private residences only with the owner's permission. Areas of natural beauty were declared out of bounds, pipelines were marked with warning signs, and six hundred signs were placed on monuments and historical places to protect them from damage. In addition, German resident officers were now appointed to assist the British resident officers when assessing damage claims and damage prevention. The German resident officer was to play an important psychological role, as troops had to constantly expect the German resident officer to pursue avoidable or willful cases of damage.[47] Germans who suffered damage were also to be calmed by the presence of a German representative when dealing with foreign troops. The British authorities also considered the German resident officer vital in preventing anger from spreading, as was demonstrated in the case of the Oldenburg resident officer, who persuaded the local German press not to report on a British tank damaging a war memorial.[48]

Three British women in front of a sign increasingly common throughout the British Zone of Occupation—"out of bounds to troops."

These drastic measures increasingly bore fruit. With the exception of Lower Saxony, "where the subject of damage caused by troops on manoeuvres or training was brought into prominence by the protest lodged by the Deputy Minister-President," the portrayal of the BAOR exercises of 1953 in the noncommunist press was mainly favorable. One local paper highlighted the "democratic behaviour" of the British officer class, who, on one occasion, entertained the German children and served them food.[49] The monthly ISD report for August 1953 also highlighted the positive impact on army initiatives on the German press and public opinion. The *Lüneburger Landeszeitung* issued a tribute to British army officers for their interest in reducing maneuver damage despite previously having "led the attack on British troops for damage on training and manoeuvres." A lengthy article now praised British officers "for the interest which they were now taking in the farmlands contained within the manoeuvre areas." The presence of British officers who inspected properties before exercises took place in order to forward local concerns to British troops "were much appreciated. They gave cause for hope that the troops involved in the manoeuvres would show similar understanding."[50]

Foreign Office attempts to minimize German protests over maneuver damage turned into a regular feature. As September 1954 saw the first full-scale NATO maneuvers to include simulated atomic weapons—exercise "Battle Royal"—maneuver damage affecting large areas once more became an issue. Again some of the British reports highlighted that neither adverse reports nor complaints were received either from the German officials or from the farmers and that "the services relations with the German population were excellent."[51] Dealing with local German officials often took place in a "friendly spirit of cooperation and give and take" regardless of the rapidly changing status and independence of the FRG: "Whilst they drive as hard a bargain as they know how, they continue to show every understanding for our needs, and I have so far observed no change in their attitude to us or to any sign of 'marching time' pending the anticipated change in our mutual status."[52]

It appears, therefore, that cooperation between the British military, aided by the resident officers, and the local German officials was becoming more successful in minimizing maneuver damage as well as German discontent. The overall impression that the British resident officer reports of 1954 convey is that in no small part due to the various efforts of both units as well as German local officials and civilians, relations between the services and the local population were better than "they have [been] for a very considerable while."[53] It was evident that while, for example, the British were introducing concrete measures to minimize maneuver damage, the German press, partly because of the appreciation of the British presence after the failure of the European Defence Community, went to great lengths to explain to the population the reason and necessity for certain maneuvers. According to the British Kreis resident officers, the situation at the end of 1954 was looking rather positive. Foreign Office initiatives and changes to BAOR behavior and practices initiated in London and Bonn clearly produced at least some local successes. The main problem was the fact that the issues at hand required constant and continued attention, and improvements did not necessarily prove long-lasting. This again highlighted the necessity to continue efforts to change BAOR behavior in the light of changing Anglo-German relations.

The ISD View of the Germans

Information Services officers frequently voiced concern that they had to continually "go over the same ground in order to keep the friendly Germans from being led into defection." Whereas British Information Services in America were dealing with "individualistic people" who were outspoken in their views, "in Germany you have a people who are not concerned with the right or wrong of a situation but are seeking alibis which will enable them always to remain on the right side of the fence."[54] Apparently it was for this reason that Germans always aimed at being liked by the British. "They will agree with you when you talk with them and will curse your guts behind your back when they are talking in suitable company."[55]

The problem according to the ISD was that there was "seldom a German who was openly Anglophile in German company." It was this characteristic that justified the continuing presence of British information officers. Furthermore, the special characteristics of Germany itself had to be considered—notably, that despite all British efforts to develop friendly personal contacts "from which we derive advantage, the general attitude has been one of distrust of the Allies."[56] This attitude was often mutual, however, as was shown by a remark by Sir Ivone Kirkpatrick. His view was that it was "neither possible nor desirable for British policy to satisfy German demands on every point and we must accept disappointments and vexation when dealing with a people so immature and unstable."[57]

The view of one ISD officer was shared by many among the British civilian staff in Germany who were tasked with the improvement of Anglo-German relations. "God knows none of us like the Germans much," but it was nonetheless important "to try and avoid some of the mistakes we

made in the time of the Weimar Republic."[58] There was considerable doubt
over the future of Anglo-German relations as well as the BAOR's role in
these. It was the perceived dangers of the German character, combined with
Federal Germany's independence, that made the 1955 change in relations
so important in the eyes of the Foreign Office and the High Commission.
However, this view needs to be considered in conjunction with the experiences made by the British administrative staff on the local levels.

The Relations of the British and German Administrations in the Länder

As established in chapter 1, the higher echelons of the British administration
not only viewed the BAOR as problematic but also had considerable doubts
about the Germans with whom they were tasked to cooperate in an Anglo-
German as well as Western alliance context. British policy toward Germany
was "positive because it was fatal to be negative about Germany. We are
all aware of the risks entailed in the present policy, but those in any other
would be much greater."[59] It has become evident that British expectations
of the future of Germany and Anglo-German relations were not necessarily positive in 1955. Yet it is also important to consider the views of those
members of the British administration working on the Land level with the
Germans and the BAOR.

In North Rhine-Westphalia the Services Liaison Section and Information
Services Division were tasked with bringing British troops and Germans
together. The suspicion that cooperation between the British and German
administrations in the British zone was going to become more and more
difficult after 1955 was confirmed in a Services Liaison Section report of
March 1954. This paper claimed that although generally the cooperation
between the Land government of North Rhine-Westphalia and the services
was good, the Germans were deliberately "dragging their feet" with regard
to "important Service requirements such as accommodation and training
grounds." Although this could partly be attributed to the upcoming *Landtag*
elections in June 1954, a far more important reason was to be found in the
fact that "they do not want to make decisions now which they might be able
to avoid making after the Occupation Statute had been repealed." The head
of the Services Liaison Section in North Rhine-Westphalia concluded that
it was time for a "showdown" to achieve at least some of the most urgent
military requirements. This was best done at a time when the British armed
services "still possess some residual authority rather than later, when our
powers will be drastically reduced.[60]

By 1955 one of the main problems for the British administration, when liaising between the armed services and German authorities, was that "the Services have used the terms 'priority' and 'urgent' so often that they ceased to mean very much to the German authorities." The Germans also could no longer be "blinded with science" and, instead of agreeing to British demands, tended to "call up technical experts to challenge decisions made on the advice of Service technicians."[61] Despite this German reluctance, the Services Liaison Section considered German attitudes toward the British positive, "and in day-to-day negotiations between the Services Liaison Section staff and the German officials there was the fullest cooperation and good will." This enthusiasm was not shared universally, as "it is however possible that the Services would not consider that they can endorse this opinion." It was considered unlikely that the services would "appreciate all the multitudinous causes of delay in the satisfaction of their bids" considering the importance of their tasks. Whereas the ISD and the High Commission expected commanding officers to be the driving force behind closer Anglo-German relations, the Services Liaison Section staff in Germany pointed out that if "the same officers are continuously frustrated in their efforts to fulfil Army requirements by German bureaucracy and reluctance this is counter-productive."[62]

A further complicating factor for the administrations of both Britain and the Federal Republic was that the devolution of power in Germany, for which the Allies themselves had been responsible, in many instances prevented the federal government from imposing its will (and therefore also policies agreed on with the British) on the Länder. The reestablishment of German self-government above local levels in the British zone had begun with the Land governments in 1946.[63] In 1949 the Basic Law of the FRG maintained the principle of federalism as a safeguard against excessive central power.[64] As a result, "extensive powers, for example in the fields of [. . .] police and local government, were vested in the states" rather than the federal level.[65] This same division of powers also applied to the relationship between the Länder and the local Kreis. "The moral therefore was that we must continue to maintain the best possible relationships with the Federal, the *Land* and the local authorities and get the best we can from all of them."[66] The head of the Services Liaison Section in North Rhine-Westphalia nonetheless concluded that, in spite of many difficulties and differences in viewpoint, the British military and the Germans had worked well together. "I do not believe that in this *Land* we shall notice an immediate change of heart or policy when sovereignty becomes a fact."[67] It is noteworthy that when considering attitudes of British administrative staff toward the German people and authorities, more positive views were prevalent on local levels compared to those on Land and national levels.

The Assessment of BAOR Attitudes by British Resident Officers

Despite the often critical view of the behavior of the armed services by the British civilian administration, there was also some praise, particularly on the "ground level." The British Kreis resident officers regularly provided detailed quarterly reports to the Land commissioners outlining political, economic, and social events in their Kreise as well as Anglo-German relations in general and relations between the services and Germans in particular. These reports provide a useful insight into local views on British actions and politics as well as Anglo-German relations. The year 1954 is particularly well documented and provides a different view of the crucial period preceding German sovereignty. The main concerns about Anglo-German relations on the local level in Germany that year were the failure of the EDC and widespread German admiration for the British foreign secretary Sir Anthony Eden and his successful efforts to reconstruct Western European defense thereafter.[68] This effort was mentioned in a large number of reports as a significant boost to Anglo-German relations on a local level, which consequently led a number of British units to go out of their way to cultivate the improved relations. The Mönchen Gladbach resident officer even worried that relations grew too cordial too quickly, thereby "bringing with it the possible danger that over-enthusiasts, on both sides, may force too quickly a plant which will ultimately have to face the cold winds which blow prosaically from the Bonn Agreement on Tax treatment of the Forces and their members."[69] The overall picture provided by resident officer reports certainly did not suggest a lack of initiative on both sides—the military and the civilian population—on local levels. The reports also highlighted, at least in some cases, the "very satisfactory" nature of contacts between British and German officials due to "the maintenance of good personal relations."[70] The impression the resident officer reports of 1954 conveyed was that, partly due to Eden's determination but also due to unit efforts, relations between the armed services and the local population were better than they had been for a considerable while.[71] This assessment, in many respects similar to that of the German authorities highlighted in chapter 2, was clearly more positive than the Foreign Office view from London.

Foreign Office Assessment
of BAOR Attitudes after 1955

Relations were nonetheless still fragile, and the gains that had been made could quickly be lost again. Especially in the context of increasing German sovereignty, the behavior of the British services was under continuous scrutiny. A 1956 account by the British embassy highlighted renewed incidents of maneuver damage and their negative consequences. Troops of the Sixth Armored Division, taking part in a night exercise, had "passed through a stretch of thirty year old forest and destroyed some two thousand trees in the Soltau area." Local German anger was sparked by the fact that "the trail of destruction was only a few yards from completely open ground," which made it hard to believe that "the tank crews were unaware of what they were doing and that the damage was not malicious or, to say the least of it, carefree." This incident sparked the resentment of the local farmers, which was further inflamed by another exercise during the next forty-eight hours. An "irate deputation of farmers" staged a demonstration outside the office of the Services Liaison officer in Soltau on 14 July and threatened to "lie down in front of the tanks unless the damage was restricted."

Although individual complaints had been common, this was the first organized protest from farmers in the area. The press, "which has of late been on the look-out for incidents involving Allied forces," without hesitation supported the view of the farmers and joined their call for the cancellation of the exercise. The British embassy in Bonn did not consider the damage to be "remarkably heavy, though in some places it is said to be rather spectacular." The Land government found itself releasing statements and "objective articles" to the press in order to aid British efforts to prevent the escalation of the problem.[72]

This was not the only clash requiring British and German efforts at national levels to defuse tensions. In March 1957 a group of fifty Scottish soldiers rampaged through the town of Lüneburg, overturning vehicles, smashing windows, and beating civilians. The military police were unable to prevent this, as they simply were "powerless."[73] "The trouble at Lüneburg" caused an outcry by the German press. The developments in Lüneburg were also reported in *The Times* on 8 August 1957. According to the article, there had been "fifty-three recorded incidents of misbehaviour since April 1," as well as a considerable rise in "more serious offences." The trouble involved a German apprentice "hit over the head with a brandy bottle," an attack on two German policemen as well as a young girl, and a woman being "molested in the park." *The Times* pointed out that "a catalogue of these incidents can be made to look unpleasant."[74] The inhabitants of the "quiet and beautiful town" were concerned that visitors might be "frightened away by lurid mental pictures of marauding bands of wild British soldiers." Despite a willingness to accept a degree of rowdy behavior by troops, locals apparently were outraged "when an aged woman visitor here for the cure is molested by a drunken British soldier." Apart from the crime itself, the problem was also a financial one, as "she leaves and tells all her friends and the Press and the place begins to get a bad name."[75]

Despite this, local opinion was judged "remarkably objective," and "soldiers will be soldiers" was considered to be the attitude by residents "to 'normal' misbehaviour—a few windows broken, singing in the streets at night and the occasional fight over a girl." Of the thirty-five hundred troops in Lüneburg, the majority were from the Welch Regiment, the Highland Light Infantry, the 8th Hussars, and the Royal Artillery. "About ninety per cent of all incidents" were attributed to alcohol. It was also believed that "the existence of a few more or less criminal types who lead others on" as well as the rivalry between Scottish and Welsh regiments were to blame.[76]

The British embassy's report of the Lüneburg disturbances was rather gloomy: "On March 1 the Welch Regiment celebrated St. David's Day by breaking a lot of windows in the town," and soon thereafter members of the Highland Light Infantry "were involved in widespread disturbances and clashes with the Military Police." The embassy counted "nearly eighty incidents (which was more than the number claimed by the German press)" between March and July, and although most of these were minor, "there were far too many trouble-makers in the Lüneburg area." The German press on this occasion was regarded as "very reasonable," as it reminded its readers of the good "discipline of British troops in general" and "their role in the defence of Germany." According to the report, there was no doubt that the Lüneburg troubles led to a decline in popularity of the BAOR throughout the entire area occupied by British troops. A recent tour through North Rhine-Westphalia had revealed that "reasonable people, who are more than satisfied with the conduct of British troops in their area, are perpetually talking about the Lüneburg affair." The damage caused by the incidents would now require a significant effort by the services to overcome, including "strong disciplinary measures as well as good public relations work."[77]

In stark contrast to the aforementioned RAF initiative, as well as previous army efforts, the behavior of some BAOR army units appeared to deteriorate rather than improve, as by 1957 the British administration repeatedly found itself having to minimize political damage over incidents involving the services. A telegram from the charge d'affaires to the commander in chief from August 1957 expressed concern "at the increasing criticism, directed against the British Forces in Germany" voiced by the German press "on account of the incidents in Lüneburg." Not only were these incidents the source of widespread negative publicity, but there were also frequent accusations that "the forces had taken inadequate steps to maintain discipline in the Lüneburg area since the New Year, that punishment of the guilty had been too light and that adequate apologies had been lacking." Although much of this criticism was "no doubt unfair and based on inadequate information," it had the potential to sour not only Anglo-German relations on a local level but also "Anglo-German relations in a wider field."[78] The incident did indeed create severe problems for both the British and German administrations involved. The Niedersachsen Land government press office reported on two cases of British soldiers robbing and assaulting German youths in the town of Lüneburg in 1957. As the number of incidents in the area had risen significantly, the local Liberal Democratic Party even demanded a complete break of relations between the town and the British troops. The perceived lack of an apology by the British officers especially aroused anger.[79]

Fear of more widespread misbehavior was created by further serious incidents in a base one hundred miles away from Lüneburg, and the chief of staff at Northern Army Group was concerned "that the indiscipline might prove catching and had decided to take decisive action to discourage unruly elements."[80] The incidents were regarded so seriously that they became the subject of numerous discussions between the British embassy and the Federal Foreign Office as well as the involvement of the War Office. The root of the trouble "was the rather injudicious decision of the War Office to put the H.L.I. [Highland Light Infantry] alongside the Welch regiment, neither of which are notable for punctilious behaviour."[81] According to an FO minute, the Rhine army's chief of staff was to send "a report on the troubles to the Secretary of State for War," the offending regiment was to be withdrawn in a month's time, and the whole future of the Lüneburg garrison itself was "under consideration." Ironically, the Rhine army was "most anxious that no hints should reach the Germans that we are considering clearing out of Lüneburg."[82] The measures taken to suppress any further trouble clearly indicated the severity of the threat the Lüneburg incident and the BAOR caused to Anglo-German relations. They also demonstrated that there were serious problems with the plan to use the BAOR as a tool to improve relations with the Germans.

Conclusion

Since 1945 relations between the British services and the (Foreign Office–led) Control Commission for Germany had generally been poor, and it may be that the widespread criticism of army officers in Germany by Foreign Office staff partly has to be seen in this light. It is evident that the Foreign Office considered that all major efforts undertaken by the civilian administration to bring British soldiers and German civilians closer together stood and fell with the attitude of local unit commanders. There were frequent complaints by local liaison officers that military personnel behaved in an utterly unacceptable manner toward Germans. According to the ISD, this situation did not improve after 1955, and it appears that the Foreign Office grew tired of attempting to improve the situation. An ISD memorandum from 1956 drew the frustrated conclusion that "our men simply do not like Germans."[83] The paper furthermore considered it best if the host country itself—through mayors, for instance—took more initiative. Frustration with the German attitudes was equally still as strong as it had been before 1955. Also if the Germans were to make more efforts, it would be better to do so "in a manner less ponderously formal than Germans usually employ, so much the better from the point of view of ready response."[84]

A resigned and frustrated ISD therefore put the blame on a continued lack of improvement on both sides. The memorandum claimed that a good many Germans did not like the British either and that it was doubtful whether a completely satisfactory solution could ever be achieved within the foreseeable future. Despite this resignation, Foreign Office fears of a deterioration of Anglo-German relations due to German independence and rearmament did not materialize. Regardless of some "disquieting signs of a resurgence of Nazism" in 1953, "the Neo-Nazis fared disastrously at the 1953 elections, a reverse from which they have never since recovered."[85]

In the meantime the Foreign Office often found itself attempting to prevent a spread of potentially negative publicity not only in Germany but also abroad. One example of this was the case of four young journalists from Commonwealth countries who had toured the British service installations and troops in Germany. Apparently, in a conversation with the British ambassador, the journalists had become "very critical of the apparent relationship between the Services and the local German population." The conversation highlighted many of the reasons for the BAOR's reluctance to establish contacts outlined in chapter 4, "like the intensity of their training, the fact they had little spare time, they were often far away from centres of population, had little incentive to learn German, little or no money for activities of this kind, to name only a few."[86] But at least some members of the ISD still thought that "the Services in Germany are in a very special position. They are the only British troops stationed in any numbers in an Allied country and I wonder whether any special thought has ever been given to the problem this presents."[87] The ISD's reply to this statement remarked that the problem of fostering contacts between the British forces in Germany and the German population was "an old one" and that "various measures" had been introduced, including "edicts sent out to the BAOR from the War Office." These apparently had very little effect, since the whole question depended upon "the frame of mind and degree of energy on the part of the British local commanders concerned." Given this fact it was "difficult to make any really constructive suggestions," and the focus may well have shifted away from improving relations between British soldiers and German civilians toward cultivating cordial relations with the new German armed forces: "In short, we have no particularly bright ideas. But I do agree with you that it is a problem which should continually be borne in mind, and I should be grateful if you would report from time to time how things are progressing."[88]

Thus, by 1956 it was evident that the ISD had run out of ideas and motivation to deal with a problem that was essentially considered unsolvable. After eight years of efforts to change BAOR attitudes and some local successes, the main problem still appeared to be the attitudes of unit commanders and high-ranking officers in small units. The British civilian administration had introduced drastic changes to how the army behaved in Germany when considering accommodation and training, but the behavior and attitude of individual officers and soldiers was more difficult to influence. And although there was no widespread anti-British unrest caused by the BAOR in Germany, from a Foreign Office perspective the idea of using the BAOR as an asset for Anglo-German relations appeared increasingly remote.

CONCLUSION

> Relations between the Services in Germany and the German
> population have always been a problem. I believe that from
> time to time the Service Ministries issue special instructions
> encouraging the forces to take more notice of the Germans in
> their areas, and senior officers stationed in Germany do their
> best. But it is at the ordinary level that relations still remain
> almost non-existent.
> —Public Relations Problems of British Services in Germany, Minute,
>   16 March 1956

This comment by a British Information Services official from 1956 aptly summarized some of the existing problems in relations between the British armed services and the Germans as well as pointing to some of the continuous efforts made in London and Bonn to foster contacts between Britons and Germans. However, "non-existent" was not always the correct term for relations between the services and Germans. As this book has demonstrated, some very real problems caused by the presence of British troops in Germany at times posed a threat to Anglo-German relations, which were dominated both by the German defeat in World War Two and the heightened Cold War tensions. As highlighted in chapter 1, the growing Cold War threat led to a continuous increase in the size of the British troop commitment during the first half of the 1950s. This not only provided further opportunities for contacts with the German population but also created the potential for greater friction at a time when London regarded the German integration into the Western system of defense as crucial.

Many of the British decision makers in London and Bonn had firsthand experience of two conflicts created by German aggression. It was the combination of the Soviet threat and the fear of a revival of German nationalism that fueled the London administration's desire to transform the BAOR. Despite both the Labour and Conservative administrations' reluctance to take part in the process of European integration, the BAOR and its relations with the German population constituted a significant element in Britain's postwar defense strategy.

The Impact of British Public Opinion
on BAOR Relations with the Germans

Whereas official British policy aimed at integrating Germany into the Western defense system and rearming the Federal Republic in the context of NATO, British public opinion was reluctant to adapt to this situation. As established in chapter 2, much of British opinion as expressed in the popular press and, to an extent, nonfictional literature still very much associated Germany with the threat of a revival of nationalism. In particular, the conservative popular press ceaselessly produced vitriolic anti-German views, and rather than addressing the changing relationship between Britain and Germany in the Cold War context, popular entertainment mainly focused on British victories in the Second World War. The swift economic revival of Germany also added to the resentment of the former enemy.

Despite these fears and resentments there was a slow but important change in attitudes. Nonfictional literature on the subject of Germany was far from unanimously anti-German, even if partly due to interference from the Foreign Office. In addition, a closer inspection of press articles of even the most hostile papers, such as the *Daily Express*, reveals at least a degree of normalization in relations through factual reporting. The image of Germany portrayed outside the popular press was often surprisingly positive. Although war films and novels generally celebrated British courage in the Second World War, they either did not portray Germans at all or characterized them not as goose-stepping Nazis but as ordinary and even decent people who were fighting on the wrong side of the war.

In postwar Britain many individual views of Germany were also shaped by personal experiences that were unrelated to the recent conflict. Contacts on individual levels between Britons and Germans were fostered through nongovernmental organizations and, for example, the twinning of towns. Of course, to argue that these changes affected large parts of the British population would be wrong; for the most part these efforts were initiated by the politicized sections of the population. But to simply assume that all British servicemen dispatched to Germany would have held anti-German views because of the recent conflict and a negative portrayal of Germany in Britain would also be too simplistic. Although some of the testimony of servicemen indicated a general antipathy to all things German, evidence has also shown that a number of young conscripts were keen on meeting Germans and exploring the country in which they were stationed. As shown in chapter 2, the impact of British public opinion of the Germans was therefore not an entirely negative factor when considering relations between

the BAOR and the Germans. The slow changes in the public perception
of Germany arguably strengthened Foreign Office plans to use the BAOR
as a tool to improve relations between the British armed services and the
German population.

"Out with the English"?
German Perceptions of the BAOR

As chapter 3 demonstrated, the German people living under the occupation
had just as diverse views of the British as the British had of them. In the immediate postwar period economic reasons compelled many Germans to in-
gratiate themselves with their occupiers. However, this slowly changed with
the advent of the "economic miracle." There is nonetheless much evidence
to support the idea that significant parts of the German population were
genuinely willing to establish good relations with the servicemen, despite
the recent conflict and a widespread antipathy to the military in general.
This was partly due to the Cold War threat but also due to an admiration
of British values and way of life. The behavior of the BAOR did not lead to
widespread protest against the stationing of British troops in Germany in
the context of the European defense system or against the financial support
of the services. As polls revealed, the British were generally considered to
be the best-behaved of all the occupation troops. Units on maneuvers were
often greeted with friendly curiosity. Despite the considerable economic
strain resulting from the presence of the BAOR on a country in the process
of rebuilding itself, the majority of German protests were aimed at changing
the conditions of occupation, not at abolishing it.

This should not distract from the fact that there was also hostility between
the Germans and the British occupying forces. German wartime experiences
often gave rise to resentment of militarism in general, particularly among
the younger generations. The human losses of the war frequently led to individual servicemen experiencing negative German attitudes. Furthermore,
German demands with regard to Allied rights and troop behavior rose with
the degree of independence of the Federal Republic. This was reflected by
a decrease in the popularity of the services in opinion polls.

The Germans placed the BAOR in a very difficult position. On the one
hand, the German population demanded adequate protection from a potential Soviet attack rather than an orderly retreat beyond the Rhine. Despite
the hopelessness that the potential conflict with Russia instilled in many
ordinary Germans who were encountered by the British services, any suggestion of troop reductions or a partial withdrawal was met with outrage.

On the other hand, there were increasing complaints about the consequences of the British troop presence, be it the requisitioning of housing, maneuver damage, or problems caused by individual soldiers. The German press was generally keen to report negative incidents involving British troops, and these quickly spread from local to national levels. Particularly the communist press used every opportunity to discredit the Allied military presence at a time when the KPD was a concern for both the federal government and the British Foreign Office. It was only drastic changes in the behavior and attitudes of troops, as well as cooperation of the BAOR with German authorities, that prevented widespread hostility among the German population. However, these fundamental changes in BAOR attitudes and behavior were not always initiated by the army itself.

The idea of strengthening cultural ties by intensifying relations with British troops was also taken up by the German government, if less enthusiastically and, as the case of the guidebook for Allied soldiers printed in German in 1956 demonstrated, also less successfully. As shown in chapter 3, the much lower levels of crime in the British Zone of Occupation partly explain the lack of interest that was apparent among the federal administration to fund measures designed to improve relations with the British. Statistics produced by the German administrations on federal and Land levels continuously highlighted the difference in behavior between the BAOR and its French and American counterparts. The German Land administrations in the British zone also often found that British behavior compared favorably to that of Canadian troops. The German federal and state archives reveal that in several cases federal requests for crime statistics were ignored by Land authorities, as they regarded the situation as satisfactory. In the context of an increasing political focus on the European Economic Community, the economic revival and political stability of the FRG, as well as the combined experiences with all Allied occupying armies, the perception of the BAOR as a threat to Anglo-German relations ceased to be a major factor for the Bonn administration by the mid-1950s. Nonetheless, the British Foreign Office continued to make efforts on all administrative levels to further improve relations between troops and civilians.

The Foreign Office and the BAOR

Due to British fears of a German flirtation with the Soviet Union in order to achieve German unification and the aim of integrating the Federal Republic into the Western family, the Foreign Office went to great lengths in order to utilize the BAOR as a tool for Anglo-German rapprochement.[1] Germany had allied itself with the Soviet Union both in 1922 and 1939, and the German integration into the anticommunist defense of Europe was crucial for the preservation of British influence in Western Europe.[2] British diplomats carefully watched out for any anti-Western tendencies, and the view of the prospects of democracy in Germany held by Foreign Office staff was often dim. The British increasingly placed their faith in Konrad Adenauer, and it was partly this support and the question of German politics in a post-Adenauer era that necessitated the exploration of all avenues to improve Anglo-German relations: "The struggle for Germany will not only be with the Russians; it will be with the Germans themselves."[3] A wide range of efforts was initiated by the Foreign Office in order to strengthen what the British high commissioner Frederick Hoyer-Millar in 1956 referred to as the "easy and cordial" relations with the Federal Republic.[4] The BAOR was to be used as a tool to develop a "sense of community" between the Western Allies and to remind the Germans "that there are other problems in the world besides German reunification."[5]

The Foreign Office in London and the High Commission in Bonn went to great lengths to achieve an improvement in relations by initiating numerous programs aimed at eradicating German grievances. Shared housing schemes for British troops and German civilians in times of great shortages were signs of goodwill introduced by the British administration and, more or less reluctantly, carried out by the BAOR. The minimization of maneuver damage, establishment of friendly press relations, organization of cultural and sports events, and severe curtailment of customs such as hunting by British troops were enforced.

There is much evidence that at least some British units (albeit RAF rather than army units) successfully planned and executed sophisticated initiatives to improve relations with local communities. However, despite the efforts of the Information Services Division, which essentially acted as a public relations agency for the BAOR, by the end of 1957 the Foreign Office had essentially given up on the idea of the BAOR as a goodwill ambassador of Great Britain: "I doubt whether we shall ever arrive at a completely satisfactory solution—at any rate, within the foreseeable future."[6] In fact, rather than hoping for better relations between soldiers and civilians, the best chance was that "things may improve when there are German forces alongside our own."[7] It was continued pessimism about the future of Germany and resignation as to the value of the BAOR that characterized the Foreign Office attitude in 1957. Both German as well as British policy makers were therefore inclined to give up on the idea of relying on the BAOR, albeit for different reasons.

However, it would be wrong to deem the efforts of the Foreign Office to improve relations between troops and Germans a failure. In fact they most likely prevented a significant deterioration of Anglo-German relations by forcing a change of attitude and preventing the spread of some of the worst behavior of British troops in the Federal Republic. Overall, the close study of German reactions to the continued British occupation has demonstrated that although by and large the majority of Germans were willing to accept foreign troops as a necessary evil, the behavior of soldiers was heavily scrutinized by the German press and frequently used as a tool for anti-Western propaganda. As noted, however, levels of crime committed by the British services were far lower than those of the other occupying powers, and only a few incidents, such as the Lüneburg case of 1957, gained notoriety on a national level. Despite German press criticism of army attitudes when handling the crisis, the British civilian administration successfully prevented further escalation. It is also important to note that although the view from the Foreign Office in London of the future of German nationalism and the value of the BAOR as a tool for improving relations may have been pessimistic, the cooperation between the British and German administrations on the Land and Kreis levels was more promising. Chapter 5 demonstrated that dealing with local German officials often took place in a spirit of give-and-take regardless of the rapidly changing status and independence of the FRG.

The BAOR and the Germans: From Enemies to Partners?

When considering the suitability of the BAOR as a tool for a rapprochement between Britons and Germans, there were several obstacles that were difficult to overcome. Arguably it was not necessarily British attitudes that stood in the way of relations but the nature of "visiting forces" in itself. As demonstrated in chapter 4, British garrisons were "by nature self-contained, geographically separated and an unnatural intrusion."[8] Units often had very busy training schedules and also suffered from severe staff shortages. Consequently the focus on relations with locals was often not a high priority when running an army that was lacking in both equipment and manpower as a first-line defense against communism. Whereas those officers in charge of organizing community relations with Germans were often far too busy, soldiers of ordinary ranks were often reluctant to establish contacts themselves. The language barrier was a major problem, and records show that Britons were not particularly eager to learn German. As a consequence, often the only contacts between Britons and Germans were between large groups of young British servicemen and Germans in local bars. This repeatedly led to mass brawls and hostility.

Army records on relations with Germans are scarce, but regimental magazines clearly show a slow change in attitudes away from an occupation power toward an army of protection. Marriages to German women were less frowned upon, and holiday visits to Germany were advertised frequently. Also German customs were increasingly featured in magazines. Despite the apathy of many Britons, successful attempts were made by troops to improve relations. In the beginning these generally involved entertaining German children and sports events. Sports events in particular were a successful means of Anglo-German rapprochement, as British troops often had to rely on German facilities and land to practice certain sports. This forced even the more reluctant units to develop contacts. Often these contacts were then picked up on by the local press, featuring them as positive examples for Anglo-German relations. That in amateur and informal sports the recent history did not matter very much and that the effort of individuals on an equal playing field counted for more than national matters made sports an ideal area for improving relations. Language barriers also counted for less in sporting events. Contacts were also often improved by the arrival of British wives and children, despite the increased pressure on the housing situation in Germany and despite FO concerns about the opinions of officers' wives.

Considering attitudes toward Germans by British officers, regular soldiers, and National Servicemen, it appears that particularly junior officers were frequently unwilling to approach Germans. As chapter 4 demonstrated, regular soldiers also often proved reluctant, whereas National Servicemen were generally more outgoing. Just as the view of the British public established in chapter 2, the views of the British soldier, forged in the crucible of war and its aftermath, were nuanced. They were sometimes hostile, sometimes indifferent, generally reluctant, but by no means an immovable obstacle that stood between the FO and the German population.

The Impact of the BAOR on Anglo-German Relations

Throughout the late 1940s and early 1950s the British administration was concerned about the potential damage the presence of the BAOR could do to the West German integration into the Western alliance system. London was also hopeful that the British armed services could be used to further Anglo-German relations. It is important to note that although servicemen caused many problems, the presence of nearly eighty thousand British troops in Germany shortly after the Second World War did not lead to a deterioration of relations. Despite a generally reluctant army, the transformation from an army of occupation to a protecting force was surprisingly successful so soon after the war. The necessary measures for this transformation were not initiated by the army but by and large were enforced by the services. What is most remarkable is the extent to which the BAOR was required to change in order to facilitate Anglo-German understanding. As demonstrated in chapter 5, it was the wide range of efforts taken, ranging from housing initiatives to avoidance of maneuver damage, that highlighted the extent of change. This in itself was remarkable only ten years after the war. The BAOR of 1957 was very different than that of 1948. Troops went to great lengths to avoid maneuver damage and in some cases shared their accommodation with Germans. Property was derequisitioned and the often luxurious conditions for British officers slowly changed. The army leadership was clearly willing to cooperate with the civilian administration in order to adapt to the changing Anglo-German relations.

However, the value of the BAOR as a tool for improving Anglo-German relations was limited. In spite of some successful efforts at unit levels, progress was slow. In the more individual contexts, anti-German sentiment still prevented closer relations. Despite a change in the portrayal of Germany in Britain and concerted efforts at all levels of the British administration, it appears that the average British "squaddie" simply refused to fulfill the diplomatic hopes placed in the BAOR. The success of the efforts to utilize the BAOR therefore lay not within a marked improvement of relations, but in preventing deterioration at a crucial time in both Anglo-German relations as well as the reemergence of the Federal Republic as a sovereign state. If the BAOR's impact on Anglo-German relations was limited, the same is equally true for the significance of local relations on the success of the Western defense against the Soviet bloc. The issues addressed in this book tended to take place in a localized and self-contained context rather than affect the wider issues of Western defense against communism.

As is evident with hindsight, British fears in the 1950s of a resurgent German nationalism proved unfounded. Doubts were certainly understandable in the light of the recent German past and continued to affect policy makers in London in the decades to come. Despite the integration of the Federal Republic into NATO and the EEC, British demands for using the BAOR to influence Germany did not disappear. As late as 1968 British observers still drew attention to the need for the BAOR to improve relations with the German public in order to restrain German politics in case of a resurgence of nationalism. The defense correspondent of *The Times* remarked in April of that year that the BAOR's role was that of an "intensely political army" that had to "continue cultivating the best possible relations with German military, official and civilian circles alike in the hopes that its relationship deter or at least defuse any rise in anti-British feeling which could readily occur under a more nationalist government."[9] Although the success of using the BAOR as a tool for Anglo-German rapprochement during the 1940s and 1950s varied, with some successes and some shortcomings, the idea of using the BAOR as a political tool clearly retained its merit.

NOTES

INTRODUCTION

1. Graham E. Watson and Richard A. Rinaldi, *The British Army in Germany: An Organizational History, 1947–2004* (Milton Keynes: Tiger Lily Publications, 2005), 1.

2. Ibid., 22.

3. Bevin Memorandum, 3 May 1946, cited in Anne Deighton, *The Impossible Peace: Britain, the Division of Germany, and the Origins of the Cold War* (Oxford: Clarendon Press, 1993), 225.

4. Patricia Meehan, *A Strange Enemy People: Germans under the British, 1945–1950* (London: Owen, 2001), 269.

5. "Within little more than half a decade [relations] deteriorated to the worst level since the end of the war." This deterioration was partly due as well to the general weakening of British relations with Europe over the European Free Trade Association (EFTA). See Sabine Lee, *Victory in Europe? Britain and Germany since 1945* (Harlow: Longman, 2001), 72. For the debate on troop costs, see, for example, Hubert Zimmermann, "The Sour Fruits of Victory: Sterling and Security in Anglo-German Relations during the 1950s and 1960s," *Contemporary European History* 9, no. 2 (2000): 225–43.

6. Anne Deighton, "Minds, Not Hearts: British Policy and West German Rearmament," in *Debating Foreign Affairs: The Public and British Foreign Policy since 1867*, ed. Christian Haase (Berlin: Philo, 2003), 78.

7. Evgenios Michail, "After the War and after the Wall: British Perceptions of Germany Following 1945 and 1989," *University of Sussex Journal of Contemporary History* 3 (September 2001): 7.

8. Deighton, "Minds, Not Hearts," 78.

9. For example, some "50,000 houses in inner London were destroyed or damaged beyond repair, with a further 66,000 in outer London. Some 288,000 more houses London-wide were seriously damaged and another two million slightly." Jerry White,

London in the Twentieth Century: A City and Its People (London: Vintage, 2008), 39.

10. Deighton, "Minds, Not Hearts," 78.

11. Matthias Schönwald, "New Friends–Difficult Friendships: Germany and Its Western Neighbours in the Postwar Era," *Contemporary European History* 11, no. 2 (2002): 318.

12. The National Archives, Foreign Office Records (hereafter, TNA, FO) 1032/1465, "Treatment of and Attitude towards the German People, 1945–1946."

13. Meehan, *Strange Enemy People*, 153.

14. TNA, FO 1014/26, "Final Report on BAOR/German Relations," Part 2, Detail, 1.b.

15. Such questions about contributions initially arose in the context of the proposed European Defence Community (EDC), later within NATO, when the BAOR formed the main element of NATO's Northern Army Group (NORTHAG).

16. Lee, *Victory in Europe*, 59.

17. TNA, FO 371/124622, C. H. Johnston, Memorandum on "Economy in our forces in Germany," 14 May 1956, iv.

18. Lee, *Victory in Europe*, 51.

19. TNA, FO 371/109787, P. Wright to Hancock, "Attitude towards the Germans of H. M. Forces stationed in Germany after ratification of the Paris Agreements," 1954.

20. Ivone Kirkpatrick, *The Inner Circle* (London: Macmillan, 1959), 236.

21. See, for example, L. V. Scott, *Conscription and the Attlee Governments: The Politics and Policy of National Service, 1945–1951* (Oxford: Clarendon Press, 1993); Roger Broad, *Conscription in Britain, 1939–1964: The Militarisation of a Generation* (London: Routledge, 2006); and Richard Vinen, *National Service: Conscription in Britain, 1945–1963* (London: Penguin, 2014).

22. David French, *Army, Empire, and Cold War: The British Army and Military Policy, 1945–1971* (Oxford: Oxford University Press, 2012), 2.

23. Watson and Rinaldi, *British Army in Germany*.

24. Deighton, *Impossible Peace*; Anne Deighton, "Cold-War Diplomacy: British Policy towards Germany's Role in Europe, 1945–49," in *Reconstruction in Post-War Germany: British Occupation and the Western Zones,* ed. Ian D. Turner (Oxford: St. Martin's, 1989), 15–36; Meehan, *Strange Enemy People*.

25. Sabine Lee, *An Uneasy Partnership: British-German Relations between 1955 and 1961* (Bochum: Brockmeyer, 1996); Daniel Gossel, *Briten, Deutsche und Europa. Die Deutsche Frage in der britischen Außenpolitik, 1945–1962* (Stuttgart: Steiner, 1999). As Gossel covers the relatively long period from 1945 to 1962, the years 1945 to 1955 are not covered in a particularly detailed manner and offer little new insight.

26. Here the memoirs of the British high commissioner to Germany, Sir Ivone Kirkpatrick, and the German ambassador to London, Hans von Herwarth, stand out. Kirkpatrick, *Inner Circle*; Hans von Herwarth, *Von Adenauer zu Brandt. Erin-*

nerungen (Berlin: Propyläen, 1990). The biography of the British military governor and high commissioner also provides useful insight. David Williamson, *A Most Diplomatic General: The Life of General Lord Robertson of Oakridge* (London: Brassey's 1996).

27. Lee, *Victory in Europe,* 51. Gottfried Niedhart goes as far as claiming that specific attempts to improve the bilateral aspect of the Anglo-German political relationship were in fact notably absent. Gottfried Niedhart, "Die Bundesrepublik Deutschland in der britischen Politik der Fünfziger Jahre: Rearmed but once again a healthy member of the Western family," *Historische Mitteilungen* 3 (1990): 186. There are nonetheless clear efforts evident on both sides to improve bilateral relations. See Lee, *Victory in Europe,* 70; Yvonne Kipp, *Eden, Adenauer und die Deutsche Frage. Britische Deutschlandpolitik im internationalen Spannungsfeld, 1951–1957* (Paderborn: Schöningh, 2002), 231.

28. Schönwald, "New Friends," 318.

29. For the discussion on how effective and wholehearted this commitment was, see Paul Cornish, "The British Military View of European Security, 1945–50," in *Building Postwar Europe,* ed. Anne Deighton (Oxford: St. Martin's, 1995), 70.

30. Angelika Volle, "Deutsch-Britische Beziehungen. Eine Untersuchung des bilateralen Verhältnisses auf der staatlichen und nichtstaatlichen Ebene seit dem Zweiten Weltkrieg," unpublished PhD thesis (Bonn: Rheinische Friedrich-Wilhelms-Universität, 1976), 41.

31. "Security for Germany" instead of "Security against Germany." Niedhart, 'Die Bundesrepublik Deutschland," 190.

32. Beatrice Heuser, "Britain and the Federal Republic of Germany in NATO, 1955–1990," in *Britain and Germany in Europe, 1949–1990,* ed. Jeremy Noakes, Peter Wende, and Jonathan Wright (Oxford: Oxford University Press, 2002), 142. On the related topic of Britain, the failure of the EDC, and German entry into NATO, see Hans Heinrich Jansen, *Grossbritannien, das Scheitern der EVG und der NATO-Beitritt der Bundesrepublik Deutschland* (Bochum: Universitätsverlag, 1992).

33. Olaf Mager, *Die Stationierung der britischen Rheinarmee. Grossbritanniens EVG-Alternative* (Baden-Baden: Nomos, 1990), 2.

34. Spencer Mawby, *Containing Germany: Britain and the Arming of the Federal Republic* (Basingstoke: Macmillan, 1999). See also Saki Dockrill, *Britain's Policy for West German Rearmament, 1950–1955* (Cambridge: Cambridge University Press, 1991); Axel Christian Azzola, *Die Diskussion um die Aufrüstung der BRD im Unterhaus und in der Presse Großbritanniens, November 1949–Juli 1952* (Meisenheim: A. Hain, 1971).

35. Deighton, "Minds, Not Hearts," 79.

36. Meehan, *Strange Enemy People,* 53.

37. FO 1014/26, cited in ibid., 156.

38. Lee, *Uneasy Partnership,* 14. For relevant press views on Germany, see also Karin Herrmann et al., eds., *Coping with the Relations: Anglo-German Cartoons from the Fifties to the Nineties* (Osnabrück: Secolo, 1988).

39. Deighton, "Minds, Not Hearts," 79.

40. Michail, "After the War"; Ruth Wittlinger, "Perceptions of Germany and the Germans in Post-War Britain," *Journal of Multilingual and Multicultural Development* 25, nos. 5/6 (2004): 453–56; R. G. Hughes, "'Don't let's be beastly to the Germans': Britain and the German Affair in History," *Twentieth Century British History* 17, no. 2 (2006): 257–83.

41. John Farquharson, "'Emotional but Influential': Victor Gollancz, Richard Stokes, and the British Zone of Germany, 1945–49," *Journal of Contemporary History* 22, no. 3 (1987): 501–519; Christian Haase, "In Search of a European Settlement: Chatham House and British-German Relations, 1920–1955," *European History Quarterly* 37, no. 3 (2007): 371–97; Rolf Breitenstein, *Total War to Total Trust. Personal Accounts of 30 Years of Anglo-German Relations* (London: Wolff, 1976); Peter Alter, "Building Bridges: The Framework of Anglo-German Cultural Relations after 1945," in Noakes et al., *Britain and Germany in Europe*. A more dated but still useful account is provided in Volle, "Deutsch-Britische Beziehungen."

42. Jill Stephenson, "Britain and Europe in the Later Twentieth Century: Identity, Sovereignty, Peculiarity," in *National Histories and European History*, ed. Mary Fulbrook (London: Boulder, 1993), 233.

43. Walter Lippmann, cited in Herrmann et al., *Coping with the Relations*, 15.

44. Richard Falcon, "Images of Germany and the Germans in British Film and Television Fictions," in *As Others See Us: Anglo-German Perceptions*, ed. Harald Husemann (Frankfurt: P. Lang, 1994), 18.

45. John Willoughby, *Remaking the Conquering Heroes: The Postwar American Occupation of Germany* (Basingstoke: Palgrave, 2001).

46. Meehan, *Strange Enemy People*.

47. John Ramsden, *Don't Mention the War* (London: Little, 2006), 246. See also C. Summers, "We had a lot of laughs," *BBC News Online*, 20 July 2004, http://news.bbc.co.uk/1/hi/world/europe/3842041.stm.

48. National Serviceman Harry Wright found the German people in the more rural town of Herford quite different and more likeable than the ones in the industrial town of Essen. See Peter Chambers and Amy Landreth, eds., *Called Up: The Personal Experiences of Sixteen National Servicemen, Told by Themselves* (London: A. Wingate, 1955), 175.

49. See B. S. Johnson, ed., *All Bull: The National Servicemen* (London: Quartet Books, 1973), 112.

50. Kipp, *Eden, Adenauer und die deutsche Frage*.

CHAPTER 1. BRITAIN, THE COLD WAR, AND THE BAOR

1. Anne Deighton, "Minds, Not Hearts: British Policy and West German Rearmament," in *Debating Foreign Affairs: The Public and British Policy since 1867*, ed. Christian Haase (Berlin: Philo, 2003), 79.

2. Noel Annan, cited in ibid., 85.

3. Deighton, "Minds, Not Hearts," 87.

4. John Ramsden, *Don't Mention the War: The British and the Germans since 1890* (London: Little, 2006), 266.

5. TNA, FO 371/118217, WG 1071/681, Minute by P. Wright, 23 June 1955.

6. Ann Lane, "Kirkpatrick, Sir Ivone Augustine (1897–1964)," *Oxford Dictionary of National Biography* (Oxford: Oxford University Press, 2004); online edition, January 2008, http://www.oxforddnb.com/view/article/34339.

7. Ivone Kirkpatrick, *The Inner Circle* (London: Macmillan, 1959), 124.

8. Lane, "Kirkpatrick."

9. Kirkpatrick, *Inner Circle*, 91.

10. Lane, "Kirkpatrick."

11. Ibid.

12. Kirkpatrick, *Inner Circle*, 222.

13. Ibid., 257.

14. Deighton, "Minds, Not Hearts," 87.

15. Kirkpatrick, *Inner Circle*, 254.

16. Charles Richardson, "Robertson, Brian Hubert, first Baron Robertson of Oakridge (1896–1974)," rev. *Oxford Dictionary of National Biography* (Oxford: Oxford University Press, 2004), online edition, January 2011, http://www.oxforddnb.com/view/article/31616.

17. Lord Longford, foreword to David Williamson, *A Most Diplomatic General: The Life of General Lord Robertson of Oakridge* (London: Brassey's, 1996).

18. Graham E. Watson and Richard A. Rinaldi, *The British Army in Germany (BAOR and After): An Organizational History, 1947–2004* (Milton Keynes: Tiger Lily Publications, 2005), 1.

19. Colin McInnes, *Hot War, Cold War: The British Army's Way in Warfare, 1945–95* (London: Brassey's, 1996), 3.

20. Ibid.

21. David French, *Army, Empire, and Cold War: The British Army and Military Policy, 1945–1971* (Oxford: Oxford University Press, 2012), 7.

22. McInnes, *Hot War, Cold War*, 4.

23. Watson and Rinaldi, *British Army in Germany*, 3.

24. Tom Hickman, *The Call-Up: A History of National Service* (London: Headline, 2004), xvi.

25. Saki Dockrill, "Retreat from the Continent? Britain's Motives for Troop Reductions in West Germany, 1955–1958," *Journal of Strategic Studies* 20, no. 3 (1997): 46.

26. McInnes, *Hot War, Cold War*, 5.

27. French, *Army, Empire, and Cold War*, 28.

28. McInnes, *Hot War, Cold War*, 5.

29. French, *Army, Empire, and Cold War*, 28.

30. Dockrill, "Retreat from the Continent?" 46.

31. McInnes, *Hot War, Cold War*, 6.

32. TNA, FO 371/76629, Memorandum, 29 January 1949, 1.

33. Ibid., 3.

34. French, *Army, Empire, and Cold War*, 28.

35. McInnes, *Hot War, Cold War*, 6.

36. Dockrill, "Retreat from the Continent?" 47.

37. TNA, FO 1030/123, Letter from Robertson to Bevin, 4 January 1949.

38. McInnes, *Hot War, Cold War*, 6.

39. Watson and Rinaldi, *British Army in Germany*, 4. Battalions were made up of between six hundred and one thousand soldiers.

40. French, *Army, Empire, and Cold War*, 29.

41. McInnes, *Hot War, Cold War*, 7.

42. Dockrill, "Retreat from the Continent?" 49.

43. McInnes, *Hot War, Cold War*, 7.

44. Watson and Rinaldi, *British Army in Germany*, 19.

45. TNA, FO 371/85220, "Strength of BAOR," 4 December 1950.

46. McInnes, *Hot War, Cold War*, 8.

47. Watson and Rinaldi, *British Army in Germany*, 22.

48. McInnes, *Hot War, Cold War*, 9.

49. Dockrill, "Retreat from the Continent?" 55; emphasis in original.

50. Ibid., 56.

51. Spencer Mawby, *Containing Germany: Britain and the Arming of the Federal Republic* (Basingstoke: Macmillan, 1999), 185.

52. Dockrill, "Retreat from the Continent?" 59.

53. Ibid., 46.

54. McInnes, *Hot War, Cold War*, 10.

55. TNA, FO 371/93375, G10110/56, Ernest Davies, "Report on Parliamentary Under-Secretary's Visit to Germany," 26 January 1951, 7.

56. Watson and Rinaldi, *British Army in Germany*, 3.

57. For a complete list of principal garrison cities in Germany, see ibid., 145.

58. Ibid., 3.

59. Ibid., 5.

60. Roy Bainton, *The Long Patrol: The British in Germany since 1945* (Edinburgh: Mainstream, 2003), 24.

61. Watson and Rinaldi, *British Army in Germany*, 19.

62. The BAOR during this period was made up from the 2nd Infantry Division, the 6th Armored Division, the 7th Armored Division, and the 11th Armored Division. A division numbered up to twenty thousand troops and was made up of several brigades, each numbering up to eight thousand men. Bainton, *Long Patrol*, 9.

63. Watson and Rinaldi, *British Army in Germany*, 24.

64. Patricia Meehan, *A Strange Enemy People: Germans under the British, 1945–1950* (London: Owen, 2001), 53.

65. Ibid.

66. Ibid.

67. TNA, FO 1032/993, "Relations between the Services and the CCG," 1948.

68. TNA, FO 1032/1095, cited in Meehan, *Strange Enemy People*, 155.

69. TNA, FO 1032/1465, cited in ibid., 152.

70. TNA, FO 1030/172, "Social Contact with Germans," Appendix A, 1.

71. TNA, FO 1014/26, "Final Report on BAOR/German Relations," Part 1, July 1948, 1.

72. TNA, FO 1032/1368, Minutes of Meeting held on 18 May 1948.

73. TNA, FO 1014/26, Memorandum on "Relations between Rhine Army and the Germans," 31 July 1948.

74. TNA, FO 1014/26, "Final Report on BAOR/German Relations," July 1948, 1.

75. Ibid.

76. Ibid.

77. Ibid.

78. TNA, FO 1014/26, "Final Report on BAOR/German Relations," Part 2, July 1948, 1.

79. Ibid., 2.

80. Ibid.

81. TNA, FO1014/26, Letter from Deputy Regional Commissioner Hamburg to Zonal Office of Educational Advisor CCG, 14 July 1948.

82. Ibid.

83. Ibid.

84. Ibid.

85. TNA, FO 1014/26, Letter from Deputy Regional Commissioner CCG Hamburg, 13 July 1948.

86. Ibid.

87. TNA, FO1014/26, Letter from Deputy Regional Commissioner Hamburg to Zonal Office of Educational Advisor CCG, 14 July 1948.

88. Meehan, *Strange Enemy People*, 53.

89. TNA, FO 1014/26, "Final Report on BAOR/German Relations," July 1948.

90. TNA, FO 1014/26, Letter from Deputy Regional Commissioner CCG Hamburg to Zonal Office of Educational Advisor CCG, 14 July 1948.

91. For an account on British attempts to regulate marriages between British civilian staff and German women, see Barbara Smith, "The Rules of Engagement: German Women and British Occupiers, 1945–1949," Wilfrid Laurier University, 2009, *Theses and Dissertations (Comprehensive)*, Paper 1072, http://scholars.wlu.ca/etd/1072.

92. TNA, FO 1032/1368, "Policy for Non-Fraternisation," Minutes of 16th Meeting, 18 May 1948.

93. TNA, FO 1013/2449, "Anglo-German Relations" Pamphlet, February 1954 Edition, 23 March 1954.

94. TNA, FO 1013/2449, Draft of "basic brief" on Anglo-German Relations, 3 February 1954.

95. Kirkpatrick, *Inner Circle*, 219.

96. TNA, FO 1013/2449, Draft of "basic brief" on Anglo-German Relations, 3 February 1954.

97. TNA, FO 1014/233, Dispatch no. 19 Headquarters CCG (BE) to Bevin, Report on Social Matters, 18 February 1948.

98. TNA, FO 1013/2449, "Anglo-German Relations" Pamphlet.

99. Sabine Lee, *Victory In Europe? Britain and Germany since 1945* (Harlow: Longman, 2001), 48.

100. Ibid., 49.

101. TNA, FO 1013/2449, Draft of "basic brief" on Anglo-German Relations, 3 February 1954.

102. TNA, FO 371/76629, FO Memorandum on "Strength of Rhine Army," Kirkpatrick to Bevin, 29 January 1949.

103. TNA, FO 1030/123, Letter from Robertson to Bevin on purpose of BAOR, 24 January 1949.

104. Ibid.

105. TNA, FO 371/93375, Ernest Davies, "Report on Parliamentary Under-Secretary's Visit to Germany," 26 January 1951.

106. Ibid.

107. Ibid.

108. TNA, FO 371/93375, Kirkpatrick (Wahnerheide) to Gainer, FO, 5 February 1951.

109. TNA, FO 800/467, Bevin to Attlee, 25 October 1950.

110. Michael Carver, "Templer, Sir Gerald Walter Robert (1898–1979)," *Oxford Dictionary of National Biography* (Oxford: Oxford University Press, 2004), online edition, http://www.oxforddnb.com/view/article/31747.

111. Ibid.

112. TNA, FO 371/109648, Personal Minute from Prime Minister to Secretary of State for War, 6 March 1954.

113. Yvonne Kipp, *Eden, Adenauer und die Deutsche Frage. Britische Deutschlandpolitik im internationalen Spannungsfeld, 1951–1957* (Paderborn: Schöningh, 2002), 231.

114. Lee, *Victory in Europe*, 7.

115. Clemes A. Wurm, "Britain and West European Integration, 1948–9 to 1955: Politics and Economics," in *Britain and Germany in Europe, 1949–1990*, ed. Jeremy Noakes, Peter Wende, Jonathan Wright (Oxford: Oxford University Press, 2002), 45.

116. TNA, FO 371/85220, Bevin to Viscount Alexander, 22 February 1950.

117. TNA, FO 371/85220, "Strength of BAOR," 4 December 1950.

118. TNA, FO 371/85220, Telegram from Kirkpatrick to FO, 6 September 1950.

119. Ibid.

120. The British Foreign Office was particularly concerned about this persistent reluctance to bear arms. Kipp, *Eden, Adenauer und die Deutsche Frage*, 76.

121. TNA, FO 371/85220, Telegram from Kirkpatrick to FO, 6 September 1950.

122. Kipp, *Eden, Adenauer und die Deutsche Frage,* 82.

123. TNA, FO 371/118217, "Future form of German nationalism: Views of Sir F. Hoyer-Millar," 8 June 1955.

CHAPTER 2. THE BRITISH

1. Patrick Major, "Britain and Germany: A Love-Hate Relationship?" *German History* 26, no. 4 (2008): 467.

2. John Farquharson, "'Emotional but Influential': Victor Gollancz, Richard Stokes, and the British Zone of Germany, 1945–49," *Journal of Contemporary History* 22, no. 3 (1987): 501.

3. Donald C. Watt, *Britain Looks to Germany: British Opinion and Policy towards Germany since 1945* (London: Wolff, 1965), 104.

4. See, for example, George H. Gallup, *The Gallup International Public Opinion Polls, Great Britain, 1937–1975* (New York: Random House, 1976).

5. Anne Deighton, "Minds, Not Hearts: British Policy and West German Rearmament," in *Debating Foreign Affairs: The Public and British Foreign Policy since 1867,* ed. Christian Haase (Berlin: Philo, 2003), 79.

6. W. Phillips Davison, cited in Angelika Volle, "Deutsch-Britische Beziehungen. Eine Untersuchung des bilateralen Verhältnisses auf der staatlichen und nichtstaatlichen Ebene seit dem Zweiten Weltkrieg," unpublished PhD thesis (Bonn: Rheinische Friedrich-Wilhelms-Universität, 1976), 73.

7. Deighton, "Minds, Not Hearts," 80.

8. Mass Observation Archive (hereafter, MOA), File 2565, 9.

9. Robert J. Wybrow, *Britain Speaks Out, 1937–87* (Basingstoke: Macmillan, 1989), 40.

10. John Ramsden, *Don't Mention the War: The British and the Germans since 1890* (London: Little, 2006) 247.

11. Evgenios Michail, "After the War and after the Wall: British Perceptions of Germany following 1945 and 1989," *University of Sussex Journal of Contemporary History* 3 (September 2001): 3.

12. MOA, File 2565, 8.

13. G. Weidenfeld, "Englisches Deutschlandbild," *Die politische Meinung* 44 (1999): 55–62.

14. Watt, *Britain Looks to Germany,* 120.

15. Wybrow, *Britain Speaks Out,* 37.

16. Watt, *Britain Looks to Germany,* 128.

17. Gallup poll, September 1954: "Do you think there is much chance that the Nazis will again become powerful in Germany?"—much chance: 40 percent; not much chance: 41 percent; undecided: 19 percent. Gallup, *Gallup International Public Opinion Polls,* 335.

18. TNA, FO 371/130857, Minute by C. P. Hope, 19 November 1957.

19. Watt, *Britain Looks to Germany*, 128.

20. TNA, FO 371/130857, Minute by J. H. Moore, 12 November 1957.

21. Watt, *Britain Looks to Germany*, 128.

22. TNA, FO 371/130857, no. 16730/IG, Minute by C. M. Rose, 4 October 1957.

23. *Daily Express*, 19 August 1954, 2.

24. *Daily Express*, 18 October 1957, 2.

25. TNA, FO 371/130857, no. 16730/IG, Minute by C. M. Rose, 4 October 1957.

26. Ibid.

27. *Daily Express*, 30 November 1954, 2.

28. A. H. Lanton, quoted in *Daily Mirror*, 28 August 1954, 2.

29. Express Diary, William Hickey, *Daily Express*, 23 March 1955, 6.

30. *Daily Mirror*, 1 July 1952, 1.

31. TNA, FO 371/130857, no. 16730/IG, Minute by C. P. Hope, 4 October 1957.

32. Ibid.

33. TNA, FO 371/130857, Minute by C. M. Rose, 8 October 1957.

34. TNA, FO 371/130857, WG1673/1, Letter from Sir Christopher Steele, Bonn, to P. F. Hancock, FO, 24 September 1957.

35. TNA, FO 371/130857, Copy of Confidential Minute from Mr. A. L. Pope to the head of Chancery, Bonn, 23 September 1957.

36. TNA, FO 371/130857, Letter from Patrick Hancock, FO to Sir Christopher Steele, Bonn, 23 October 1957.

37. Ibid.

38. Louis Heren was the *Times* correspondent in Bonn from 1955 to 1960, "the best war correspondent of his generation and a proper *Times* man." Philip Howard, "Heren, Louis Philip (1919–1995)," *Oxford Dictionary of National Biography* (Oxford: Oxford University Press, 2004), online edition, January 2011, http://www.oxforddnb.com/view/article/58200.

39. Watt, *Britain Looks to Germany*, 127.

40. TNA, FO 371/130857, Minute by J. H. Moore, 12 November 1957.

41. Ibid.

42. TNA, FO 371/130857, Minute by C. P. Hope, 19 November 1957.

43. TNA, FO 371/130857, Minute by P.H.G. Wright, 14 November 1957.

44. TNA, FO 371/130857, Minute by C. P. Hope, 19 November 1957.

45. Audrey Whiting, "Yellow Bellies—by Order," *Sunday Pictorial*, January 1957.

46. Ibid.

47. Ibid.

48. Bundesarchiv Koblenz (hereafter, BK), B145/610, Letter from Eric Peterson c/o Birkbeck College to Dr. Adenauer, 27 January 1957.

49. BK, B145/610 Letter from Herr von Dziembowski, Auswärtiges Amt to Eric Peterson, 7 March 1957.

50. Ramsden, *Don't Mention the War*, 262.

51. Robert M. Cassidy, "The British Army and Counterinsurgency: The Salience of Military Culture," *Military Review*, May-June 2005, http://usacac.army.mil/CAC/milreview/download/English/MayJun05/cassidy.pdf.

52. BBC [Written Archives Centre], Reference Card A/132/P A81379, 4,000C, 17-1-57, 112, Commentary: "German Re-unification again: by Lord Strang," 4 March 1957, Julia de Beausobre, "A Matter of Conscience, A talk on letter written shortly before their execution, by some Germans who defied Hitler," 24 December 1956.

53. BBC, Reference Card A/132/P A69044 5,000C, 29-6-54, 111, Peter Stern, "The Dilemma of the German Novel," 29 December 1956.

54. BBC, T4/57 Documentaries, "Special Enquiry on Germany, 1954–1955," Memorandum from Anthony de Lotbiniere to Imlay Newbiggin-Watts, 18 February 1955.

55. BBC, T4/57, "Special Enquiry on Germany, The Federal Republic," 2, 18 April 1955.

56. Ibid., 3.

57. BBC, T4/57, DOC VR/55/190, Norman Swallow, Audience Research Report, "Special Enquiry," 6 May 1955.

58. BBC, T4/57, FC 1051/75, Memorandum from FO to Office of UK High Commissioner, Germany, 9 January 1955.

59. BBC, T4/57, PB 10110/1, Letter from A.C.E. Malcolm, FO London, to Tangye Lean, BBC, 2 October 1952.

60. *The Listener* 42, no. 1074, W. N. Ewer, "Democracy on Trial again in Germany," 25 August 1949, 298.

61. *The Listener* 53, no. 1367, Geoffrey Barraclough, "Germany Ten Years After," 12 May 1955, 829.

62. E. M. Butler's account of his visit to Bonn University aimed at finding out "what the young men and women of Germany, [. . .] were really thinking and feeling about life, [. . .] their deep, almost unconscious reaction to the situation in which they find themselves." *The Listener* 40, "The Faust Legend and the Youth of Germany," 1 July 1948, 16.

63. *The Listener* 53, no. 1367, Terence Prittie, "What Do the Youth of Germany Want?" 28 April 1955, 734.

64. Ibid.

65. Alistair Horne, prologue to *Back into Power: A Report on the New Germany* (London: Parrish, 1955).

66. Richard Davenport-Hines, "Russell, (Edward Frederick) Langley, second Baron Russell of Liverpool (1895–1981)," *Oxford Dictionary of National Biography* (Oxford: Oxford University Press, 2004), online edition, http://www.oxforddnb.com/view/article/31636.

67. Patricia Meehan, *A Strange Enemy People : Germans under the British, 1945–1950* (London: Owen, 2001), 269.

68. Davenport-Hines, "Russell."

69. TNA, FO 371/109733, *Daily Express*, 11 August 1954.

70. Ibid.

71. *Daily Mirror*, 12 August 1954, 9.

72. Watt, *Britain Looks to Germany,* 128.

73. TNA, FO 371/109733, CW1671/9, Memorandum by F. A. Warner, 11 August 1954.

74. TNA, FO 371/109733 CW1671/10(1), Minute by F. A. Warner to Sir Frank Roberts, 11 August 1954: "In view of the fuss occasioned by the banning of Lord Russell's book on war criminals, you might just like to be reminded that there are two other books connected with Germany, the publication of which H.M.G. are at present seeking to influence."

75. TNA, FO 371/109733, CW1671/9, Memorandum by F. A. Warner, 11 August 1954.

76. TNA, FO 371/109733, CW1671/10, Letter from A. M. Palliser to I. Kirkpatrick, 10 August 1954.

77. TNA, FO 371/109733, Letter from Goldstream to Russell, 23 July 1954.

78. TNA, FO 371/109733, *The Observer*, 22 August 1954, "Note by the Lord Chancellor's Office," 5.

79. Ibid.

80. Ibid., 8.

81. TNA, FO 371/109733, CW1671/21, Letter to A.A.S. Stark, 1 November 1954.

82. Wendy Webster, "From Nazi-Legacy to Cold War: British Perceptions of European Identity, 1945–1964," in *European Identity and the Second World War*, ed. Michael Wintle and Menno Spiering (Basingstoke: Palgrave, 2011), 104.

83. Annedore Leber, *Conscience in Revolt* (London: Vallentine, 1957).

84. TNA, FO 371/109733, CW1671/18, Letter from E.J.W. Barnes to F. A. Warner, Western Department FO, 8 September 1954.

85. Ibid.

86. Robert Birley in Leber, *Conscience in Revolt*, vi.

87. TNA, FO 371/109733, CW 1671/22, Letter from Norman Wymer to Anthony Eden, 28 October 1954.

88. TNA, FO 371/109733, Minute by T.R.M. Sewell, 2 November 1954.

89. TNA, FO 371/109733, Draft from Private Secretary to Norman Wymer, November 1954.

90. TNA, FO 371/109733, Minute by P. Hancock, 3 November 1954.

91. Ramsden, *Don't Mention the War*, 265.

92. Alexander P. Scotland, *The London Cage* (London: Evans Bros., 1957). The book was eventually published in 1957 and heavily censored.

93. TNA, FO 371/109733, CW1671/10(1), Minute F. A. Warner to Sir Frank Roberts, 11 August 1954.

94. Ibid.

95. David Lodge, *Ginger, You're Barmy: An Uncompromising Novel of Army Life* (London: Penguin, 1970), 178.

96. Wybrow, *Britain Speaks Out*, 36.

97. Nicholas Monsarrat, *The Cruel Sea* (London: Knopf, 1951), 236.

98. Ibid., 238.

99. Ibid., 240.

100. Ibid., 238.

101. John Ramsden, "Re-focusing 'the People's War': British War Films of the 1950s," *Journal of Contemporary History* 33, no.1 (1998): 36.

102. Wybrow, *Britain Speaks Out*, 45.

103. Paul Brickhill, *Reach for the Sky: The Story of Douglas Bader* (London: Collins, 1954), 291.

104. Ibid., 287.

105. Ibid., 336.

106. Ibid., 354.

107. Penny Summerfield, "Dunkirk and the Popular Memory of Britain at War, 1940–1958," *Journal of Contemporary History* 45 (2010): 797.

108. Ibid., 796.

109. Ibid., 797.

110. Ramsden, "Re-focusing 'the People's War,'" 37.

111. Ibid., 39.

112. Brickhill, *Reach for the Sky*, 304.

113. Ramsden, "Re-focusing 'the People's War,'" 39.

114. George Orwell, "Boys' Weeklies," in George Orwell, *Inside the Whale and Other Essays* (Harmondsworth: Penguin, 1968), 188.

115. Ibid.,196.

116. *The Hotspur*, issues 557–701 (London: D. C. Thompson, 1947–1950).

117. Colin Seymour-Ure, "Hulton, Sir Edward George Warris (1906–1988)," rev. *Oxford Dictionary of National Biography* (Oxford: Oxford University Press, 2004), online edition, May 2011, http://www.oxforddnb.com/view/article/40161.

118. James Chapman, "Onward Christian Spacemen: Dan Dare—Pilot of the Future as British Cultural History," *Visual Culture in Britain* 9, no. 1 (2008): 55.

119. Ibid., 66.

120. David Kynaston, *Austerity Britain, 1945–51* (London: Bloomsbury, 2007), 504–506.

121. *Valiant*, issues 1–20, London, IPC Magazines, October 1962–February 1963.

122. Nicholas Pronay, "The British Post-Bellum Cinema: A Survey of the Films Relating to World War II Made in Britain between 1945 and 1960," *Historical Journal of Film, Radio, and Television* 8, no. 1 (1988): 39.

123. John Walker, ed., *Halliwell's Film Guide*, 8th ed. (London: Harper Collins, 1991), 1213, 225, 1028.

124. Richard Falcon, "Images of Germany and the Germans in British Film and Television Fictions," in *As Others See Us: Anglo-German Perception*, ed. Harald Husemann (Frankfurt: P. Lang, 1994), 18.

125. Guy Cumberpatch notes "that in a corpus of 370 British and American films (or rather film synopses) produced between 1929 and 1989, German characters were four times as likely to be portrayed negatively as positively." Quoted in Falcon, "Images of Germany," 8.

126. According to John Ramsden, the overall number of British War films for the decade of the 1950s was around eighty, including those dealing with Japan and other theaters of war. For a list of these films, see Ramsden, "Re-focusing 'the People's War,'" 62.

127. Walker, *Halliwell's*, 983.

128. Peter Baker, editor of *Films and Filming*, cited in Ramsden, "Re-focusing 'the People's War,'" 41.

129. Ramsden, "Re-focusing 'the People's War,'" 40.

130. Wybrow, *Britain Speaks Out*, 45.

131. The British film encyclopedist Leslie Halliwell aptly described the film as an "understated British war epic with additional scientific interest and good acting and model work, not to mention a welcome lack of love interest." Walker, *Halliwell's*, 261.

132. Ramsden, "Re-focusing 'the People's War,'" 42.

133. Walker, *Halliwell's*, 949.

134. National Army Museum (hereafter, NAM), File no. 2006-12-77-82, Letters from National Serviceman Cpl. Malcolm Barker, Queen's Royal Regiment, to his mother, 15 September 1952.

135. Walker, *Halliwell's*, 287.

136. His curiosity was further heightened by the fact that two of the former German generals interviewed by Brigadier Desmond Young, the author of *Rommel*, lived in Iserlohn, the town where he was stationed. A fellow conscript offered to show their residences to him. NAM 2006-12-77-82, 12 October 1952.

137. Patrick Major, "'Our Friend Rommel': The Wehrmacht as 'Worthy Enemy' in Postwar British Popular Culture," *German History* 26, no. 4 (2008): 521.

138. Hugh Trevor-Roper, cited in Major, "'Our Friend Rommel,'" 524.

139. Ramsden, *Don't Mention the War*, 306.

140. Walker, *Halliwell's*, 822.

141. Falcon, "Images of Germany," 19.

142. Ramsden, *Don't Mention the War*, 306.

143. Wybrow, *Britain Speaks Out*, 52. Incidentally, Halliwell was less enthusiastic. "A sympathetic view of a German hero [...] is the most notable feature of this disappointingly patchy and studio-bound war epic, with too many actors in ill-defined bit parts, too undisciplined a storyline, and too confusing scenes of battle." Walker, *Halliwell's*, 85.

144. *The Times*, Wednesday, 26 July 1950, 8, and 26 March 1953, 12.

145. *The Daily Telegraph*, cited in Ramsden, *Don't Mention the War*, 308.

146. Halliwell characterized the film as a "competent transcription of a bestselling book, cleanly produced and acted; a huge box office success." Walker, *Halliwell's*, 254.

147. Walker, *Halliwell's*, 254.

148. Ramsden, "Re-focusing 'the People's War,'" 51.

149. Ibid., 53.

150. *Kinematograph Weekly*, 12 April 1951, 22 December 1955, cited in Ramsden, "Re-focusing 'the People's War,'" 53.

151. Ramsden, "Re-focusing 'the People's War,'" 42.

152. Ramsden, *Don't Mention the War*, 318.

153. Geoffrey Gorer, *Exploring English Character* (New York: Criterion, 1955), 93.

154. Ibid., 88.

155. Ibid.

156. Walker, *Halliwell's*, 410.

157. MOA, File 2565, 9.

158. See, for example, Ramsden, *Don't Mention the War*, 325.

159. *The Reading Citizen*, June 1947, 6.

160. Margaret Brown, "Towns That Build Bridges," *History Today* 48, no. 8 (1998).

161. Reginald Peck, "How the Germans Live," *The Listener* 40, 2 December 1948, 843.

162. Ibid.

163. Anthony Mann, *Comeback: Germany, 1945–1952* (London: Macmillan, 1980), 193.

164. Ibid., 194.

165. Ibid.

166. Horne, *Back into Power*, 235.

167. Ibid., 245.

168. Ibid., 246.

169. Ibid., 247.

170. Richard Weight, "Losing the Peace: Germany, Japan, America, and the Shaping of British National Identity in the Age of Affluence," in *An Affluent Society? Britain's Post-War "Golden Age" Revisited*, ed. Lawrence Black and Hugh Pemberton (Aldershot: Ashgate, 2004), 205.

171. R. V. Jones, "The German Challenge to Britain," *The Listener* 40, no. 1412, 19 April 1956, 440; emphasis by Robertson in original.

172. David Kynaston, *Family Britain, 1951–57* (London: Bloomsbury, 2009), 616.

173. Jones, "German Challenge to Britain," 440.

174. Peter Hennessey, *Having It So Good: Britain in the Fifties* (London: Allen Lane, 2006), 389.

175. *Daily Mirror*, 7 August 1957, 4.

176. Kynaston, *Family Britain*, 171.

177. Brickhill, *Reach for the Sky*, 291.

CHAPTER 3. THE GERMANS

1. [Landesarchiv Niedersachsen], NI, Nds. 100 Acc. 60/55 Nr 1142 27, *Die Welt*, 6 October 1952.

2. TNA, FO 371/93379, *Frankfurter Allgemeine Zeitung*, 30 March 1951.

3. NRW [Hauptstaatsarchiv, Düsseldorf, Ministerialarchiv], NW 115/174, *Ruhr Nachrichten*, 16 February 1951.

4. TNA, FO 371/85226, Monthly Report of Land Commissioner North Rhine-Westphalia Bishop to High Commissioner, December 1949, 2.

5. TNA, FO 1013/2439, Letter Deputy Land Commissioner W. J. Bate to Land Commissioner on "Military Accommodation Programme and Allied/German Relations Generally," 19 March 1952.

6. NRW, NW 115/174.

7. See, for example, Jeffry Diefendorf, *In the Wake of War: The Reconstruction of German Cities after World War Two* (Oxford: Oxford University Press, 1993).

8. TNA, AIR (Air Ministry) 48/223, 129, cited in Patricia Meehan, *A Strange Enemy People: Germans under the British, 1945–1950* (London: Owen, 2001), 35.

9. According to one German newspaper report, all in all "the Allies had under requisitioning over 16,000 houses, 11,000 plots of land, and 679 barracks, over 13,000 flats, over 8,000 single rooms, 1,200 hotels, and 600 restaurants"; NRW, NW 115/174, *Kölnische Rundschau*, 16 July 1951.

10. Meehan, *Strange Enemy People*, 138.

11. The Allies had returned 14,000 houses, 13,000 flats, 1,600 hotels and restaurants, and 3,900 office buildings by 1951. NRW, NW 115/174, *Stuttgarter Nachrichten*, 18 August 1951.

12. See, for example, Meehan, *Strange Enemy People*, and Volker Koop, *Besetzt. Britische Besatzungspolitik in Deutschland* (Berlin: Be.bra, 2007).

13. Koop, *Besetzt*, 91.

14. Ibid., 99.

15. Commander-in-Chief and Military Governor, Air Marshal Sir Sholto Douglas, quoted in Meehan, *Strange Enemy People*, 137.

16. Koop, *Besetzt*, 152.

17. TNA, FO 1013/2451, British Resident Düsseldorf Report, 30 September 1954.

18. Jeremy Bastin, *The History of the 15th/19th The King's Royal Hussars, 1945–1980* (Chichester: Keats House, 1981), 52.

19. TNA, CAB 129/82, C. P. (56) 157, on "Forces Conditions of Service in Germany: Memorandum by the Chancellor of the Exchequer," 27 June 1956.

20. TNA, CAB 129/82, C .P. (56) 155, "Forces' Conditions of Service in Germany: Memorandum by the Secretary of State for War," 25 June 1956.

21. TNA, FO 1013/2451, British Resident Düsseldorf Report, 30 September 1954.

22. NRW, NW 115/174, *Frankfurter Allgemeine Zeitung*, 3 January 1951.

23. NRW, NW 115/174, *Rheinische Post*, 3 January 1951.

24. One example in North Rhine-Westphalia was the *Notgemeinschaft der Besatzungsbetroffenen* (Hardship Association of Those Affected by Occupation), expanded in 1951 to *Schutzverband der Besatzungsbetroffenen Düsseldorf und Umgebung* (Association for the Protection of Those Affected by Occupation in Düsseldorf and Surrounding Areas), NRW, NW 115/174.

25. NRW, NW 115/174, *Rheinische Post*, 11 January 1951.

26. Ibid.

27. NRW, NW 115/174, Head of Press Office (Chef der Pressestelle), 9 February 1952.

28. NRW, NW 115/175, *Die Welt*, 22 April 1953.

29. NRW, NW 115/175, *Freie Presse*, 27 April 1953.

30. NRW, NW 115/175, Chef der Pressestelle, 31 January 1952.

31. NRW, NW 115/175, *Ruhr Nachrichten*, 29 May 1953.

32. NRW, NW 115/175, Chef der Pressestelle, 26 May 1952.

33. David Kynaston, *Austerity Britain*, (London: Bloomsbury, 2007), 122–23.

34. NRW, NW 115/175, *Westfalenpost*, 12 November 1955.

35. NRW, NW 115/175, *Abendpost*, 10 January 1956.

36. NRW, NW 115/174, *Freie Presse*, 27 January 1951.

37. Stadtarchiv Bad Oeynhausen, B II 18, cited in "Lübbecke und die Britische Kontrollkommission 1945," *Lübbecke Kompakt*, http://www.luebbecke.de.

38. NRW, NW 115/174, *Freie Presse*, 27 January 1951.

39. Lance Corporal Gordon Cox, RAMC Bielefeld, cited in Roy Bainton, *The Long Patrol: The British in Germany since 1945* (Edinburgh: Mainstream, 2003), 61.

40. TNA, FO 1013/2439, Letter Deputy Land Commissioner W. J. Bate to Land Commissioner on "Military Accommodation Programme and Allied/German Relations Generally," 19 March 1952.

41. NRW, NW 115/174, *Rheinische Post*, 2 July 1951.

42. NRW, NW 115/175, *Der Nordwestspiegel*, 3 June 1954, 3.

43. TNA, FO 1010/171, Report on Damage Caused by Training in the Reinsehlen Training Area, 1951.

44. TNA, FO 953/1424, Information Services Quarterly Report, 30 July 1953.

45. TNA, FO 1013/1978, Translated copy of KPD pamphlet, Siegen, 1951 (emphasis added to translation in red pencil presumably by British officer).

46. NRW, NW 115/173, *Volksecho*, 18 March 1950.

47. NRW, NW 115/173, *Die Zeit*, 30 March 1950.

48. NRW, NW 115/173, *Westfalenpost*, 20 March 1950.

49. NRW, NW 115/173, *Süddeutsche Zeitung*, 26 March 1950.

50. NRW, NW 115/173, Radio Sender Leipzig, 28 March 1950.

51. NRW, NW 115/173, *Westdeutsche Allgemeine Zeitung*, 30 March 1950.

52. NRW, NW 115/173, Radio NWDR, 27 March 1950, NW 115/173, *Westdeutsches Tageblatt*, 28 March 1950.

53. NRW, NW 115/173, *Westfälische Nachrichten*, 5 April 1950.

54. NRW, NW 115/173, *Der Mittag*, 9 May 1950.

55. NRW, NW 115/173, *Rheinische Post*, 10 May 1950.

56. Alistair Horne, *Back into Power: A Report on the New Germany* (London: Parrish, 1955), 194–95.

57. Ibid., 191.

58. TNA, FO 371/109264, "Annual Political Report for 1953," Hoyer-Millar to Eden, 15 March 1954, 2.

59. NI, Nds. 50 Acc. 96/88 Nr 167/3.

60. NI, Nds. 50 Acc. 96/88 Nr 167/3 Wirtschaftsminister Seebohm to Ministerpräsident Kopf, 30 June 1953.

61. NI, Nds. 50, Nr 248 Teil 2, 254, *Wolfenbütteler Zeitung*, 7 November 1952.

62. NI, Nds. 50 Nr 248 Teil 2, 253, Letter from Lord Blandford, 8 November 1952.

63. Ibid.

64. Ibid.

65. NI, Nds. 50 Nr 248 Teil 2, 248, Letter from Mr. Lieberkuehn to Niedersachsen, Minister for Food, Agriculture, and Forestry, 11 November 1952.

66. Ibid., 250.

67. NI, Nds. 50 Nr 248 Teil 2, 257, Bericht Nr 104.

68. NI, Nds. 50 Nr 248 Teil 2, 265, Vermerk, 17 January 1953.

69. TNA, FO 953/1423, Information Services Quarterly Report, December 1952.

70. NI, Nds. 50 Acc. 96/88 Nr 163/3, *Lüneburger Landeszeitung*, 25 September 1952.

71. Horne, *Back into Power*, 134.

72. TNA, FO 1013/2075, Hamburg Public Safety Report, Public Safety Branch, Land Commissioner's Office, 28 June 1954.

73. TNA, FO 1013/2075, Public Safety Reports, Special Police Corps Monthly Letter, April 1954.

74. Ibid.

75. Ibid.

76. NI, Nds. 100, Acc. 60/55, Nr 1142, 2, Letter from Dora Dittmann to Canadian Camp Commander Hannover, 10 September 1952.

77. Ibid., 58.

78. Ibid., 60.

79. Bundesarchiv, Koblenz (hereafter, BK), 145/610, *Vancouver Sun*, 12 October 1956, "Germans Snipe at Canadian Troops: 'Go home, Canucks' Is Attitude Overseas Soldiers Run up Against."

80. Ibid.

81. BK, B145/610, Bericht Nr 191/56 Konsulat der Bundesrepublik, Vancouver.

82. NRW, NW 115/175, *Rheinische Post*, 08 April 1952.

83. NRW, NW 115/173, *Düsseldorfer Nachrichten*, 7 June 1950.

84. NRW, NW 115/175, *Rheinische Post*, 08 April 1952.

85. Politisches Archiv des Auswärtigen Amts, Berlin (hereafter, AA), B86/937, 507/81/38/2, Deutscher Städtetag an Auswärtiges Amt, Stimmungsbericht des Städteverbands Baden Württemberg, Dr. Krebsbach, 9 January 1960, 4.

86. AA, B86/937, 507/81/20/6, 211-81-24-1-2360/56, Aufzeichnung vom 6 Juli 1956, Graf von Baudini an Bundesminister des Innern, der Verteidigung und der Justiz.

87. AA, B86/937 MB 1531/56, List of crimes compiled by Minister President of Baden Württemberg, 18 July 1956.

88. TNA, FO 371/124625, Letter from Chancery British Embassy Bonn to Western Department Foreign Office, 31 July 1956.

89. NI, Nds. 100 Acc. 2000/034 Nr 8, 9.

90. Sexual offenses by British soldiers rose from fifteen to eighteen; those committed by Belgians rose from two to three; and those by Canadians decreased from six to one. Violent crimes committed by British soldiers rose from forty-six to sixty; those committed by Canadians decreased from eighteen to thirteen; and those by Belgians rose from eleven to twelve. NRW, NW 179/1336, 1.

91. NRW, NW 179/1336, 1–3, Letter from Interior Minister to Minister President NRW, 5 September 1956.

92. NRW, NW 179/1336, 7, Letter from Ministerialrat Dr. Kordt, 29 September 1956.

93. NRW, NW 179/1336, 51, Letter from Herr Biernat to Mr. Plaice, 17 December 1956.

94. NRW, NW 179/1336, 49, *Rheinische Post*, 29 December 1956.

95. NRW, NW 179/1336, 11, Letter from Ministerialrat Dr. Kordt, 29 September 1956.

96. Ibid.

97. NRW, NW 179/1336, 49, *Rheinische Post*, 29 December 1956.

98. NI, Nds. 100 Acc. 2000/034 Nr 8, 122–30.

99. Ibid., 130.

100. Ibid.

101. Ibid.

102. Ibid., 152.

103. TNA, FO 371/130776, WG1195/16 Minute from British Embassy, Bonn, to FO, London, 12 August 1957.

104. Ibid.

105. Bastin, *King's Royal Hussars*, 51.

106. Ibid., 100.

107. Ibid., 60.

108. David Finlay Clark, *Stand by Your Beds! A Wry Look at National Service* (Glasgow: Dunfermline, 2006), 168.

109. Sir Robert Birley, Educational Advisor to the British Military Government, cited in Peter Alter, "Building Bridges: The Framework of Anglo-German Cultural Relations after 1945." In *Britain and Germany in Europe*," ed. Jeremy Noakes, Peter Wende, and Jonathan Wright (Oxford: Oxford University Press, 2002), 341.

110. See, for example, *Neue Zeitung*, 27 November 1951, cited in BK, B145/610/250-2-2, Einladung von Angehörigen der Besatzungsmacht durch deutsche Familien zu Weihnachten, 1951–1956.

111. Ibid.

112. NRW, NW 115/174, *Rheinische Post*, 26 May 1951.

113. Ibid.

114. NRW, NW 179/685, "Wegweiser für alliierte Soldaten in Deutschland," November 1956.

115. NRW, NW 179/685, 33, Letter from Minister for Economics and Transport to Minister President of North Rhine-Westphalia, 22 January 1957.

116. NRW, NW 179/685, 36, Letter dated 8 February 1957.

117. BK, B145/60, 250-4.

118. BK, B145/60, 250-4, Letter from J. M. Fisher, British Embassy, Bonn, to Hanns Küffner, Presse-und Informationsamt der Bundesregierung, Bonn, 16 May 1958 (my emphasis).

119. BK, B136/5528, 4-24109-2175/57, "Begegnungsstätten der Soldaten der alliierten Einsatzkräfte mit der deutschen Bevölkerung und deutschen Soldaten," 21 March 1957.

120. BK, B136/5528, 4-24109-3274/57II Brief Dr. Globke an Emil Kemmer, 2 September 1957.

121. BK, B145/610, 250-2.

122. BK, B145/610, 211-81-24-03/3620/56, "Aufzeichnung über die Besprechung am 28 September 1956 im Auswärtigen Amt über Übergriffe von amerikanischen Soldaten gegenüber der deutschen Zivilbevölkerung." See also BK, B250/80 D10216/56 "Beziehungen zwischen der deutschen Bevölkerung und Angehörigen der Stationierungsstreitkräfte," 29 September 1956.

123. BK, B145/610, 250-1-III, "Rundbrief betr. Arbeitskreis zur Verbesserung der Beziehungen zwischen der deutschen Bevölkerung und Angehörigen der Stationierungsstreitkräfte; Verschiebung einer geplanten Sitzung im November 1957."

124. BK, B145/610, 301-81-24-3/1364/62, "Schnellbrief Auswärtiges Amt an Bundesministerien des Innern und der Verteidigung," 15 June 1962.

CHAPTER 4. THE SOLDIERS, THE AIRMEN, AND THE GERMANS

1. NRW, NW 115/175, *Westdeutsches Tageblatt*, 14 February 1952.

2. TNA, FO 800/467, File 176 Ger/48/43, Secretary of State's conversation with General Robertson, 27 July 1948.

3. TNA, FO 371/104044, COS Committee Report COS (53)376, Copy of Minute from Chairman, Commanders-In-Chief Committee, British Forces, Germany to Secretary, Chiefs of Staff Committee, 4 August 1953.

4. TNA, FO 371/104044, COS Committee Report COS (53)376, "The Effect of the Present Reinforcement Policy on the Operational Plans of the British Forces in Germany," 4 August 1953, Annex, 10.

5. Ibid., 3.

6. Ibid., 4.

7. Ibid.

8. TNA, FO 800/467, Memorandum Alexander to Attlee, 14 February 1948.

9. TNA, FO 371/104044, COS Committee Report, Annex, 4.

10. Ibid., 5.

11. Ibid., 10.

12. Ibid., 10–11.

13. Ibid., 7.

14. Royal Signals Museum (hereafter, RSM), File no. 936.1, David Horsfield, Personal account of time as Commander Royal Signals 2 Infantry Div. BAOR 1956–1959 (1985).

15. NRW, NW 115/173, *Westdeutsche Allgemeine*, 3 October 1950.

16. Alan Tizzard, Tank Commander in the 10th King's Hussars at Iserlohn, 1950, quoted in Tom Hickman, *The Call-Up: A History of National Service* (London: Headline, 2004), 133.

17. Glyn Jones, quoted in ibid., 134.

18. RSM, File no. 938.1/7, 1, Brigadier C. T. Honeybourne, OBE, Account of 7th Armored Division, Royal Signals, October 1954–November 1956.

19. Durham Record Office (hereafter, DRO), D/Wn 20/468/1(2), Letter from Anne Watson to W. I. Watson, 1st Battalion Durham Light Infantry, 6 June 1950.

20. Second Lieutenant Tony Thorne, stationed in Brunswick, cited in Hickman, *The Call-Up*, 137.

21. Trevor Royle, *The Best Years of Their Lives: The National Service Experience, 1945–1963* (London: Deutsch, 2002), 145.

22. A "Gaststube" often served both as a bar and a restaurant. Jeremy Bastin, *The History of the 15th/19th the King's Royal Hussars, 1945–1980* (Chichester: Keats House, 1981), 52.

23. *The Wire* 3, no. 2 (February 1949): 117.

24. TNA, DEFE 11/64 163A 412/42, Letter from E. Shinwell to John Strachey M.P., 2 May 1951.

25. Bastin, *King's Royal Hussars*, 59.

26. Sgt. S. H. Harcourt, *The Wire* 3, no. 2 (February 1949): 117.

27. David McNeill, RAF Coastal Command, cited in Royle, *Best Years*, 146.

28. As described by, for example, Private J. E. Booth, 4th Infantry Workshop REME, stationed in Duisburg between 1950 and 1951, cited in Roy Bainton, *The Long Patrol: The British in Germany since 1945* (Edinburgh: Mainstream, 2003), 48.

29. NAM 2006-12-77-82, National Serviceman Corporal Malcolm Barker, Queen's Royal Regiment, in a letter to his mother, 26 May 1953.

30. Royal Artillery Museum (RAM), "Annual Historical Returns, 16 Regiment RA, 1951–1955."

31. Ibid., 15 September 1952.

32. Ibid., 26 December 1952.

33. Ibid.

34. K.O. Airey, Royal Artillery, stationed at Bielefeld in 1947–1948, cited in Bainton, *Long Patrol*, 67.

35. NAM 2006-12-77-82, Malcolm Barker, letter to mother, 22 November 1952.

36. NAM 2002-02-901-18, Lt. Col. Anthony Gervase Ryshworth-Hill, MC, Diary entry, 20 July 1954.

37. NAM 2002-02-901-15, Ryshworth-Hill, Diary entry, 11 July 1951.

38. NAM 2002-02-901-18, Ryshworth-Hill, Diary entry, July 1954.

39. Ibid., 5 December 1955.

40. Imperial War Museum, Southwark (hereafter, IWM), IWM Interview, file no. 26546, 01/2003, Martyn Highfield, GSO2 Staff Officer, to CRA, HQ, BAOR, 1950–51, served with 77 HAA Regt. 1952–55.

41. IWM interview, file no. 19898, 10 November 1998, Frederick Hunn, NCO, served with 4th Hussars, 1953–55, and 12th Lancers, 1955–58, in Germany.

42. RSM, File no. 936.1, Peter Baldwin—My Life.

43. David Findlay Clark, *Stand by Your Beds! A Wry Look at National Service* (Glasgow: Dunfermline, 2006), 157.

44. Ibid.

45. Ibid., 158.

46. Ibid., 159.

47. Ibid., 165.

48. Ibid., 166.

49. Sergeant Hugh Martin, Army Education Corps, stationed at Finkenwerder between 1950 and 1952, cited in Bainton, *Long Patrol*, 64.

50. IWM interview, file no. 18477, 28 July 1998, Francis Leon Collett, served with 1st Bn Royal Tank Regt. Detmold, 1950–1952, as a regular soldier.

51. Ibid.

52. National Serviceman Ian Carr, cited in B. S. Johnson, ed., *All Bull: The National Servicemen* (London: Quartet Books, 1973), 112.

53. Ibid.

54. Tony Thorne, *Brasso, Blanco, and Bull* (London: Robinson, 1998), 149.

55. Royle, *Best Years*, 146.

56. Thorne, *Brasso, Blanco, and Bull*, 151.

57. See, for example, Tony Thorne's recollection of a formal reception with the German mayor of Brunswick and his wife. Thorne, *Brasso, Blanco, and Bull*, 204.

58. NAM 2006-12-77-82, Malcolm Barker, in a letter to his mother, 6 July 1952.

59. Ibid., 14 July 1952.

60. National Serviceman J. G. Booth, 8th Armored Brigade, stationed in Verden between 1955 and 1957, cited in Bainton, *Long Patrol*, 44.

61. Patricia Meehan, *A Strange Enemy People: Germans under the British, 1945–1950* (London: Owen, 2001), 135.

62. *The Times,* 15 October 1946, Letters to the Editor, Ruth Elford, "British Wives in Germany."

63. *The Times,* 17 October 1946, Letters to the Editor, BAOR wife, "British Wives in Germany."

64. Meehan, *Strange Enemy People,* 137.

65. *The Sapper* 2, no. 9 (1956): 204.

66. *The Wire* 3, no. 2 (1949), Mrs. E. M. Pitt, "Life in the BAOR: Wives' Viewpoints," 117.

67. *The Wire* 3, no. 1 (1949): 37.

68. NI, Nds. 100 Acc. 2000/034 Nr 8 Report Oberstadtdirektor Hameln, 13 June 1956.

69. *The Sapper* 51, no. 605 (1946): 91.

70. *The Sapper* 54, no. 644 (1949): 162.

71. *The Wire* 3, no. 2 (1949): 117.

72. TNA, WO 216/484, General Harding to War Office, 1952.

73. *The Wire* 3, no. 8 (1949): 468.

74. Clark, *Stand by Your Beds,* 167.

75. Hickman, *The Call-Up,* 197.

76. Ian Carr, cited in Johnson, *All Bull,* 113.

77. Signalman Dennis Pell, 11th Air Formation Signals Regiment, stationed at Fassberg in 1948, cited in Bainton, *Long Patrol*, 65.

78. Ibid.

79. TNA, FO 371/118158, Letter from C. H. Johnston, UK High Commission, Bonn, to P. F. Hancock, Western Department, FO, 4 February 1954.

80. TNA, FO 1042/8, Ambassador's Military Committee: Brief for the Ambassador for his Meeting with the Commanders-In-Chief on 22 November 1956.

81. TNA, FO 1042/8, "Ambassador's Military Committee: Minutes of a Meeting held at the British Embassy, Bonn, 1 February 1956."

82. See, for example, *The Wire* 3, no. 2 (1949): 91: "It was in this atmosphere of goodwill and good humour that 3 Air Support Signals Unit [. . .] organised parties for German children."

83. Tony Mason and Eliza Riedi, *Sport and the Military: The British Armed Forces, 1880–1960* (Cambridge: Cambridge University Press, 2010), 220.

84. "Foreign Office Correspondence over Army Football in Occupied Zones, 1946," TNA, FO 371/55626, cited in Mason and Riedi, *Sport and the Military,* 207.

85. Mason and Riedi, *Sport and the Military,* 176.

86. TNA, FO 1013/2451, British Resident Report Mönchen Gladbach, December 1954.

87. TNA, FO 1013/2451, British Resident Münster, Quarterly Report, June 1954.

88. Ibid., December 1954.

89. TNA, FO 1013/2451, British Resident Recklinghausen, Quarterly Report, June 1954.

90. Ibid., March 1954.

91. Royal Engineers Museum (hereafter, REM), Royal Engineers Drag Hunt BAOR Meets, 1957–1958.

92. Ibid.

93. DRO, D/DLI 2/2/107, Minutes of Mess Meetings of 2nd BN Durham Light Infantry, 5 May 1954.

94. An article in the August 1949 issue describes the German tradition of *Richtfest* as a "festival to mark the completion of the skeleton of a building"; *The Sapper* 55, no. 648 (1949): 6.

95. *The Sapper* 57, no. 678 (1952): 10.

96. *The Sapper* 2, no. 9 (1956): 229.

97. *The Sapper* 3, no. 6 (1956): 151.

98. TNA, FO 953/1791, "'Review of Press Liaison Officer Organisation' produced by the Command Information Office HQ 2nd Tactical Air Force for the period July–December 1956, 12 February 1957."

99. TNA, FO 953/1791, "2nd Half-Year Review of 2nd TAF Press Liaison Officer Organisation, July 1956–December 1956."

100. TNA, FO 953/1791, "'Review of Press Liaison Officer Organisation.'"

101. Ibid.

102. Ibid.

103. Ibid., 4.

104. Ibid., 5.

105. Ibid.

106. Ibid., 6.

107. Ibid., 8.

108. Ibid., 9.

109. Ibid.

110. Ibid., 7.

111. Ibid.

112. Ibid., 10.

113. Ibid.

114. Ibid., 11.

115. Ibid.

116. Ibid., 12.

117. Ibid.

118. Ibid., 13.

119. Ibid.

120. BK, B145/610 250E IV 13 639/56, Letter British Information Services, British Embassy, Bonn, J. M. Fisher to Dr. Krause-Brewer, Bundespresseamt, Bonn, 15 December 1956.

CHAPTER 5. "HOW THE ARMY OF A DEMOCRATIC NATION SHOULD BEHAVE"

1. TNA, FO 953/1285 PC1013/15, "Report on the Role of Information Services in Germany," 15 May 1952.

2. Ibid.

3. Ibid.

4. TNA, FO 953/1286, Dispatch no. 187, from Sir Ivone Kirkpatrick to Anthony Eden, 22 July 1952.

5. TNA, FO 953/1285, Dispatch from Kirkpatrick to Eden, 9 June 1952.

6. Ibid.

7. Ibid.

8. Ibid.

9. Ibid.

10. TNA, FO 953/1285, Report on ISD role in Germany, R. Chaput de Saintonge, 16 May 1952.

11. Ibid.

12. Ibid.

13. TNA, FO 371/130777, WG 1196/30, Memorandum on "The German Army," 7 November 1957.

14. TNA, FO 953/1285, Dispatch from Kirkpatrick to Eden, Annex D, 9 June 1952.

15. Jörg Friedrich, The Fire: The Bombing of Germany, 1940–1945 (New York: Columbia University Press, 2006), 180.

16. Ibid., 182.

17. TNA, FO 1013/2427, *Die Welt,* 28 February 1952.

18. TNA, FO 1013/2427, *Die Welt,* 29 February 1952.

19. TNA, FO 1013/2427, *Die Welt,* 28 February 1952.

20. TNA, FO 1013/2427, Memorandum by Colonel Darley, "General Comments on Herford Plan," February 1952.

21. Ibid.

22. TNA, FO 1013/2439, Letter from Deputy Land Commissioner W. J. Bate to Land Commissioner on "Military Accommodation Programme and Allied/German Relations Generally," 19 March 1952.

23. Ibid.

24. TNA, FO 1013/2449, Letter from Services Relations Advisor Major-General Dalton to Office of Land Commissioner North Rhine-Westphalia, 3 February 1954.

25. TNA, FO 1013/2449, Letter from Services Relations Advisor Major-General Dalton to Commander-in-Chief of Belgian Forces, 12 May 1954.

26. TNA, FO 1013/2449, Letter from British Resident in Düsseldorf, H.G. Bird, to Land Commissioner's Office North Rhine-Westphalia, 28 May 1954.

27. TNA, FO 1013/2449, "Anglo-German Relations" Pamphlet, February 1954 edition, 23 March 1954, 2.

28. Ibid., 4.

29. Ibid.

30. Ibid.

31. TNA, FO 1013/2439, Letter from Deputy Land Commissioner W. J. Bate to Land Commissioner on "Military Accommodation Programme and Allied/German Relations Generally," 19 March 1952.

32. Ibid.

33. TNA, FO 371/109733, FO Minute from Wright to Hancock, 16 December 1954.

34. Ibid.

35. TNA, FO 1010/171, British Resident Lüneburg to Deputy Land Commissioner, 4 June 1952.

36. TNA, FO 1010/171, "Report on Damage Caused by Training in the Reinsehlen Area," May 1951.

37. TNA, FO 371/104044, Letter from Chancery of High Commissioner to Foreign Office, 29 August 1953.

38. TNA, CAB 129/49, C. (52) 23 "Political Situation in the German Federal Republic: Memorandum by the Secretary of State for Foreign Affairs," 7 February 1952.

39. TNA, FO 371/104044, Letter from Chancery of High Commissioner to Foreign Office, 29 August 1953.

40. TNA, FO 371/104044, Foreign Office Minute, 14 August 1953.

41. TNA, FO 371/104044, Letter from Chancery of High Commissioner to Foreign Office, 29 August 1953.

42. Ibid.

43. TNA, FO 371/104044, Brigadier Gibson to Brigadier Mitchell, HQ 1 Corps BAOR, 15 May 1952.

44. TNA, FO 371/104044, Letter from Chancery of UK High Commissioner to Central Department FO, 15 August 1953.

45. Ibid.

46. Ibid.

47. NI, NDS 50, Acc. 96/88, Nr 166/2 Letter from Deputy Land Commissioner H. F. Piper to Interior Minister Niedersachsen, 25 August 1953.

48. NI, NDS 50, Acc. 96/88, Nr 166/2 Letter Interior Minister Niedersachsen, 29 October 1953.

49. TNA, FO 953/1424, Information Services Quarterly Report, 30 July 1953.

50. TNA, FO 953/1424, Information Services Monthly Report for August 1953.

51. TNA, FO 1013/2451, British Resident Herford, Quarterly Report, 23 June 1954.

52. TNA, FO 1013/2451, British Resident Düsseldorf Report, 30 September 1954.

53. TNA, FO 1013/2451, British Resident Recklinghausen, Quarterly Report, September 1954.

54. TNA, FO 953/782, Minute from R. A. Chaput de Saintonge to C.F.A. Warner, 4 May 1950.

55. Ibid.

56. TNA, FO 953/1285, Dispatch Ivone Kirkpatrick to Anthony Eden, 9 June 1952.

57. TNA, FO 953/1286, PC1013/26, Comments on Memorandum about "The Role of British Information Services in Germany," Dispatch no. 187, 22 July 1952.

58. TNA, FO 371/118207, C. B. Ormerod, British Information Services, New York, to P. Mennell, ISD, London, 5 April 1955.

59. TNA, FO 371/118207, Western Department of FO Minute by P. Wright, 23 April 1955.

60. TNA, FO 1013/2452, Quarterly Report Services Liaison Section to Land Commissioner, 31 March 1954, 1.

61. TNA, FO 1013/2452, Field Sections' Quarterly Report to Land Commissioner NRW, 31 December 1953, 2.

62. TNA, FO 1013/2452, Quarterly Report, Services Liaison Section, September 1954, 1.

63. Donald C. Watt, *Britain Looks to Germany* (London: Wolff, 1965), 76. "In July 1946 the British zone was reshaped by the combining of the two provinces of North Rhine and Westphalia into a single *Land*. The states of Hannover, Oldenburg, Brunswick and Schaumburg-Lippe formed the *Land* of Lower Saxony. The two Hanseatic cities of Hamburg and Bremen were also turned into *Länder*." Patricia Meehan, *A Strange Enemy People: Germans under the British, 1945–1950* (London: Owen, 2001), 260.

64. Sabine Lee, *Victory in Europe? Britain and Germany since 1945* (Harlow: Longman, 2001), 38.

65. Ivone Kirkpatrick, *The Inner Circle* (London: Macmillan, 1959), 216.

66. TNA, FO 1013/2452, Quarterly Report Services Liaison Section to Land Commissioner, September 1954, 2.

67. Ibid., 1.

68. TNA, FO 1013/2451, British Resident Arnsberg, Quarterly Report, 14 December 1954.

69. TNA, FO 1013/2451, British Resident Report Mönchen Gladbach, December 1954.

70. TNA, FO 1013/2451, British Resident Arnsberg, Quarterly Report, 3 June 1954.

71. TNA, FO 1013/2451, British Resident Recklinghausen, Quarterly Report, September 1954.

72. TNA, FO 371/124637, WG12010/1, British Embassy Bonn to FO, 24 July 1956.

73. NI, Nds. 100, Acc. 2000/034, Nr 8, 26.

74. *The Times*, 8 August 1957, cited in TNA, FO 371/130776.

75. Ibid.

76. Ibid.

77. TNA, FO 371/130776, WG1195/16 Minute from British Embassy, Bonn, to FO, London, 12 August 1957.

78. TNA, FO 371/130776, WG1195/14, Telegram to Headquarters Northag, 8 August 1957.

79. NI, Nds. 50, Acc. 96/88, Nr 165/2, "Pressebericht Pressestelle Hannover," 6 August 1957.

80. TNA, FO 371/130776 WG1195/16 Minute from British Embassy, Bonn, to FO, London, 12 August 1957.

81. TNA, FO 371/130776 WG1195/16 Minute from British Embassy, Bonn, to FO, London, 12 August 1957.

82. TNA, FO 371/130776, WG1195/15, FO Minute from P. F. Hancock to Sir F. Hoyer-Millar, 8 August 1957.

83. TNA, FO 953/1662, "Public Relations Problems of British Services in Germany and Co-Operation with the German Services," J. M. Fisher to R. A. Chaput de Saintonge, 16 March 1956.

84. Ibid.

85. Kirkpatrick, *Inner Circle,* 252–53.

86. TNA, FO 953/1662, "Public Relations Problems,' J. M. Fisher to Chaput de Saintonge, 16 March 1956.

87. Ibid.

88. TNA, FO 953/1662, Chaput de Saintonge to Fisher, 6 July 1956.

CONCLUSION

1. TNA, FO 371/103666, C1071/67, Memorandum, "The Problem of Germany."

2. Yvonne Kipp, *Eden, Adenauer und die Deutsche Frage. Britische Deutschlandpolitik im internationalen Spannungsfeld, 1951–1957* (Paderborn: Schöningh, 2002), 39.

3. TNA, FO 371/118217, WG 1071/681, Minute, 23 June 1955.

4. TNA, FO 371/124488, Hoyer-Millar to Lloyd, 31 January 1956.

5. TNA, PREM 11/1334, cited in Kipp, *Eden, Adenauer und die Deutsche Frage,* 241.

6. TNA, FO 953/1662, PC 1181/16, German Information Department Minute, 9 April 1956.

7. Ibid.

8. TNA, FO 953/1662, "Public Relations Problems of British Services in Germany," Minute, 16 March 1956.

9. Charles Douglas-Home, "Rhine Army's Relations with the German People," *The Times,* 3 April 1968, 11.

BIBLIOGRAPHY

Unpublished Primary Sources

Archives

BBC Written Archives Centre, Reading
    T4/57, Documentaries, "Special Enquiry on Germany, 1954–1955"
    Reference Card A/132/P A69044 5,000C, 29-6-54, 111
    Reference Card A/132/P A81379, 4,000C, 17-1-57
Bundesarchiv, Koblenz (BK)
    Bundeskanzleramt
        B136/5528 Begegnungsstätten für alliierte und deutsche Soldaten sowie Zivilisten (Laufzeit 1957)
            4-24109-2175/57 Begegnungsstätten der Soldaten der alliierten Einsatzkräfte mit der deutschen Bevölkerung und deutschen Soldaten, 21 March 1957
            4-24109-3274/57II Brief Dr. Globke an Emil Kemmer, 2 September 1957
    Presse-und Informationsamt der Bundesregierung
    B145/610
        211-81-24-03/3620/56 Aufzeichnung über die Besprechung am 28 September1956 im Auswärtigen Amt über Übergriffe von amerikanischen Soldaten gegenüber der deutschen Zivilbevölkerung
        250-1-III Rundbrief betr. Arbeitskreis zur Verbesserung der Beziehungen zwischen der deutschen Bevölkerung und Angehörigen der Stationierungsstreitkräfte, 6 November1957
        250-2 Verhältnis der deutschen Bevölkerung gegenüber den alliierten Truppen in Deutschland, August 1956–November 1957, Bd. 1
        250-2-2 Einladung von Angehörigen der Besatzungsmacht durch deutsche Familien zu Weihnachten, 1951–1956
        250-4 Wegweiser für alliierte Soldaten, Bd. 1, 26.11.1956–December 1958

250-80 D10216/56 Beziehungen zwischen der deutschen Bevölkerung
und Angehörigen der Stationierungsstreitkräfte, 29 September 1956

250 E IV 13 639/56 British Information Services, British Embassy
Bonn, J. M. Fisher to Dr. Krause-Brewer, Bundespresseamt Bonn,
15 December 1956

301-81-24-3/1364/62, Schnellbrief Auswärtiges Amt an Bundesministerien des Innern und der Verteidigung, 15 June 1962.

Durham Record Office (DRO), Durham

D/DLI 2/2/107 The Durham Light Infantry, Minute Book of Mess Meetings,
19 October 1945–24 April 1955

D/Wn 20/468/1–3 Letters from Anne Watson to W. I. Watson, 1st Battalion
Durham Light Infantry, 6–8 June 1950

Imperial War Museum (IWM), Southwark

IWM Interviews

Number 18477, Francis Leon Collett, Production Date 28 July 1998

Number 19898, Frederick Hunn, Production Date 10 November 1998

Number 26546, Martyn Highfield, Production Date January 2003

Landesarchiv Niedersachsen, Hannover (NI)

Nds. 50 Staatskanzlei

Nds. 50 Acc. 96/88

Nr 163/3 Artikel *Lüneburger Landeszeitung*, 25 September 1952

Nr 165/2 Pressebericht Pressestelle Hannover, 6 August 1957

Nr 166/2 Brief von Deputy Land Commissioner H. F. Piper an Innenministerium Niedersachsen, 25 August 1953

Nr 166/2 Brief Innenminister Niedersachsen an Beauftragten des
Bundeskanzlers für die mit der Vermehrung der alliierten Truppen
zusammenhängenden Fragen, 29 October 1953

Nr 167/3 Brief Wirtschaftsminister Seebohm an Ministerpräsident
Kopf, 30 June 1953

Nds. 50 Nr 248 Teil 2, Artikel *Wolfenbütteler Zeitung*, 7 November 1952

Brief Herr Lieberkuehn an Minister für Ernährung, Land-und Forst-
wirtschaft, 11 November 1952

Bericht Nr. 104

Brief Lord Blandford, 8 November 1952

Nds. 100 Innenministerium

Nds. 100 Acc. 60/55 Nr 1142 Brief Dora Dittmann an Kanadischen Camp
Commander Hannover, 10 September 1952

Nds. 100 Acc. 2000/034 Nr 8 Report Oberstadtdirektor Hameln, 13
June 1956

Landesarchiv Nordrhein-Westfalen, Düsseldorf (NRW)

Hauptstaatsarchiv, Düsseldorf

NW 115/173 Besatzung, 1950

NW 115/174 Besatzung, 1951

NW 115/175 Besatzung, 1949–1951

NW 179/685 Wegweiser für alliierte Soldaten in Deutschland, November 1956

NW 179/1336 Zwischenfälle mit alliierten Streitkräften

Mass Observation Archive (MOA), University of Sussex

 File 2565 Attitudes to the German People, 1948

The National Archives (TNA), Kew

 Cabinet Records

  CAB 129 Cabinet: Memoranda

   CAB 129/49, 1952 January 1–February 20

   CAB 129/82, 1956 January 22–August 1

 Foreign Office Records (FO)

  FO 371 General Correspondence

   FO 371/76629 Strengths of Occupation Forces in Germany, 1949

   FO 371/85220 Strengths of Occupation Forces in Germany, 1950

   FO 371/85226 Monthly Reports of the Land Commissioner Nordrhein Westfalen

   FO 371/93375 Western Allies' Move from Occupation toward Partnership with the Federal Republic of Germany, 1951

   FO 371/93379 Western Allies' Move from Occupation toward Partnership with the Federal Republic of Germany, 1951

   FO 371/103666 Political exchanges leading towards Four-Power talks on the future of Germany, 1953

   FO 371/104044 Build-up of strategic DM currency reserves: effect of reinforcement policy regarding UK troops in the FRG; establishment of tripartite understanding on military exercises in the FRG, 1953

   FO 371/109264 Annual political report on Federal Republic of Germany (FRG) for 1953

   FO 371/109648 Appointment of C-in-C, Northern Army Group; enforcement of Off Limits orders, 1954

   FO 371/109733 Problem over publication of Lord Russell of Liverpool's book *The Scourge of the Swastika*: publication of other books about FRG and the war, 1954

   FO371/109787 Attitude of HM Forces in Germany toward Germans after ratification of Paris Agreements, 1954

   FO 371/118158 Political situation and events in Federal Republic of Germany and political parties in Federal Parliament, 1955

   FO 371/118207 UK Policy toward Germany, 1955

   FO 371/118217 Future form of German nationalism: views of Sir F. Hoyer-Millar, 1955

   FO 371/124488 Review of Events in FRG in 1955, 1956

   FO 371/124622 Strength of UK Armed Forces in FRG, 1956

   FO 371/124625 Behavior of Allied troops in FRG, 1956

FO 371/124637 Damage caused by BAOR training exercises in FRG, 1956

FO 371/130776 UK armed forces in FRG, 1957

FO 371/130777 Defense of FRG, 1957

FO 371/130857 Attitude of British press to FRG, 1957

FO 800 Various Ministers' and Officials' Papers

FO 800/467 Private Papers Ernest Bevin: Germany 1948–1951

FO 953 Information Policy Department and Regional Information Departments

FO 953/782 Report on information services in Germany, 1950

FO 953/1285 Purpose and activities of British Information Services in the FRG, 1952

FO 953/1286 Purpose and activities of British Information Services in the FRG, 1952

FO 953/1423 Information Services quarterly reports from Germany, 1953

FO 953/1424 Information Services quarterly reports from Germany, 1953

FO 953/1662 Activities of British Information Services in FRG, 1956

FO 953/1791 Activities of British Information Services in FRG, 1957

FO 1010 CCG, Lower Saxony Region

FO 1010/171 Claims for compensation in respect of training and maneuver damage: part 1, 1950–1952

FO 1013 CCG, North Rhine-Westphalia Region

FO 1013/1978 Maneuver rights, Siegen: vol. 1, 1951

FO 1013/2075 Public Safety Reports, 1954

FO 1013/2427 Sharing of requisitioned accommodation with Germans, 1951–1952

FO 1013/2439 Accommodation policy general: vol. 2, 1951–1952

FO 1013/2449 Services relations with Germans policy, 1954

FO 1013/2451 British Residents: quarterly reports, 1954

FO 1013/2452 Field section quarterly reports to Land Commissioner, 1954

FO 1014 CCG, Hansestadt Hamburg

FO 1014/26 CCG relationship with Germans, 1948

FO 1014/233 British policy to Germans, 1949

FO 1030 CCG, Various Private Office Papers and Administration and Local Government Branch Files

FO 1030/123 British Army of the Rhine (BAOR): strengths, organization, and dispositions, 1948–1949

FO 1030/172 Social contact with Germans, 1946–1947

FO 1030/253 Future Policy in Germany, 1949–1950

FO 1032 CCG, Military Sections and Headquarters Secretariat

FO 1032/993 Relations between services and CCG, 1948

FO 1032/1465 Treatment of and Attitudes towards the German People, 1945–1946

FO 1032/1368 Non-fraternization policy: vol. 2, 1947–1948

FO 1042 Embassy, Bonn, West Germany: General Correspondence

FO 1042/8 Ambassador's Military Committee, 1956

War Office Records

WO 216 Office of the Chief of the Imperial General Staff

WO 216/484 Visit of General Harding C-in-C BAOR to England, 1952

Ministry of Defense Files

DEFE 11 Chiefs of Staff Committee

DEFE 11/64 Occupation forces in Europe, 1951–1952

National Army Museum (NAM), Chelsea

NAM 2002-02-901-15 Private Diary of Lt. Col. Anthony Gervase Ryshworth-Hill, MC, March 1951–April 1952

NAM 2002-02-901-18 Private Diary of Lt. Col. Anthony Gervase Ryshworth-Hill, MC, April 1954–December 1955

NAM 2006-12-77-82 Letters from National Serviceman Cpl. Malcolm Barker, Queen's Royal Regiment, to his mother, 1952–1953

Politisches Archiv des Auswärtigen Amts, Berlin (AA)

Referat 507: Rechtsfragen der Stationierung ausländischer Truppen

Bestand B 86/937, Betreff: Truppenvertrag

507-/81/20/6 Arbeitskreis zur Verbesserung der Beziehungen zwischen Streitkräften und Zivilbevölkerung

507-/81/38/2 Deutscher Städtetag an Auswärtiges Amt

Royal Artillery Museum (RAM), Woolwich Arsenal

"Annual Historical Returns, 16 Regiment RA, 1951–1955"

Royal Engineers Museum (REM), Gillingham, Kent

Royal Engineers Drag Hunt Meets, 1957–1958

Royal Signals Museum (RSM), Blandford

936.1 Peter Baldwin—My Life

936.1 Horsfield, David, Personal Account of Time as Commander Royal Signals 2 Inf Div BAOR 1956–1959 (1985)

938.1/7 7th Signals Regiment, October 1954–November 1956, Account by Brigadier C. T. Honeybourne, OBE

Published Primary Sources

Newspapers

British
  Daily Express
  Daily Mail
  Daily Mirror

    The Reading Citizen
    Sunday Pictorial
    The Times
German
    Abendpost
    Düsseldorfer Nachrichten
    Freie Presse
    Lüneburger Landeszeitung
    Neue Zeitung
    Frankfurter Allgemeine Zeitung
    Kölnische Rundschau
    Der Mittag
    Der Nordwestspiegel
    Rheinische Post
    Stuttgarter Nachrichten
    Süddeutsche Zeitung
    Ruhr Nachrichten
    Die Welt
    Westdeutsche Allgemeine Zeitung
    Westdeutsches Tageblatt
    Volksecho
    Westfalenpost
    Westfälische Nachrichten
    Wolfenbütteler Zeitung
    Die Zeit

Periodicals

    The Listener
    The Sapper
    The Wire

Comics

    The Hotspur
    Valiant

Published Secondary Sources

Alter, P. "Building Bridges: The Framework of Anglo-German Cultural Relations after 1945." In Noakes et al., *Britain and Germany in Europe*, 327–46.
Azzola, Axel Christian. *Die Diskussion um die Aufrüstung der BRD im Unterhaus und in der Presse Großbritanniens, November 1949–Juli 1952*. Meisenheim: A. Hain, 1971.

Bainton, Roy. *The Long Patrol: The British in Germany since 1945.* Edinburgh: Mainstream, 2003.

Bastin, Jeremy. *The History of the 15th/19th the King's Royal Hussars, 1945–1980.* Chichester: Keats House, 1981.

Breitenstein, Rolf. *Total War to Total Trust: Personal Accounts of 30 Years of Anglo-German Relations: The Vital Role of Non-Governmental Organizations.* London: Wolff, 1976.

Brickhill, Paul. *Reach for the Sky: The Story of Douglas Bader.* London: Collins, 1954.

Broad, Roger. *Conscription in Britain, 1939–1964: The Militarisation of a Generation.* London: Routledge, 2006.

Brown, Margaret. "Towns That Build Bridges." *History Today* 48, no. 8 (1998). Online edition, http://www.historytoday.com/margaret-brown/towns-build-bridges.

Carver, Michael. "Templer, Sir Gerald Walter Robert (1898–1979)." *Oxford Dictionary of National Biography.* Oxford: Oxford University Press, 2004. Online edition, http://www.oxforddnb.com/view/article/31747.

Cassidy, Robert M. "The British Army and Counterinsurgency: The Salience of Military Culture." *Military Review* (May–June 2005). http://usacac.army.mil/CAC/milreview/download/English/MayJun05/cassidy.pdf.

Chambers, Peter, and Amy Landreth, eds. *Called Up: The Personal Experiences of Sixteen National Servicemen.* London: A. Wingate, 1955.

Chapman, James. "Onward Christian Spacemen: Dan Dare—Pilot of the Future as British Cultural History." *Visual Culture in Britain* 9, no. 1 (2008): 55–79.

Clark, David Findlay. *Stand by Your Beds! A Wry Look at National Service.* Glasgow: Dunfermline, 2006.

Cornish, Paul. "The British Military View of European Security, 1945–1950." In *Building Postwar Europe: National Decision-Makers and European Institutions, 1948–63,* edited by Anne Deighton, 70–86. Oxford: St. Martin's, 1995.

Davenport-Hines, Richard. "Russell, (Edward Frederick) Langley, second Baron Russell of Liverpool (1895–1981)." *Oxford Dictionary of National Biography.* Oxford: Oxford University Press, 2004. Online edition, http://www.oxforddnb.com/view/article/31636.

Deighton, Anne. "Cold-War Diplomacy: British Policy towards Germany's Role in Europe, 1945–49." In *Reconstruction in Post-War Germany: British Occupation and the Western Zones,* edited by Ian D. Turner, 15–34. Oxford: St. Martin's, 1989.

———. *The Impossible Peace: Britain, the Division of Germany, and the Origins of the Cold War.* Oxford: Clarendon Press, 1990.

———. "Minds, Not Hearts: British Policy and West German Rearmament." In *Debating Foreign Affairs: The Public and British Policy since 1867,* edited by Christian Haase, 78–96. Berlin: Philo, 2003.

Diefendorf, Jeffry. *In the Wake of War: The Reconstruction of German Cities after World War Two.* Oxford: Oxford University Press, 1993.

Dockrill, Saki. *Britain's Policy for West German Rearmament, 1950–1955.* Cambridge, Cambridge University Press, 1991.

———. "Retreat from the Continent? Britain's Motives for Troop Reductions in West Germany, 1955–1958." *Journal of Strategic Studies* 20, no. 3 (1997): 45–70.

Falcon, Richard. "Images of Germany and the Germans in British Film and Television Fictions." In *As Others See Us: Anglo-German Perceptions*, edited by Harald Husemann, 7–28. Frankfurt: P. Lang, 1994.

Farquharson, John. "'Emotional but Influential': Victor Gollancz, Richard Stokes, and the British Zone of Germany, 1945–49." *Journal of Contemporary History* 22, no. 3 (1987): 501–519.

French, David. *Army, Empire, and Cold War: The British Army and Military Policy, 1945–1971*. Oxford: Oxford University Press, 2012.

Friedrich, Jörg. *The Fire: The Bombing of Germany, 1940–1945*. New York: Columbia University Press, 2006.

Gallup, George H. *The Gallup International Public Opinion Polls, Great Britain, 1937–1975*. New York: Random House, 1976.

Gorer, Geoffrey. *Exploring English Character*. New York: Criterion, 1955.

Gossel, Daniel. *Briten, Deutsche und Europa. Die Deutsche Frage in der britischen Außenpolitik, 1945–1962*. Stuttgart: Steiner, 1999.

Haase, Christian. "In Search of a European Settlement: Chatham House and British-German Relations, 1920–55." *European History Quarterly* 37, no. 3 (2007): 371–97.

Hennessey, Peter. *Having It So Good: Britain in the Fifties*. London: Allen Lane, 2006.

Herrmann, Karin, Harald Husemann, and Lachan Moyle, eds. *Coping with the Relations: Anglo-German Cartoons from the Fifties to the Nineties*. Osnabrück: Secolo, 1988.

Herwarth, Hans von. *Von Adenauer zu Brandt. Erinnerungen*. Berlin: Propyläen, 1990.

Heuser, Beatrice. "Britain and the Federal Republic of Germany in NATO, 1955–1990." In Noakes et al., 141–62. *Britain and Germany in Europe*.

Hickman, Tom. *The Call-Up: A History of National Service*. London: Headline, 2004.

Horne, Alistair. *Back into Power: A Report on the New Germany*. London: Parrish, 1955.

Howard, Philip. "Heren, Louis Philip (1919–1995)." *Oxford Dictionary of National Biography*. Oxford: Oxford University Press, 2004. Online edition, January 2011, http://www.oxforddnb.com/view/article/58200.

Hughes, R. G. "'Don't let's be beastly to the Germans': Britain and the German Affair in History." *Twentieth Century British History* 17, no. 2 (2006): 257–83.

Jansen, Hans-Heinrich. *Grossbritannien, das Scheitern der EVG und der NATO-Beitritt der Bundesrepublik Deutschland*. Bochum: Universitätsverlag, 1992.

Johnson, B. S., ed. *All Bull: The National Servicemen*. London: Quartet Books, 1973.

Kipp, Yvonne. *Eden, Adenauer und die Deutsche Frage. Britische Deutschlandpolitik im internationalen Spannungsfeld, 1951–1957*. Paderborn: Schöningh, 2002.

Kirkpatrick, Ivone. *The Inner Circle*. London: Macmillan, 1959.

Koop, Volker. *Besetzt. Britische Besatzungspolitik in Deutschland*. Berlin: Be.bra, 2007.

Kynaston, David. *Austerity Britain, 1945–51*. London: Bloomsbury, 2007.

———. *Family Britain, 1951–57*. London: Bloomsbury, 2009.

Lane, Anne, "Kirkpatrick, Sir Ivone Augustine (1897–1964)." *Oxford Dictionary of National Biography*. Oxford: Oxford University Press, 2004. Online edition, January 2008, http://www.oxforddnb.com/view/article/34339.

Leber, Annedore. *Conscience in Revolt*. London: Vallentine, 1957.

Lee, Sabine. *An Uneasy Partnership: British-German Relations between 1955 and 1961*. Bochum: Brockmeyer, 1996.

———. *Victory in Europe? Britain and Germany since 1945*. Harlow: Longman, 2001.

Lodge, David. *Ginger, You're Barmy: An Uncompromising Novel of Army Life*. London: Penguin, 1970.

Mager, Olaf. *Die Stationierung der britischen Rheinarmee. Grossbritanniens EVG-Alternative*. Baden-Baden: Nomos, 1990.

Major, Patrick. "Britain and Germany: A Love-Hate Relationship?" *German History* 26, no. 4 (2008): 457–68.

———. "'Our Friend Rommel': The Wehrmacht as 'Worthy Enemy' in Postwar British Popular Culture." *German History* 26, no. 4 (2008): 520–35.

Mann, Anthony. *Comeback: Germany, 1945–1952*. London: Macmillan, 1980.

Mason, Tony, and Eliza Riedi. *Sport and the Military: The British Armed Forces, 1880–1960*. Cambridge: Cambridge University Press, 2010.

Mawby, Spencer. *Containing Germany: Britain and the Arming of the Federal Republic*. Basingstoke: Macmillan, 1999.

McInnes, Colin. *Hot War, Cold War: The British Army's Way in Warfare, 1945–95*. London: Brassey's, 1996.

Meehan, Patricia. *A Strange Enemy People: Germans under the British, 1945–1950*. London: Owen, 2001.

Michail, Evgenios. "After the War and after the Wall: British Perceptions of Germany following 1945 and 1989." *University of Sussex Journal of Contemporary History* 3 (September 2001). Online edition, https://www.sussex.ac.uk/webteam/gateway/file.php?name=3-michail-after-the-war-and-after-the-wall&site=15.

Monsarrat, Nicholas. *The Cruel Sea*. London: Knopf, 1951.

Niedhart, Gottfried. "Die Bundesrepublik Deutschland in der britischen Politik der Fünfziger Jahre: Rearmed but once again a healthy member of the Western family." *Historische Mitteilungen* 3 (1990): 181–92.

Noakes, Jeremy, Peter Wende, and Jonathan Wright, eds. *Britain and Germany in Europe, 1949–1990*. Oxford: Oxford University Press, 2002.

Orwell, George. *Inside the Whale and Other Essays*. Harmondsworth: Penguin, 1968.

Pronay, Nicholas. "The British Post-Bellum Cinema: A Survey of the Films Relating to World War II Made in Britain between 1945 and 1960." *Historical Journal of Film, Radio, and Television* 8, no. 1 (1988): 39–54.

Ramsden, John. *Don't Mention the War: The British and the Germans since 1890*. London: Little, 2006.

————. "Re-focusing 'the People's War': British War Films of the 1950s." *Journal of Contemporary History* 33, no. 1 (1998): 35–63.

Richardson, Charles. "Robertson, Brian Hubert, first Baron Robertson of Oakridge (1896–1974)." rev. *Oxford Dictionary of National Biography*. Oxford: Oxford University Press, 2004. Online edition, January 2011, http://www.oxforddnb.com/view/article/31616.

Royle, Trevor. *The Best Years of their Lives: The National Service Experience, 1945–1963*. London: Deutsch, 2002.

Schönwald, Matthias. "New Friends–Difficult Friendships: Germany and Its Western Neighbours in the Postwar Era." *Contemporary European History* 11, no. 2 (2002): 317–32.

Scotland, Alexander P. *The London Cage*. London: Evans Bros., 1957.

Scott, L. V. *Conscription and the Attlee Governments: The Politics and Policy of National Service, 1945–1951*. Oxford: Clarendon Press, 1993.

Seymour-Ure, Colin. "Hulton, Sir Edward George Warris (1906–1988)," rev. *Oxford Dictionary of National Biography*. Oxford: Oxford University Press, 2004. Online edition, May 2011, http://www.oxforddnb.com/view/article/40161.

Smith, Barbara. "The Rules of Engagement: German Women and British Occupiers, 1945–1949." Wilfrid Laurier University, 2009. *Theses and Dissertations (Comprehensive)*. Paper 1072. http://scholars.wlu.ca/etd/1072.

Stadtarchiv Bad Oeynhausen, B II 18. Cited in "Lübbecke und die Britische Kontrollkommission 1945." *Lübbecke Kompakt*, http://www.luebbecke.de.

Stephenson, Jill. "Britain and Europe in the Later Twentieth Century: Identity, Sovereignty, Peculiarity." In *National Histories and European History*, edited by Mary Fulbrook, 230–54. London: Boulder, 1993.

Summerfield, Penny. "Dunkirk and the Popular Memory of Britain at War, 1940–1958." *Journal of Contemporary History* 45 (2010): 788–811.

Summers, C. "We had a lot of laughs." *BBC News Online*, 20 July 2004, http://news.bbc.co.uk/1/hi/world/europe/3842041.stm.

Thorne, Tony. *Brasso, Blanco, and Bull*. London: Robinson, 1998.

Vinen, Richard. *National Service: Conscription in Britain, 1945–1963*. London: Penguin, 2014.

Volle, Angelika. "Deutsch-Britische Beziehungen. Eine Untersuchung des bilateralen Verhältnisses auf der staatlichen und nichtstaatlichen Ebene seit dem Zweiten Weltkrieg." Unpublished PhD thesis. Bonn: Rheinische Friedrich-Wilhelms-Universität, 1976.

Walker, John, ed. *Halliwell's Film Guide*. 8th ed. London: Harper Collins, 1991.

Watson, Graham E., and Richard A. Rinaldi. *The British Army in Germany (BAOR and After): An Organizational History, 1947–2004*. Milton Keynes: Tiger Lily Publications, 2005.

Watt, Donald C. *Britain Looks to Germany: British Opinion and Policy towards Germany since 1945*. London: Wolff, 1965.

Webster, Wendy. "From Nazi-Legacy to Cold War: British Perceptions of European Identity, 1945–1964." In *European Identity and the Second World War,* edited by Michael Wintle and Menno Spiering, 92–110. Basingstoke: Palgrave, 2011.

Weidenfeld, G. "Englisches Deutschlandbild." *Die politische Meinung* 44 (1999): 55–62.

Weight, Richard. "Losing the Peace: Germany, Japan, America, and the Shaping of British National Identity in the Age of Affluence." In *An Affluent Society? Britain's Post-War "Golden Age" Revisited*, edited by Lawrence Black and Hugh Pemberton, 203–222. Aldershot: Ashgate, 2004.

White, Jerry. *London in the Twentieth Century: A City and Its People.* London: Vintage, 2008.

Williamson, David. *A Most Diplomatic General: The Life of General Lord Robertson of Oakridge.* London: Brassey's, 1996.

Willoughby, John. *Remaking the Conquering Heroes: The Postwar American Occupation of Germany.* Basingstoke: Palgrave, 2001.

Wittlinger, Ruth. "Perceptions of Germany and the Germans in Post-War Britain." *Journal of Multilingual and Multicultural Development* 25, nos. 5/6 (2004): 453–65.

Wurm, Clemens A. "Britain and West European Integration, 1948–9 to 1955: Politics and Economics." In Noakes et al., *Britain and Germany in Europe,* 27–47.

Wybrow, Robert J. *Britain Speaks Out, 1937–87.* Basingstoke: Macmillan, 1989.

Zimmermann, H. "The Sour Fruits of Victory: Sterling and Security in Anglo-German Relations during the 1950s and 1960s." *Contemporary European History* 9, no. 2 (2000): 225–43.

INDEX

Adenauer, Konrad: dismissal as mayor of Cologne, 34; focus of British policy, 153; 1957 state visit to Britain, 46; radio broadcast on value of BAOR, 94; relationship with British High Commissioner, 16; target of communist propaganda, 79, 81

Alexander, Viscount Albert Victor, 35

Allied Control Council, 15

Allied High Commission, 15, 30

Anglo-German Association, 93, 135

Anglo-German Relations, 132–33

atomic bomb, 18

Attlee, Clement, 18, 33

Bad Oeynhausen, 22, 77, 93

Bader, Douglas, 55–56

BAOR troop, enlisted ranks: attitudes towards Germany, 4, 28, 108–9, 154; contacts with Germans, 47, 69, 85, 104, 108–9; German views of, 87–89, 90–91; off duty activities, 104; sexual relationships with German women, 111–12

BAOR troops, officers: attitudes towards Germany, 26, 28, 106, 125, 131–34; Foreign Office view of, 146–47; German views of, 69, 71, 81, 138, 145; and German women, 111–12; incidents caused by, 83–85; living conditions in Germany, 74, 77

Barraclough, Geoffrey, 49

Beaverbrook, Lord, 43, 46, 51

Beaverbrook press, 43, 49, 54, 89

Belgium, 22, 115, 121

Berlin: blockade, 3, 18, 39, 41, 87; cost of occupation, 33

Besatzungsverdrängte organizations, 75–76

Bevin, Ernest, 1, 14, 18, 33, 35

Blitz, the, 3, 6

British Air Forces of Occupation, 1, 36. *See also* Royal Air Force

British Broadcasting Corporation (BBC): cooperation with Foreign Office, 49; 1955 television documentary on Germany and audience response, 48–49; radio reporting on Germany, 47–48

British Control Commission: attempts to improve Anglo-German relations, 4, 25, 28, 113, 130; formation and organizational structure, 23–24; relations with and attitude towards BAOR, 9, 24, 26–28; withdrawal, 27–29

British Commonwealth, 35, 146

British Expeditionary Force, 17

British Military Governor, 4

British Zone of Occupation: British troop deployment and bases, 1–2, 6, 22–23; bomb damage, refugees and lack of accommodation, 72–73; civilian administration, 23, 29, 128; reestablishment of German self-government, 141

Brussels Pact, 18

Buchenwald concentration camp, 52

Buffs, The (Royal East Kent Regiment), 7, 104

Canada: Canadian press reports, 86; Canadian troops, 86, 132, 152

PETER SPEISER is a lecturer in history at the University of Westminster.

THE HISTORY OF MILITARY OCCUPATION

The University of Illinois Press
is a founding member of the
Association of American University Presses.

Composed in 10/13 Sabon
by Lisa Connery
at the University of Illinois Press
Manufactured by Sheridan Books, Inc.

University of Illinois Press
1325 South Oak Street
Champaign, IL 61820-6903
www.press.uillinois.edu